Knowing JESUS *Intimately*

A Relationship of Love-motivated, Spirit-empowered Obedience

Knowing JESUS *Intimately*

A Relationship of Love-motivated, Spirit-empowered Obedience

Stephen E. Canup

Special thanks to Rev. Don Castleberry,
Founder, Freedom in Jesus Prison Ministries

Published by:
Freedom in Jesus Prison Ministries
www.fijm.org | *info@fijm.org*

Acknowledgements

Everyone needs a mature spiritual mentor and trusted accountability partner. I love and appreciate Don Castleberry for fulfilling this role for me. His trust, time and commitment to me have been invaluable. He has become one of my very best friends.

Rev. Don Castleberry is the Founder of Freedom in Jesus Prison Ministries. Learn more about this anointed prison ministry at *www.fijm.org* or, write to Freedom in Jesus Prison Ministries, P.O. Box 939, Levelland, TX 79336. You may e-mail us at *info@fijm.org*

Special thanks to Kevin Williamson for cover creation, layout and design assistance. For inquiries about his work, contact Kevin at *kevin@kevinwilliamsondesign.com*

Appreciation is also expressed for printing and shipping services through Perfection Press. For information contact Robert Riggs, *rriggs@printedtoperfection.com*

Table of Contents

Preface

One of the best truths I find myself often stating is, "Of my own self I can do nothing, but with God all things are possible". How many times have I told the Holy Spirit this fact as He continued to urge me and prepare me to sit down to begin this book? Why have I hesitated until now?

In large part, I feel unqualified to write anything at all, but I am reminded that God uses the weak and foolish things of this world to shame or confound the wise and strong (1 Corinthians 1:27). Facing this daunting topic, in many ways I feel weak and foolish. After all, I do not hold a degree in Theology, have not attended a Seminary, do not pastor a mega-church, and have only really been truly saved since 2009.

To the world I am very much an unknown author although over 500,000 copies of my previous four books are widely distributed for free in prisons and jails across America. It is true that I am an ordained and licensed minister of the Gospel of Jesus Christ, but I almost exclusively speak to and write for people who are in some form of bondage–that is, addictions of every kind, depressed, suicidal, lonely, bipolar, poor self-image, self-destructive, prideful, sexually immoral, lawbreakers, etc.–whether they are living in "the free world", or incarcerated behind steel bars and razor wire. Certainly, these are people who are even now like I once was.

I guess my main qualification is that I have been a radical lover and follower of Jesus since the day I went "all in" in 2009 on a prison bunk. Once I began to comprehend the love and forgiveness of God the Father demonstrated towards me, and the price Jesus paid on my behalf, I began to seek God with all my heart. The Holy Spirit gave me a hunger and thirst for the Word of God and I wanted to spend almost every hour of every day learning more about the Father, Son and Holy Spirit.

My God-given motivational gifts are teaching and encouraging although I did not know then what they were called and where to find them in the Bible (Romans 12:6-8). Even while I was still in prison, my purpose and passion began to quickly manifest in sharing what God was teaching me with all those who were still in bondage with me and who would listen or read what I was learning and sharing through my writing and research. I want everyone to walk in the freedom only God can provide, and fully experience the abundant life Jesus came to give us (John 10:10).

This passion for learning and sharing more about God's Word and the Gospel of Jesus Christ continued after my release when I almost immediately became a full-time volunteer for Freedom in Jesus Prison Ministries under its founder, Don Castleberry, in 2011, and by whom I was ordained and licensed in 2012. Starting with 10-12 men in 2011 in one prison, our Christian Discipleship Teachings are now mailed every three months to about 7,000 prisoners in over 1,200 facilities across the country. As of early 2023, the Holy Spirit has taught, encouraged and equipped me to write over 60 detailed teachings on 40 topics mailed to those on our discipleship mailing list.

So, all that being said, why am I writing this book? I feel an urgency in my soul and spirit to share one of the most startling truths I was ever led to consider. One day as I was re-reading the book of Matthew I was struck with the importance of Matthew 7:21-23. On that day a few years ago, I could say with certainty that "I know Jesus", but was I certain that "Jesus knew me"?

Brothers and sisters in Christ, it is crucial that you personally have a clear revelation, on this side of eternity, of whether or not Jesus knows you! I believe we are in the last seconds of the last minutes of the last hours of "the Last Days". Run to Jesus. Cling to Him. Know Him intimately!

No-one is guaranteed tomorrow, and we can never know when we will take our last breath in this world and our next breath in front of Jesus (see 2 Corinthians 5:6-10). **When you see Him will you hear, *"Well done good and faithful servant"*, or *"Depart from Me, I never knew you"*?**

I pray this book helps you know for sure which of these phrases you will hear before you ever step into eternity. Please ask the Holy Spirit to reveal these truths to you...

Introduction

According to the Bible, we know of only two basic statements a person will hear when they face Jesus in Heaven.

In a parable concerning the Kingdom of Heaven in Matthew 25:14-30, Jesus related that the master would say to the obedient, good stewards, ***"Well done, good and faithful servant...Enter into the joy of your lord."*** Certainly, this is what we all hope to hear.

However, earlier in the same gospel, in Matthew 7:21-23, to those who called Him "Lord", Jesus said, ***"I never knew you. Away from me you evildoers."*** These are people who said they knew Jesus but were startled and surprised to hear that Jesus did not "know" them!

This clear distinction in possible statements that one might hear upon seeing Jesus in Heaven should strike a healthy fear of the Lord into every person who identifies as a "Christian" and professes to know Jesus.

You say, "I know Jesus", but most critically, does "Jesus know you"?

I remember the day the Holy Spirit brought this to my attention. While reading through the book of Matthew the words of Jesus saying ***"I never knew you"*** almost leapt off the page at me. I stopped, read it again, and said aloud, "This is something I never want to hear!" Previously I had only considered the phrase, ***"Well done, good and faithful servant"*** as something every "Christian" who made it into Heaven and faced Jesus would hear.

I asked the Holy Spirit how a person could ever know on this side of eternity which statement they would hear? To my way of thinking it is crucial to have this assurance before leaving this life. Wouldn't you agree?

As I researched and examined several related scriptures, the Holy Spirit led me to examine the meanings behind the Greek word translated as "knew" that Jesus used when he is quoted as saying, ***"I never knew you"***. As we will learn more later, this word includes the meaning of an intimacy of relationship. One must have an intimate, ongoing, personal relationship with Jesus to receive the welcome we all want to hear, ***"Well done, good and faithful servant"***.

My next question for the Holy Spirit was, "What does the Word indicate as being important in distinguishing whether someone just 'knows about Jesus' versus having an intimate personal relationship with Him?"

As I studied, and will later share with you in more detail, the key distinguishing factor is for us to have a heart that increasingly desires to be obedient to the Word, and is quick to genuinely repent when we miss it. This commitment to ongoing obedience is motivated by a real love for Jesus, and grows continually in response to us comprehending and receiving the unconditional love of the Father. The Holy Spirit makes God's love ever more real to us daily thereby inspiring and empowering our obedience; and, gently convicting us to repent when we are disobedient.

Please re-read the previous paragraph and make note that **the key distinguishing factors are love-motivated, Spirit-empowered obedience**

and repentance. That is, we will not be satisfied to just hear the Word, or know what it says, rather we will want to **obey** it (see James 1:22). Out of our growing love for God, and in recognition of our growing comprehension of His unconditional love for us, and for what He's done in and through Jesus, we will want to do our best to please Him in every way (see Colossians 1:9-14). **Our lives are so rewarding when our hearts are love-motivated and Spirit-empowered to obey and serve Him in genuine humility and joyful thankfulness!**

As we move ahead in this book, I will be sharing with you much of what God has been teaching me relative to developing and maintaining an intimacy of personal relationship with Jesus! In addition to discussing key concepts in this regard, I will be attempting to suggest practical applications to our daily lives, especially with regard to love, obedience and the Holy Spirit.

I pray that God will touch our hearts and anoint each of us to desperately desire and pursue our goal of knowing Jesus intimately. I am certain you agree with me, we all want to hear ***"Well done good and faithful servant"*** when we meet Jesus face to face!

What Will You Hear When You See Jesus?

Christianity is not about "religion". Jesus did not come to establish new rules, rites and religious orders. He came to restore us to **an intimate, personal relationship** with our Heavenly Father through His Holy Spirit working in and through our surrendered, submissive, obedient lives. Are you pursuing daily an intimacy of personal spiritual relationship with Him?

It is not enough to claim that we "know about" Jesus, or that we once said a prayer "accepting" Jesus as Savior, but did not ever really repent and turn from our old life. It is important that He really becomes our Lord and Master, and that we surrender to His Holy Spirit leadership. **Our lives should demonstrate evidence of a heart that is set on doing our best to obey Him, and quick to genuinely repent when we don't. We must desire to foster a deep, abiding intimacy of ongoing spiritual relationship with God, having a mindset focused on pleasing Him, not the world.**

From my study of the gospels, it seems we will only hear one of two things when we stand before Jesus: ***"Well done, good and faithful servant, enter in to My Joy"***, or, ***"Depart from Me, I never knew you, worker of lawlessness."*** It is crucial that Jesus says He knows you!

If you were to ask a person if they know Jesus, the large majority of the world would say "Yes". In fact, they really mean they "know about" Jesus. They know who Jesus is; that is, they have heard about Him, but they do not really have a "relationship" with Him.

Those who attend church, including many who have said a prayer of salvation, would mainly say they "know Jesus", but their lives do not reflect the proof of an intimacy of relationship with Him. Jesus said you can tell a tree by its fruit. With this group of people, it is more about religion, or following a set of rules and religious practices, than it is about an ongoing relationship.

Then, there is a core minority, a "remnant", who are certain they have an intimate relationship with Jesus. Their lives demonstrate to others that they have a heart that wants to be obedient to God, and they are quick to repent when they miss the mark.

Why is this a very important distinction?

Because, when we get to Heaven we will hear one of two important phrases from Jesus. These are:

"Well done, good and faithful servant."

Or,

"Depart from Me. I never knew you."

Are you certain which of these two phrases Jesus will say to you?

You might respond, "No, I am not certain, what makes the difference? What is the deciding factor? How can I know which phrase He will use for me?"

Study this carefully... knowing and applying the answer could very well determine your eternity.

In the three parables discussed below, the people who appeared before

Him all thought they knew Him, yet one group is turned away because He says He does not "know" them!

You might say you know Jesus, but are you certain today that Jesus KNOWS you?

In the following scriptures, I have emphasized key words and phrases.

THE PARABLE OF THE TEN VIRGINS

Matthew 25: 1-13 "At that time the kingdom of heaven will be like ten
virgins who took their lamps and went out to meet the bridegroom. 2
Five of them were foolish and five were wise. 3 The foolish ones took
their lamps but did not take any oil with them. 4 The wise ones, however, took oil in jars along with their lamps. 5 The bridegroom was a long
time in coming, and they all became drowsy and fell asleep.

6 "At midnight the cry rang out: 'Here's the bridegroom! Come out to
meet him!'

7 "Then all the virgins woke up and trimmed their lamps. 8 The foolish
ones said to the wise, 'Give us some of your oil; our lamps are going out.'

9 "'No,' they replied, 'there may not be enough for both us and you.
Instead, go to those who sell oil and buy some for yourselves.'

10 "But while they were on their way to buy the oil, the bridegroom
arrived. The virgins who were ready went in with him to the wedding
banquet. And the door was shut.

11 "Later the others also came. 'Lord, Lord,' they said, 'open the door
for us!'

12 "But he replied, 'Truly I tell you, ***I don't know you***.'

13 "Therefore keep watch, because you do not know the day or the hour."

Here we read about ten virgins who knew the Bridegroom and were waiting for his return. In the Jewish bridal custom, the bride and her friends had always to be dressed and ready to respond immediately to the surprise midnight cry of the groom's arrival. In this parable, five were fully ready and were welcomed in to the bridal feast, but the other five had not been obedient in staying prepared. Since oil is often a reference to the Holy Spirit, could it also be that these five were unprepared because they did not have the indwelling presence of the Holy Spirit meaning they were not truly "born again"?

Clearly they thought they had a personal relationship, but did they? In spite of them addressing him as "Lord", the Bridegroom said, "I don't know you", and the five foolish ones who were disobedient and unprepared were turned away. Can you imagine their shock and disappointment?

THE NARROW DOOR

Luke 13:22-27 22 "Then Jesus went through the towns and villages,
teaching as he made his way to Jerusalem. 23 Someone asked him, 'Lord,
are only a few people going to be saved?'

"He said to them, 24 'Make every effort to enter through the narrow door, because many, I tell you, will try to enter and will not
be able to. 25 Once the owner of the house gets up and closes the
door, you will stand outside knocking and pleading, 'Sir, open the door for us.'

"But he will answer, '***I don't know you or where you come from***.'

26 "Then you will say, 'We ate and drank with you, and you taught in our streets.'

[27] "But he will reply, '***I don't know you or where you come from. Away from me, all you evildoers!***'"

Again, in this passage, those left outside after the door had been closed thought they had a personal relationship which would allow entry. That is, they had previously spent some time eating and drinking with, and listening to, the owner of the house. In this scriptural section, the owner is harsher than the Bridegroom had been with the foolish virgins saying not only that he didn't know them, but that he didn't even know where they came from. He called out their disobedience by calling them "evildoers".

In both passages above, the Greek word translated as **"know"** is **"oida"** (#3857 in The Strongest NIV Exhaustive Concordance). This Greek word carries these shades of meaning: *"to know, to possess information, recognize, realize, to come to know, to understand, to be able to use knowledge".*

So, in both previous parables, the Bridegroom and owner of the house are emphatically stating that no personal relationship actually existed with the ones who were turned away! Don't you know that this was surely met with surprise, disappointment, and perhaps even horror?

But wait... the next example is even worse.

In this passage, which starts with the heading "True and False Disciples" Jesus distinguishes even further.

TRUE AND FALSE DISCIPLES

Matthew 7:21-23 "Not everyone who says to me, 'Lord, Lord,' will enter the kingdom of heaven, but only the one who does the will of my Father who is in heaven. 22 Many will say to me on that day, 'Lord, Lord, did we not prophesy in your name and in your name drive out demons and in your name perform many miracles?' 23 Then I will tell them plainly, ***'I never knew you. Away from me, you evildoers!"***

Again, these are people who called Jesus "Lord" and thought they had a relationship with Him. They had even done many religious works in His Name. Yet again Jesus very specifically referred to their disobedience when He called them "evildoers". Perhaps they also had the wrong heart motivation when they did things they thought were serving Him?

In this last parable, the Greek word translated as **"knew"** above is **"ginosko"** (#1182 in The Strongest NIV Exhaustive Concordance) This Greek word carries these shades of meaning: "*to know, to come to know, recognize, understand; to have sexual relations*". This implies a deeper level of spiritual intimacy

Interestingly, this is the same basic definition of the Hebrew word "yada" which the King James Version translated in Genesis 4:1 that "Adam ***knew*** his wife..." So we can infer, that this type of "knowing" is not just possessing knowledge of, but **it is "knowing" in a more intimate sense**. Similarly, in Matthew 1:25, the same meaning accompanies the statement that Joseph "knew her not" (KJV) or, "had no union with Mary until after she gave birth" (NIV).

So, from these three parables we learn that it is not enough for us to simply know about Jesus, or even for us to say, we know Jesus. The type of "knowing" we are talking about comes from an intimate, personal relationship with Him. That is, Jesus must know us intimately.

Interestingly, immediately after this last parable, in Matthew 7:24, Jesus teaches, "Therefore everyone who ***hears these words of mine and puts them into practice*** is like a wise man who built his house on the rock." Jesus is connecting our personal relationship with Him to our obedience.

This is similar to what He says in John 10:27-28, "My sheep listen to my voice; ***I know them***, and they follow me. ***I give them eternal life***, and ***they*** shall never perish; no one will snatch ***them*** out of my hand." The word translated as "know" is the same Greek word Ginosko, #1182, as we saw in Matthew 7:21-23, so it is an intimacy of knowing.

How then does Jesus say he intimately knows His sheep? They listen to His voice, and they follow Him. We can infer that those who are His sheep are trained to hear his commands and obey them. He gives ***them*** eternal life!

In other words, Jesus intimately knows those who obey Him! Our obedience is a direct indication that we really know Jesus and that He intimately knows us. This is the key.

OTHER RELEVANT SCRIPTURE PASSAGES

Let's examine closely other scriptures which provide more insight and clarification for knowing Jesus and Him knowing us. I have emphasized key words and phrases that characterize how God expects us to respond to Him, and therefore these truths would certainly impact how we live as "born again" believers:

Luke 6:46 "Why do you call me, 'Lord, Lord,' and do not do what I say?"

1 John 2:3-6, 17 "**We know that we have come to know him if we keep his commands.** Whoever says, 'I know him,' but does not do what he commands is a liar, and the truth is not in that person. But **if anyone obeys his word**, love for God is truly made complete in them. This is how we know we are in him: Whoever claims to live in him must live as Jesus did ... [17] The world and its desires pass away, but **whoever does the will of God** lives forever."

1 John 3:6 "No one who lives in him keeps on sinning. **No one who continues to sin has either seen him or known him**."

1 John 3:24 "**The one who keeps God's commands lives in him, and he in them**. And this is how we know that he lives in us: We know it by the Spirit he gave us."

1 John 4:7-8 "Dear friends, let us love one another, for love comes from God. **Everyone who loves has been born of God and knows God. Whoever does not love does not know God**, because God is love."

John 14:6-7, 15-17, 21, 23-24 Jesus answered, "I am the way and the truth and the life. No one comes to the Father except through me. **If you really know me**, you will know my Father as well. From now on, you do know him and have seen him."... [15] "**If you love me, keep my commands**. And I will ask the Father, and he will give you another advocate to help you and be with you forever— the Spirit of truth. The world cannot accept him, because it neither sees him nor knows him. **But you know him, for he lives with you and will be in you**... "[23] Jesus replied, "**Anyone who loves me will obey my teaching.** My Father will love them, and we will come to them and make our home with them. Anyone who does not love me will not obey my teaching. These words you hear are not my own; they belong to the Father who sent me."

John 8:31-32 "To the Jews who had believed him, Jesus said, '**If you hold to my teaching**, you are really my disciples. **Then you will know the truth**, and the truth will set you free.' "

John 8:54-55 Jesus replied, "If I glorify myself, my glory means nothing. My Father, whom you claim as your God, is the one who glorifies me. Though you do not know him, I know him. If I said I did not, I would be a liar like you, but **I do know him and obey his word**."

Luke 8:21 He replied, "My mother and brothers are **those who hear God's word and put it into practice.**"

Mark 3:35 "**Whoever does God's will** is my brother and sister and mother."

Romans 8:9 "You, however, are not in the realm of the flesh but are in the realm of the Spirit, if indeed the Spirit of God lives in you. And **if anyone does not have the Spirit of Christ, they do not belong to Christ.**"

Matthew 19:17 "Why do you ask me about what is good?" Jesus replied. "There is only One who is good. **If you want to enter life, keep the commandments.**"

Revelation 3:20 "Here I am! I stand at the door and knock. **If anyone hears my voice and opens the door**, I will come in and eat with that person, and they with me."

2 Timothy 2:19 "Nevertheless, God's solid foundation stands firm, sealed with this inscription: **'The Lord knows those who are his,'** and, **'Everyone who confesses the name of the Lord must turn away from wickedness.'**"

2 Peter 1:3-8 "His divine power has given us everything we need for a godly life **through our knowledge of him** who called us by his own glory and goodness. Through these he has given us his very great and precious promises, so that through them you may participate in the divine nature, **having escaped the corruption in the world caused by evil desires.**

"For this very reason, make every effort to add to your faith goodness; and to goodness, knowledge; and to knowledge, self-control; and to self-control, perseverance; and to perseverance, godliness; and to godliness, mutual affection; and to mutual affection, love. **For if you possess these qualities in increasing measure, they will keep you from being ineffective and unproductive in your knowledge of our Lord Jesus Christ.**"

Galatians 4:8-9 "Formerly, when you did not know God, you were slaves to those who by nature are not gods. **But now that you know God—or rather are known by God**—how is it that you are turning back to those weak and miserable forces? Do you wish to be enslaved by them all over again?"

1 Corinthians 8:3 "**But whoever loves God is known by God.**"

Luke 14:26 "If anyone comes to me and does not hate father and mother, wife and children, brothers and sisters—yes, even their own life—**such a person cannot be my disciple.**"

Jeremiah 9:23-24

"This is what the Lord says:

'Let not the wise boast of their wisdom
or the strong boast of their strength
or the rich boast of their riches,
but let the one who boasts boast about this:
that they have the understanding to know me,
that I am the Lord, who exercises kindness,
justice and righteousness on earth,
for in these I delight,'
declares the Lord."

John 17:3 "**Now this is eternal life: that they know you**, the only true God, and Jesus Christ, whom you have sent."

John 3:36, NASB "He who believes in the Son has eternal life; but **he who does not obey the Son will not see life**, but the wrath of God abides on him."

Brothers and sisters in Christ, please note the emphasis above on love, obedience and the Holy Spirit. This is crucial. **An intimate relationship with Jesus is marked by love-motivated, Spirit-empowered obedience.**

PURSUING RELATIONSHIP AND REST IN GOD

Centuries ago Augustine wrote, "You made us for Yourself, and our heart is restless until it rests in You." Jesus said, "Come to me, all you who are weary and burdened, and I will give you rest."

Something deep inside that was always missing before is finally made complete in a genuine relationship with Jesus; and, through His Spirit we will be filled with His rest, peace, joy and righteousness. We should always want to know Him better and more intimately.

Dr. Charles Stanley, has written, "To fellowship with God – to talk to Him and listen to Him as you study the Bible, pray, and worship Him – is to get to know Him better. He has 'betrothed' (or engaged) His people to Himself for one reason: to let Himself be known.

"When you develop your relationship with God and discover more about His holy character, He illuminates your heart and mind, giving you a greater desire to know Him more intimately – and leaving your fleshly desires behind in the process. Your worldly desires simply cannot compare to the deep comfort, joy, and fulfillment that God offers you. Rather, you see the things that you acquire outside of His will turning to ashes, while the blessings He gives you endure and satisfy your soul."

Dr. Tony Evans wrote, "Our fundamental problem as Christians is not really obedience. Our problem is keeping our love for Christ fervent, for love makes obedience a delight. A decline in obedience is the outgrowth of a decline in love."

In *The Jeremiah Study Bible*, when expounding upon Matthew 21:28-32, Dr. David Jeremiah wrote, "Jesus does not count what people profess with their lips as obedience; only their deeds matter. An obedience that brings a person into vital, intimate, personal relationship with Christ is one that consistently performs what it professes."

PRACTICAL APPLICATION

What does "an intimate relationship" look like? Let's say we wanted to pursue a deeper relationship with someone. There are a number of things we would do to cultivate and foster that relationship. Here are some methods we would employ in our daily life with the other person, and how they might then be related to cultivating an intimate relationship with God:

- Practicing daily communication – Do I have an attitude of ongoing prayer/conversation with God?

- Desiring to spend time together – Do I want to be alone with God daily?

- Trusting the other – Do I trust the Father to lead me daily by His Spirit?

- Accepting direction, guidance and correction – How do I respond to advice and chastisement?

- Wanting to learn more about the other – Do I desire to study what He reveals about Himself in the Bible?

- Desiring to please the other – Do I have a heart that always tries to please the Father?

- Loving the other deeply – Do I love Him enough to want to do my best to always obey Him?

- Sacrificing for the other – Will I lay my own life down for my Father and put Him first in everything?

- Committing to the other forever – Do I operate daily with eternity uppermost in my mind?

Certainly, we should pursue an intimate relationship with God with the same strategies and even more dedication than we would with another person. As we have seen, it can make an eternal difference for us.

TAKEAWAY HIGHLIGHT

It is not enough to "know about" Jesus.

It is not enough to say you know Jesus, but continue to live rebelliously and defiantly in disobedience.

Knowing Jesus in an intimate way will be evidenced by a life of Spirit-empowered obedience. This is an obedience that is motivated by increasingly understanding and receiving God's love.

Jesus said, "My sheep hear my voice, I know them, and they follow Me." (John 10:27)

Live your life in such a way so that when you get to Heaven, you will hear Jesus say, **"Well done, good and faithful servant! You have been faithful with a few things; I will put you in charge of many things. Come and share your master's happiness!"** (Matthew 25:23)

You do not want to hear Him say, **"I never knew you. Away from me, you evildoers!"** (Matthew 7:23)

Let's learn more about love-motivated, Spirit-empowered obedience...

Love–motivated, Spirit–empowered Obedience

In Matthew 22:37-38, when asked about the greatest commandment, Jesus replied: "'Love the Lord your God with all your heart and with all your soul and with all your mind.' This is the first and greatest commandment." Our love for God increases in direct proportion to how much we comprehend and receive His great love for us!

In John 14:15, Jesus said, "If you love me, you will obey my commands." Implied in this passage is that the love you have for God actually empowers your obedience through the Holy Spirit. That is, my love for Jesus actually enables me to keep His commands. Jesus actually explains how.

The very next verse introduces the disciples to the gift the Father and the Son would give His true disciples (verses 16-18): "And I will ask the Father, and he will give you another advocate to help you and be with you forever— the Spirit of truth. The world cannot accept him, because it neither sees him nor knows him. But you know him, for he lives with you and will be in you. I will not leave you as orphans; I will come to you."

Jesus never asks us to do something that is impossible. He does not leave us alone to try to figure things out for ourselves. The Father and the Son gave us a Helper, the Holy Spirit, to empower everything in our Christian walk as long as we daily surrender to His leadership. God Himself helps us love Him with all our heart, mind, soul and strength.

Part of the role of the Holy Spirit is to make practical and real everything the Father and the Son have made available to us. The most valuable, priceless, unconditional, amazing, eternal thing they have made available to us is their love!

LOVE-BASED OBEDIENCE

Craig Denison whose daily devotional, "First15 Devotional" (*www.first15.org*), is one I read often, had this to say about love-based obedience:

"For much of my life I feared the thought of obedience, especially to the almighty, all-knowing and all-powerful Creator of the universe. I couldn't seem to find a way to consistently choose him over myself. I couldn't seem to be able to live for his affections over those of the world. As hard as I would try in various seasons, I just couldn't be obedient.

"What I didn't realize about God's command to be obedient was the process by which I could grow in obedience. God will take our obedience however he can get it because he wants us to enjoy the incredible fruits of his perfect will, but his desire is always to love us to a place that our obedience would be a natural overflow of our love for him. He longs for us to live a lifestyle of love-based obedience.

"John 14:15 says very simply, *"If you love me, you will keep my commandments."* Jesus' words here are a promise. If we truly love him, we will keep his commandments. If we truly have love in our hearts, we can't help but be obedient to him. I long to grow to the place where I am so in love with Jesus that I long to choose him in every situation. I long to be a servant so in love with my King that I would die for him or anyone else he asked me to.

"The love of God is so real, so powerful and so transformational that it can mold and shape us into people who no longer live for this temporal world but seek first an everlasting, invisible Kingdom. If we will simply be people who let God love us in every moment, we will naturally be people who are obedient to God's perfect will for us."

FIND DELIGHT AND ACCEPTANCE IN GOD

Craig Denison, "First15 Devotional" (www.first15.org), also wrote this about every person's desire to be accepted and bring delight to another: "Our Father created all of us with a desire to be delighted in by *him*. The Creator of all things, the only one who knows everything about you, longs for you to know that he deeply enjoys you. You, just being fully you, are loved. You, with all your failures, victories, sins, and quirks are loved by God. God made you the way he did for a reason! He savors talking with you, and watching you work. He longs for you to live the life he's laid out for you and experience the fullness of joy he has richly provided you. Of course he hates when we sin. He can't possibly approve of something we're doing that's harmful to us and others. But even in our failure God pursues us. Even in rebellion God longs for us to turn our hearts toward him so that he can run out to meet us and clothe us with grace. Out of his unconditional love, he wants to throw a celebration in honor of restored relationship with you (see Luke 15:11-32).

"Seek fulfillment for your desire to be delighted in in the arms of your loving Father. See him as your Father running out to meet you that you might be fully loved by him. Let his love sink into the depths of your heart that your desire to be delighted in may be fully satisfied in him."

Dr. Charles Stanley said, "When we have a holy, respectful fear of the Lord, our desire changes from satisfying ourselves to serving our God. Pleasing Him is not a chore; rather, it becomes a joy done out of humility and thankfulness."

RESPONDING TO GOD'S LOVE

After I got saved in prison in 2009, the two Bible passages I identified with most were the ones concerning Jonah running from God (Jonah 1:1 – 4:11), and about the prodigal son turning his back on his father to live his life on his own terms (Luke 15:11-32). Many of us who have been in prison could probably relate to both of these. Do you?

As a young man I felt God had a call on my life to fulfill His purpose but I wanted to "do my own thing" so I ignored Him. After having been raised in a Christian home and regularly attending the Baptist Church, I turned my back on God when I went to college. In my pride, I foolishly thought I could run my own life and didn't need God. For most of the next 40 years, I did things my own way, almost never went to church, and I very rarely read the Bible.

After I went to prison at age 56, I finally got past my pride enough to admit to God that apparently I was not doing such a great job of "running my own life". I told God, "After all, look where I ended up!" Through humility and broken-ness I repented to God and asked Him to forgive me. Though I never heard an audible voice, I felt deep in my spirit that He welcomed me home with wide-open arms (see Luke 15:17-24). In my heart, I felt His love and forgiveness in a way that seemed to fill the emptiness deep inside that had been haunting me so long.

As I received Jesus as my Savior, and began to understand His finished work at the Cross, including His death, burial and resurrection, I began to understand the demonstration of love that enabled Him to sacrifice Himself willingly for me even while I was still a sinner (Romans 5:8). God loves us so very much that He paid the ultimate price to save us so we could make a free will choice to have an intimate relationship with Him (John 3:16-21).

It is the love, kindness and goodness of God that continually motivates us to be obedient, and to genuinely repent when we are disobedient (Romans 2:4-11). Our Father's love is unconditional, unlimited, undeserved, and eternal. He accepts us just as we are but He loves us too much to leave us that way! There is nothing we can do to make Him love us any more than He already does; and, thankfully, there is nothing we can do to make Him love us any less! He just wants us to use our free will daily to choose to love Him. The more we believe and receive His great love the more we will joyfully obey Him.

Also, the more we experience and comprehend His great love for us, the easier it becomes to love others. After all, Jesus said all the commandments can be met by loving God with all our heart, mind, soul and strength; and, loving others as we love ourselves.

God will always love you, and He will never leave you or forsake you. Knowing and fully receiving His love motivates us to want to please Him. He is looking for those who have a heart that wants to be obedient (2 Chronicles 16:9a), and is quick to repent when we miss it (2 Peter 3:9). The Holy Spirit gives us the power to obey.

SOME RELEVANT SCRIPTURE PASSAGES

Luke 15:17-24 "When he came to his senses, he said, 'How many of my father's hired servants have food to spare, and here I am starving to death! I will set out and go back to my father and say to him: Father, I have sinned against heaven and against you. I am no longer worthy to be called your son; make me like one of your hired servants.' So he got up and went to his father.

"But while he was still a long way off, his father saw him and was filled with compassion for him; he ran to his son, threw his arms around him and kissed him.

"The son said to him, 'Father, I have sinned against heaven and against you. I am no longer worthy to be called your son.'

"But the father said to his servants, 'Quick! Bring the best robe and put it on him. Put a ring on his finger and sandals on his feet. Bring the fattened calf and kill it. Let's have a feast and celebrate. For this son of mine was dead and is alive again; he was lost and is found."

Romans 5:8 "But God demonstrates his own love for us in this: While we were still sinners, Christ died for us."

John 3:16-21 "For God so loved the world that he gave his one and only Son, that whoever believes in him shall not perish but have eternal life. For God did not send his Son into the world to condemn the world, but to save the world through him. Whoever believes in him is not condemned, but whoever does not believe stands condemned already because they have not believed in the name of God's one and only Son. This is the verdict: Light has come into the world, but people loved darkness instead of light because their deeds were evil. Everyone who does evil hates the light, and will not come into the light for fear that their deeds will be exposed. But whoever lives by the truth comes into the light, so that it may be seen plainly that what they have done has been done in the sight of God."

Romans 2:4 "...Or do you show contempt for the riches of his kindness, forbearance and patience, not realizing that God's kindness is intended to lead you to repentance?"

Psalm 103:11-12 "For as high as the heavens are above the earth, so great is his love for those who fear him; as far as the east is from the west, so far has he removed our transgressions from us."

Jeremiah 31:3 "I have loved you with an everlasting love; I have drawn you with unfailing kindness."

Hebrews 13:5-6 "Keep your lives free from the love of money and be content with what you have, because God has said, 'Never will I leave you; never will I forsake you.' So we say with confidence, 'The Lord is my helper; I will not be afraid. What can mere mortals do to me?'"

2 Chronicles 16:9 "For the eyes of the Lord range throughout the earth to strengthen those whose hearts are fully committed to him..."

2 Peter 3:9 "The Lord is not slow in keeping his promise, as some understand slowness. Instead he is patient with you, not wanting anyone to perish, but everyone to come to repentance."

TAKEAWAY HIGHLIGHT

God will always love you, and He will never leave you or forsake you. Knowing and fully receiving His love motivates us to want to please Him. He is looking for those who have a heart that wants to be obedient (2 Chronicles 16:9a), and is quick to repent when we miss it (2 Peter 3:9). The Holy Spirit gives us the power to obey.

PRACTICAL APPLICATION

Spend a few minutes intentionally and unhurriedly focusing on how far the Lord has already brought you. Tell Him you are grateful for the plan He has for you. Think about what it means to be forever unconditionally, perfectly loved by the Father. Thank Him and Jesus for giving you their Holy Spirit to make this love real and practical to you. Tell Him you unconditionally surrender to His love and leadership. Ask the Holy Spirit to empower love-motivated obedience in your life today and forever.

WANT TO KNOW MORE?

Write to us to request the discipleship teaching entitled "God's Love for You". Mail it to: Freedom in Jesus Prison Ministries, Attn: Teachings, P.O. Box 939, Levelland, TX 79336.

Let's consider some other principles of obedience...

Principles of Obedience

As we have been considering love-motivated obedience, we will want to expand our understanding of obedience as an overarching principle in the Bible. One of our dear prison ministers and close friend, Carol Breeden, graduated to Heaven in 2020. Here is something she wrote on obedience that seems especially relevant to our goal of learning more about pursuing an intimacy of personal relationship with Jesus:

"This may not be your favorite subject; however, I have found that the more I walk in obedience to His Word, the more peaceful my life is. You see, there was a time in my life when I would read His Word but didn't understand it. So many times when I made daily choices, those choices would be against His Word and I was not even aware of my disobedience. That is very displeasing to God. Not only was God displeased, but I suffered the consequences of my wrong choices, not even understanding what was happening. That, my friend, is like looking into a mirror at myself, and then turning away and forgetting what I looked like.

"So it is important that we study His Word, and it is important that we understand it. How can we be a "doer" of His Word if we do not understand what His Word means? God has a beautiful plan for each of us, and He shares in His Word what He expects from us. The more I understand His plan, the more grateful I become. And the more grateful I become, the more I love Him. And the more I love Him, the more I want to walk in obedience.

"Our heavenly Father loves us. He doesn't want us to follow a list of "do's and don'ts" out of fear for what will happen if we don't. He wants us to love Him in return. And because we love Him, we walk in obedience to His Word. If you have children, would you want them to be afraid of you? Would you want them to obey you out of fear? No, I believe you would want them to obey you because they love you and they realize that you are looking out for their best interests–that you are making decisions on their behalf based on what you think is best for them. That is what our Father has done, you know. He has set principles into motion for our protection. When we obey those principles, it will be well with our souls!

"God does not want us to just go through the motions of loving Him. He wants genuine love. We can sometimes pretend with our "friends" to care for them just so we can get from them what we want. But that is not a loving relationship, and it will soon turn sour. Likewise, your heavenly Father knows what is in your heart. Do you know what is in your heart? Do you really love Him? Jesus said, '*If you love me, then keep My commandments.*' Obedience is better than sacrifice."

As I thought about this phrase, "obedience is better than sacrifice" (see 1 Samuel 15:22), it occurs to me to emphasize that man-made religious rituals are not effective. What honors God is a heart that is set on obeying Him, and is quick to repent when we miss the mark in rebellion.

BLESSINGS FOLLOW OBEDIENCE

When I was released from prison, Freedom in Jesus Ministries' Founder, Don Castleberry, began mentoring me about our Christian journey – a journey leading to the very presence of God. We can experience His Presence in this life. We do not have to die first. But in the process, God never advances us any further than our last act of disobedience. Think about this–His best for us lies on the other side of our obedience.

A.W. Tozer, in *Experiencing the Presence of God*, wrote, "Which is more important to a Christian, believing or obeying? For the sparrow flying through the air, both wings are equally important. With only one it is impossible to fly. So we must believe God's Word and obey it. By these two wings, a man will rise to God in faith and humble obedience to the Lord Himself...very few Christians are prepared to go with God all the way. They go part of the way and then improvise. They follow the Lord until things look a little sticky and then they say, 'Well, there's no use to get radical about this and be a fanatic. I think I can reason this out for myself.'...The result is, of course, luke-warmness, which God will spew out of His mouth."

David Wilkerson wrote, "No matter who you are, if you harbor a secret sin you will experience continual disturbances in your life, your home and family, your work. Confusion, worry, and fears will replace your peace and strength."

I remember times in the past when I needed God to do something, and I thought I was waiting on Him. I learned, however, that He was waiting on me! Waiting for what? He wanted first my obedience in a certain area of my life I had been selfishly withholding. Once I surrendered that area to Him, His blessings were released, and I experienced more of His Presence daily.

In a devotional, *100 Days of Prayer for a Righteous Man*, I read, "Are you ready, willing, able, and anxious to receive God's blessings? Then obey Him. And you can rest assured that when you do your part, He'll do His part!"

Ask the Holy Spirit to show you any areas in which you are not presently obedient. Then surrender them fully to God. His blessings are waiting for you!

"Only he who believes is obedient, and only he who is obedient believes." (Dietrich Bonhoeffer)

SOME RELEVANT SCRIPTURE PASSAGES

Micah 6:8 – "He has shown you, O mortal, what is good. And what does the Lord require of you? To act justly and to love mercy and to walk humbly with your God."

Joshua 22:5–"But be very careful to keep the commandment and the law that Moses the servant of the Lord gave you: to love the Lord your God, to walk in obedience to him, to keep his commands, to hold fast to him and to serve him with all your heart and with all your soul."

John 14:23 "Jesus replied, 'If anyone loves me, he will obey my teaching. My Father will love him, and we will come to him and make our home with him.'"

I John 5:2-4 "This is how we know that we love the children of God: by loving God and carrying out his commands. This is love for God: to obey his commands. And his commands are not burdensome, for everyone born of God overcomes the world. This is the victory that has overcome the world, even our faith."

Proverbs 13:13 "He who scorns instruction will pay for it, but he who respects a command is rewarded."

I John 2:17 "The world and its desires pass away, but the man who does the will of God lives forever."

Deuteronomy 26:16-19 "The LORD your God commands you this day to follow these decrees and laws; carefully observe them with all your heart and with all your soul. You have declared this day that the LORD is your God and that you will walk in his ways, that you will keep his decrees, commands and laws, and that you will obey him. And the LORD has declared this day that you are his people, his treasured possession as he promised, and that you are to keep all his commands. He has declared that he will set you in praise, fame and honor high above all the nations he has made and that you will be a people holy to the LORD your God, as he promised."

John 15:14–"Jesus said, 'You are my friends if you do what I command.'"

John 14:15 – "Jesus said, 'If you love me, keep my commands.'"

I John 3:24 – "The one who keeps God's commands lives in him, and he in them. And this is how we know that he lives in us: We know it by the Spirit he gave us."

I John 2:3-4 – "We know that we have come to know him if we keep his commands. Whoever says, 'I know him,' but does not do what he commands is a liar, and the truth is not in that person."

Titus 1:16 – "They claim to know God, but by their actions they deny him. They are detestable, disobedient and unfit for doing anything good."

Deuteronomy 28:1-14 "If you fully obey the LORD your God and carefully follow all his commands I give you today, the LORD your God will set you high above all the nations on earth. All these blessings will come upon you and accompany you if you obey the LORD your God: You will be blessed in the city and blessed in the country. The fruit of your womb will be blessed, and the crops of your land and the young of your livestock—the calves of your herds and the lambs of your flocks. Your basket and your kneading trough will be blessed. You will be blessed when you come in and blessed when you go out. The LORD will grant that the enemies who rise up against you will be defeated before you. They will come at you from one direction but flee from you in seven. The LORD will send a blessing on your barns and on everything you put your hand to. The LORD your God will bless you in the land he is giving you. The LORD will establish you as his holy people, as he promised you on oath, if you keep the commands of the LORD your God and walk in his ways. Then all the peoples on earth will see that you are called by the name of the LORD, and they will fear you. The LORD will grant you abundant prosperity—in the fruit of your womb, the young of your livestock and the crops of your ground—in the land he swore to your forefathers to give you. The LORD will open the heavens, the storehouse of his bounty, to send rain on your land in season and to bless all the work of your hands. You will lend to many nations but will borrow from none. The LORD will make you the head, not the tail. If you pay attention to the commands of the LORD your God that I give you this day and carefully follow them, you will always be at the top, never at the bottom. Do not turn aside from any of the commands I give you today, to the right or to the left, following other gods and serving them."

TAKEAWAY HIGHLIGHT

A.W. Tozer, in Experiencing the Presence of God, wrote, "Which is more important to a Christian, believing or obeying? For the sparrow flying through the air, both wings are equally important. With only one it is impossible to fly. So we must believe God's Word and obey it. By these two wings, a man will rise to God in faith and humble obedience to the Lord Himself."

PRACTICAL APPLICATION

Prayerfully consider any areas in your life where you are not being obedient. Ask the Holy Spirit to bring these to mind. He will not do it to condemn you (Romans 8:1) but to gently convict you of righteousness (John 16:8-11). In your Christian journey do you feel stuck, unable to move forward? The areas of disobedience brought to your mind by the Holy Spirit may be your roadblocks. God wants you to deal with them, fully surrender, and move forward. Trust Him.

WANT TO KNOW MORE?

Write to us to request the two discipleship teachings on "Obedience". Mail it to: Freedom in Jesus Prison Ministries, Attn: Teachings, P.O. Box 939, Levelland, TX 79336.

In order to be obedient, we must surrender and submit...

Surrender and Submission

An intimate personal relationship with Jesus not only requires us to surrender and repent when the Holy Spirit draws us to receive Jesus as Savior, but we must willingly submit to Jesus as Lord of our lives. We have to reach a point where we finally realize we cannot save ourselves and surrender to the only One Who can.

If we let Him, the Holy Spirit's leadership on a daily basis teaches us to make Jesus Lord of our lives and enables us to yield to His plan for our lives. We must allow Him to re-make us into the person He has always planned for us to be. As we submit to Him daily, He will show us the fullness of the abundant life Jesus came to give us (John 10:10).

The best picture of submission is one of clay in a potter's hands. The potter transforms the clay from a shapeless handful of ugly mud into an exquisite object of beautiful art. The potter is totally in charge of the transformation, and the end product is determined in large part by his patience and skill. As followers of Jesus, we can be sure we have the best Master Potter!

In Isaiah 64:8 we read, "Yet, O LORD, you are our Father. We are the clay, you are the potter; we are all the work of your hand." This is illustrated in Jeremiah 18:1-6, "This is the word that came to Jeremiah from the LORD: 'Go down to the potter's house, and there I will give you my message.' So I went down to the potter's house, and I saw him working at the wheel. But the pot he was shaping from the clay was marred in his hands; so the potter formed it into another pot, shaping it as seemed best to him. Then the word of the LORD came to me: 'O house of Israel, can I not do with you as this potter does?" declares the LORD.' Like clay in the hand of the potter, so are you in my hand..."

Paul writes about the need for us to allow God to mold us as He sees fit, and accept the result knowing in His wisdom He shapes us for His purpose. Romans 9:20-21 says, "But who are you, O man, to talk back to God? Shall what is formed say to him who formed it, `Why did you make me like this?' Does not the potter have the right to make out of the same lump of clay some pottery for noble purposes and some for common use?"

Sometimes God allows extreme circumstances, like prison or other hardships of life, to get our attention. Often these may come as a consequence of poor choices made by ourselves or others, but they are best viewed as opportunities for positive change. To be transformed, a piece of clay must be soft so it will yield. We must consciously and willingly submit to God.

Regardless of how bad a mess we have made of our lives, and how far we may have run away from God, we are never so broken or so lost that God cannot find us, joyfully accept our returning to Him (Luke 15:32), make us a new creation (II Cor. 5:17) and establish His plan for our lives (Jer. 29:11-14a). However, we must be *gratefully humble, prayerfully submissive and faithfully obedient*. In *humility* we must recognize we cannot re-make ourselves and be *grateful* He can. In *submission* we must *prayerfully* put ourselves in His hands and patiently allow

Him to form us, and subject us to the hardening fire of trials and circumstances. We must be always *faithful* in *obedience* to follow His instructions so that we will experience the best of His intentions as He accomplishes His will through us, forming us into the image of His Son (Rom. 8:29).

Pastor Adrian Rogers said, "Your fear of God should not be that He will put His hand on you, but that He will take it off."

In an article entitled "The Potter's Hands" Dr. David Jeremiah wrote, "Sometimes we think we're unusable, unredeemable. We've done something for which we feel shame and guilt, and we think God can no longer do much with us. Our problems are occasionally of our own making, and our pain arises from our own stupidity...If you're under some sort of pressure right now, visualize the skillful hands of the divine Potter using it for good in your life...You can trust His dexterous and expert fingers not to harm, but to help you...God can take our sins and shame and spin them into a design that glorifies Him."

Dr. James MacDonald in his article, "The Potter's Wheel", asks us to "Picture a potter's wheel. The potter spins the turnstile and shapes a mound of clay into a vase, a cup, or a dish. By applying the appropriate pressure from his hands, he works the clay into a work of art. Now picture your life on that wheel. God's hand is purposeful, the pressure is the right amount in the right places. Is it sometimes painful? Almost always. Do you want to resist the process? Naturally you do. But will you trust that He will bring a good result through your being yielded to Him?"

As an ex-convict I can relate to the term "surrender". Can you? However, in this case we surrender completely to the Lordship of Jesus, and to the Potter's hands for **our** benefit – in fact, for our freedom rather than our captivity or incarceration. In an article entitled "Reasons to Surrender", Dr. Charles Stanley writes, "Yielding to Him means following His way in attitude, words, thoughts, and deeds – and doing so unapologetically, unwaveringly, fearlessly."

Complete surrender and willing submission are keys to love-motivated obedience leading to an intimate personal relationship with Jesus. Have you truly surrendered to the Hands of our Potter?

SOME RELEVANT SCRIPTURE PASSAGES

John 10:10 Jesus said, "The thief comes only to steal and kill and destroy; I have come that they may have life, and have it to the full."

Romans 8:28-29 "And we know that in all things God works for the good of those who love him, who have been called according to his purpose. For those God foreknew he also predestined to be conformed to the image of his Son, that he might be the firstborn among many brothers and sisters."

Jeremiah 29:11-14 "For I know the plans I have for you," declares the Lord, "plans to prosper you and not to harm you, plans to give you hope and a future. Then you will call on me and come and pray to me, and I will listen to you. You will seek me and find me when you seek me with all your heart. I will be found by you," declares the Lord, "and will bring you back from captivity. I will gather you from all the nations and places where I have banished you," declares the Lord, "and will bring you back to the place from which I carried you into exile."

Romans 9:20-21 "But who are you, a human being, to talk back to God? Shall what is formed say to the one who formed it, 'Why did you make me like this?' Does not the potter have the right to make out of the same lump of clay some pottery for special purposes and some for common use?"

Isaiah 64:8 "Yet you, Lord, are our Father. We are the clay, you are the potter; we are all the work of your hand."

Jeremiah 18:1-6 "This is the word that came to Jeremiah from the Lord: 'Go down to the potter's house, and there I will give you my message.' So I went down to the potter's house, and I saw him working at the wheel. But the pot he was shaping from the clay was marred in his hands; so the potter formed it into another pot, shaping it as seemed best to him. Then the word of the Lord came to me. He said, 'Can I not do with you, Israel, as this potter does?' declares the Lord. Like clay in the hand of the potter, so are you in my hand, Israel."

TAKEAWAY HIGHLIGHT

Complete surrender and willing submission are keys to love-motivated obedience leading to an intimate personal relationship with Jesus.

PRACTICAL APPLICATION

Spend some time thinking about the fact that our Father God already sees in His mind's eye what He wants to make of you. He already knows the full, perfect and complete plan He desires for you. Will you let Him have His way completely, or will you hold back? Tell Him you trust Him enough to be patient during the progression of His creative work in you. Your intimacy of relationship is directly related to how much you willingly surrender and submit.

WANT TO KNOW MORE?

Write to us to request the two discipleship teachings on "Surrender and Submission". Mail it to: Freedom in Jesus Prison Ministries, Attn: Teachings, P.O. Box 939, Levelland, TX 79336.

Are you sure you know Jesus? An intimate relationship with Jesus starts the minute we repent, surrender, believe the Gospel, and are born again...

ARE YOU SURE YOU KNOW JESUS?

God's Forgiveness of Us

Our relationship with God begins when we believe and receive God's forgiveness of us, and truly repent by turning from our old way of life. Surely, all of us know we need plenty of forgiveness! Amen?

I was saved as a young boy in a Baptist church where my family attended. However, for most of my life I did not attend church or make any serious attempt to follow Jesus. If you have ever previously read my testimony, you will remember that I sinned more and more, indulged in many addictions, and descended into depravity after God turned me over to my own desires and reprobation. I was guilty of almost everything Paul describes about this condition in Romans 1:18-32. Eventually my sin landed me in prison with a total of six years to do.

Having been in an emotional and mental state of severe and frequently suicidal depression for years, I believed for the longest time the lie of the enemy that there was no hope of anything ever getting better. Additionally, I believed his lie that I had gone too far and done too much for God to forgive me. I was overcome with guilt, regret, remorse and shame. Have you felt this way?

RBC Ministries, in their booklet on "The Forgiveness of God" says, "If we believe our emotions, we may feel we have gone too far. Our self-contempt seems deserved. But there's hope. God wants us to believe in His ability to forgive sins we cannot forget. God is angry at sin, but His anger is not a denial of His love...The truth is that His love is equal to His anger, and because of His love He found a way to show mercy. He sent His Son Jesus.

"God's justice–which demanded punishment for sinners–was satisfied by Jesus. The payment for our sin came at heaven's expense...God built a two-lane bridge of mercy and justice over the chasm of sin separating us and Him. When Jesus was crucified, God accepted the sacrifice as sufficient payment for our sin. Justice was satisfied...Three days later, Christ rose bodily from the dead. By the miracle of the resurrection He showed heaven's acceptance of His sacrifice.

"Our sin was forgiven. Our guilt was removed. By one man, once and for all! Because of the unlimited scope of Christ's death on the cross, we have received forgiveness not only for past sins, but for all sins – past, present, and future...The moment we trust Christ as Savior, we are given immunity from punishment. The issue is settled: Our case is closed and God will not open the files of our guilt again. Just as the courts of earth honor the principle of double jeopardy, heaven will not judge twice those whose sins have been punished in Christ. We will not be tried again for the sins He bore in our place."

Jesus was made sin with our sinfulness, so that we could be made righteous with His righteousness. God declares as righteous all those who appeal to the death of Christ as payment for their sin. No sin is excluded. We are saved by faith alone in Christ alone. There is nothing in the entire universe more powerful than the Blood of Jesus that takes away our sin. When we do not deny the Spirit–and thereby accept by faith what Jesus did for us–there is no sin (and no sinner) beyond God's love and forgiveness.

In an article entitled, "The Forgiveness of our Sins", Dr. Charles Stanley wrote, "Based on the authority of the Bible, I can tell you without reservation that God loves you, and He forgives everyone who trusts Christ as Savior. Scripture says:

- With His blood, Jesus paid our entire sin debt and obtained our full pardon (Matt. 26:28). Every sin—without exception—is covered (Col. 2:13-14).
- Forgiveness is given to everyone who believes in Jesus (Acts 10:43) and remains available to all believers (1 John 1:9).
- Our pardon for sin is based on the riches of our Father's grace, which always exceeds the offense (Eph. 1:7; Rom. 5:20).
- God doesn't count past, present, or future sins against us (Rom. 8:1; 2 Cor. 5:19).

"To reconcile us to Himself, God sent His Son to die in our place. He accepted Christ's sacrifice as payment in full for our transgressions. He offers forgiveness solely on the basis of our relationship with Jesus, not on our behavior. Because of our faith in Christ's completed work on the cross, we can be assured that we have received and will continue to receive His divine mercy.

"Scripture assures us that no transgression is beyond the scope of God's pardon. This isn't license to sin—far from it! Divine forgiveness should instead motivate a passion for holiness. If you're struggling to accept God's forgiveness, reread the verses above, and be thankful for such a great gift."

The Bible is filled with declarations of God's love and forgiveness. Your sins are not excluded. This was a major realization for me. I knew I could start over. I found present and eternal hope, and freedom, in Jesus! Receive God's forgiveness.

SOME RELEVANT SCRIPTURE PASSAGES

I John 1:9 "If we confess our sins, he is faithful and just and will forgive us our sins and purify us from all unrighteousness."

II Chronicles 7:14 "...if my people, who are called by my name, will humble themselves and pray and seek my face and turn from their wicked ways, then will I hear from heaven and will forgive their sin and will heal their land."

Colossians 2:13 "When you were dead in your sins and in the un-circumcision of your sinful nature, God made you alive with Christ. He forgave us all our sins..."

Psalm 103:11-12 "For as high as the heavens are above the earth, so great is his love for those who fear him; as far as the east is from the west, so far has he removed our transgressions from us."

Micah 7:18-19 "Who is a God like you, who pardons sin and forgives the transgression of the remnant of his inheritance? You do not stay angry forever but delight to show mercy. You will again have compassion on us; you will tread our sins underfoot and hurl all our iniquities into the depths of the sea."

Psalm 32:1-5 "Blessed is he whose transgressions are forgiven, whose sins are covered. Blessed is the man whose sin the LORD does not count against him and in whose spirit is no deceit. When I kept silent, my bones wasted away through my groaning all day long. For day and night your hand was heavy upon me; my strength was sapped as in the heat of summer. Then I acknowledged my sin to you and did not cover up my iniquity. I said, 'I will confess my transgressions to the LORD'— and you forgave the guilt of my sin."

Other passages: John 3:16; Psalm 130:3-4; Psalm 86:5; Proverbs 28:13; Jeremiah 31:34; Isaiah 44:22; Isaiah 55:6-7.

TAKEAWAY HIGHLIGHT

The Bible is filled with declarations of God's love and forgiveness. Your sins are not excluded. Our relationship with God begins when we believe and receive God's forgiveness of us, and truly repent by turning from our old way of life.

PRACTICAL APPLICATION

Think about how many sinners in the Bible we are given examples of that God forgave. Do you sometimes wonder if God can really forgive and utilize you? Look what He did for others:

Adam and Eve – The first humans to sin also became the first to experience God's forgiveness (Gen. 3).

Moses – Although he murdered an Egyptian in anger, God chose him to deliver His people from slavery; to take them to the promised land; to spend time personally in God's presence; and, to become known as a "friend of God" (Ex. 2,3,33,34).

Aaron – Although he was involved in making a golden calf, Aaron later was head of the priesthood (Ex. 32; Lev. 8).

Aaron and Miriam – When they opposed Moses' God-given authority, Miriam was stricken with leprosy. But they confessed and were forgiven and cleansed (Num. 12).

Eliphaz, Bildad, Zophar – These men falsely accused Job and misrepresented God, but they were forgiven (Job 42).

Rahab – This Jericho prostitute turned to the Lord of Israel and became part of Jesus' family tree (Josh. 2; Matt. 1:5).

David – Although he was guilty of murder and adultery, David repented and confessed his sin. He was spoken of as a man after God's own heart (II Sam. 11-12; Ps. 51).

Matthew – This tax collector with a bad reputation became Christ's disciple (Matt. 9:9-13).

A Criminal – When he cried out to Jesus on the cross, this thief was welcomed into paradise (Lk. 23:40-43).

Peter – Though he denied Christ three times, Peter became a pillar in the church (Mk. 14:66-72; Jn. 21:15-19).

A Woman Caught in Adultery – Her accusers backed away and Christ forgave her sins (John 8:1-11).

Paul – Killer of Christians and self-confessed "chief of sinners", Paul is a prime example of the grace of God (Acts 9; I Tim. 1:15).

Corinthian Believers – Once they were idolaters, adulterers, homosexuals, thieves, greedy, slanderers, and swindlers, but then they experienced God's forgiveness (I Cor. 6:9-11).

Spend a few minutes re-reading these examples. God can still utilize you. He has a plan for your life. What He did for others, He will do for you!!!

WANT TO KNOW MORE?

Write to us to request the discipleship teaching on "God's Forgiveness of Us". Mail it to: Freedom in Jesus Prison Ministries, Attn: Teachings, P.O. Box 939, Levelland, TX 79336.

An intimate relationship with Jesus starts the minute we truly repent, surrender, believe the Gospel, and are born again. Have you ever truly repented and turned from your lifestyle of sin?

True Repentance

The Bible is very clear that true repentance is required for effective salvation. There are many scriptures in both the Old and New Testaments stressing the importance of true repentance. The Bible says to "Repent, and believe the Gospel"; "Repent, and be saved"; and, "Repent, and be baptized." Are you certain that you have come to salvation by way of true repentance?

A decision to accept Jesus as Savior is not effective if it does not lead to a change of direction – away from sin, towards God. Repentance is not an emotion – for example, not the feeling of "I am sorry", or, "I feel bad about what I've done" – rather, it is a decision. It is like deciding to make a "U-turn" on a highway. You are then headed in the opposite direction from where you were going. Someone in true repentance does not just say "I'm sorry I did that"; they will also live a different life demonstrating a new mind-set of "I won't do it again".

The Greek words translated as "repentance" in the New Testament mean "to think differently", "a reversal of a decision", "to change your mind", "to turn about in opinion", "to turn about from an intended way", and to change "attitudes, thoughts and behaviors concerning the demands of God for right living". Similarly, Webster's dictionary defines "repent" as "to turn from sin and resolve to reform one's life".

There are over 70 scriptures about repentance. Some of them include: Psalm 51:17; Matthew 3:1-2, 11; Matthew 4:17; Mark 1:4, 14-15; Mark 6:12; Luke 5:32; Luke 15:7; Acts 2:38; Acts 3:19; Acts 11:18; II Corinthians 7:9-10; II Timothy 2:25, II Peter 3:9; and, Revelation 3:19.

True repentance is not just a change of mind. It is also a change of attitude and heart. It involves a Godly sorrow and regret because of personal sin, and results in a radical break with sin. J.C Ryle said, "The beginning of the way to heaven is to feel that we are on the way to hell". Dr. Charles Stanley said, "An unrepentant man or woman is not condemned by God (to hell), rather has chosen to remain in the company of all those condemned by their own free will".

In the Old Testament, Psalm 51, David gives us a great example of an attitude of true repentance. He has a "broken spirit and contrite heart" (Psalm 51:17) over his actions of adultery and murder surrounding his affair with Bathsheba. David knew he could not come to God with his own self-righteousness; rather, he approached God with a broken heart and a spirit willing to change. Lydia Reimer writes, "Repentance tears down the wall of separation that stands between us and God. It prepares us for His presence." Be sure to read all of Psalm 51 carefully to get a more complete understanding of David's exemplary approach to repentance.

The parable about the prodigal son in Luke 15:11-24, is one of best teachings of Jesus that illustrates the kind of repentance it takes to go home to the Father. The "U-turn" occurs in verse 17 where it says "he came to himself", or "he came to his senses". He made a decision to turn around and go home. Then he took action by getting up out of his mess and actually going along the road home – in a different direction than when he left home earlier when "he set off for a distant country and there squandered his wealth in wild living" (Luke 15:13).

Bible teacher R.B. Thieme, Jr. writes, "What does it mean to come to yourself? It means to look at life from the biblical perspective: to face up to the situation as it really exists; to recognize the sins in your own life; to stop rationalizing or justifying your sins; to stop blaming God or someone else (operation patsy) and to actually acknowledge your sin – to recognize that you are wrong and contrary to the Word of God."

In *Mere Christianity*, author C.S. Lewis is describing the "hole" we find ourselves in before we come to our senses like the prodigal son. "Now what sort of 'hole' had (he) got himself into? He had tried to set up on his own, to behave as if he belonged to himself. In other words, fallen man is not simply an imperfect creature who needs improvement: he is a rebel who must lay down his arms. Laying down your arms, surrendering, saying you are sorry, realizing that you have been on the wrong track and getting ready to start life all over again from the ground floor – that is the only way out of our 'hole'. This process of surrender – this movement full speed astern (in the opposite direction) – is what Christians call repentance."

In summary, "true repentance" involves a real change of heart, leading to a complete change of mind, which in turn leads to a change of direction–away from sin and toward the Father. It is like making a U-turn when you are going the wrong way down a one-way street. You realize in your mind that you are headed the wrong way, and you have a change of heart that makes you want to turn completely around to go in the correct but opposite direction. There will be visible evidence of the change, and you will resolve not to turn back around the wrong way.

In our new direction, if we temporarily stumble, we do not let the enemy's lies convince us to turn permanently back to our old direction. Instead, we quickly confess our sin (1 John 1:9), and we allow the

Holy Spirit to empower and encourage us to get up and continue on the right path towards the Father. True repentance has evidence of a permanently changed direction, and a significantly changed life.

If you ever prayed a prayer of salvation before but nothing ever changed about the direction of your life, I strongly suggest to you that you did not repent. If you did not repent, you did not get saved! God heard your words but He read your heart. If you were not ready to turn from your old way of living and do your best to follow Jesus, then you did not repent. In your mind you may have wanted the benefits of salvation, but in your heart you were not really willing to allow Jesus to be the Lord of your life.

Has true repentance changed your direction? Have you made a "U-turn"? If not, please "run to God with repentance in one hand and praise in the other" (Tommy Tenney). Like me, you will be glad you did!!!

SOME RELEVANT SCRIPTURE PASSAGES

Isaiah 30:15 "For thus the Lord God, the Holy One of Israel, has said, 'In repentance and rest you will be saved, in quietness and trust is your strength.'"

Acts 3:19 "Therefore repent and return, so that your sins may be wiped away, in order that times of refreshing may come from the presence of the Lord."

Romans 2:4 "Do you think lightly of the riches of His kindness and tolerance and patience, not knowing that the kindness of God leads you to repentance?"

James 4:8 "Draw near to God and He will draw near to you. Cleanse your hands, you sinners; and purify your hearts, you double-minded."

1 John 1:9 "If we confess our sins, He is faithful and righteous to forgive us our sins and to cleanse us from all unrighteousness."

Luke 5:32 "I have not come to call the righteous but sinners to repentance."

Luke 15:7 "I tell you that in the same way, there will be more joy in heaven over one sinner who repents than over ninety-nine righteous persons who need no repentance."

Luke 24:47 "Repentance for forgiveness of sins would be proclaimed in His name to all the nations, beginning from Jerusalem."

2 Corinthians 7:9-10 "I now rejoice, not that you were made sorrowful, but that you were made sorrowful to the point of repentance; for you were made sorrowful according to the will of God, so that you might not suffer loss in anything through us. For the sorrow that is according to the will of God produces a repentance without regret, leading to salvation, but the sorrow of the world produces death."

2 Peter 3:9 "The Lord is not slow about His promise, as some count slowness, but is patient toward you, not wishing for any to perish but for all to come to repentance."

Mark 1:15 "The time is fulfilled, and the kingdom of God is at hand; repent and believe in the gospel."

Ezekiel 18: 21-22 "If the wicked man turns from all his sins which he has committed and observes all My statutes and practices justice and righteousness, he shall surely live; he shall not die. All his transgressions which he has committed will not be remembered against him; because of his righteousness which he has practiced, he will live."

TAKEAWAY HIGHLIGHT

True repentance involves a real change of heart, leading to a complete change of mind, which in turn leads to a change of direction–away from sin and toward the Father. In our new direction, if we temporarily stumble, we do not let the enemy's lies convince us to turn permanently back to our old direction. Instead, we quickly confess our sin (1 John 1:9), and we allow the Holy Spirit to empower and encourage us to get up and continue on the right path towards the Father. True repentance has evidence of a permanently changed direction, and a significantly changed life.

PRACTICAL APPLICATION

Take some quiet time to consider if you have truly repented of your old ways. Are you cooperating with the Holy Spirit as He leads you daily on the right path? Was there ever a time when you were truly sorrowful for your sin and told God about it? Did you change your direction away from sin to determinedly walk towards God? When you stumble do you get up quickly, repent and keep headed the right direction?

WANT TO KNOW MORE?

Write to us to request the discipleship teaching on "Repentance". Mail it to: Freedom in Jesus Prison Ministries, Attn: Teachings, P.O. Box 939, Levelland, TX 79336.

An intimate relationship with Jesus starts the minute we truly repent, surrender, believe the Gospel, and are born again. Have you believed the Gospel of Jesus Christ and been born again?

The Gospel of Jesus Christ

The Apostle Paul, in Romans 1:16, wrote, "For I am not ashamed of the gospel, because it is the power of God that brings salvation to everyone who believes: first to the Jew, then to the Gentile."

But what exactly is the gospel to which Paul is referring?

It is the Gospel of Jesus Christ. I found a good summary at *www. GotQuestions.org* which I present here in the following five paragraphs:

"The word *gospel* means 'good news,' so the gospel of Christ is the good news of His coming to provide forgiveness of sins for all who will believe (Colossians 1:14; Romans 10:9). Since the first man's sin, mankind has been under the condemnation of God (Romans 5:12). Because everyone breaks God's perfect law by committing sin, everyone is guilty (Romans 3:23). The punishment for the crime of sin is physical death (Romans 6:23) and then an eternity spent in a place of punishment (Revelation 20:15; Matthew 25:46). This eternal separation from God is also called the "second death" (Revelation 20:14–15).

"The bad news that all are guilty of sin and condemned by God is countered by the gospel, the good news of Jesus Christ. God, because of His love for the world, has made a way for man to be forgiven of their sins (John 3:16). He sent His Son, Jesus Christ, to take the sins of mankind on Himself through death on a cross (1 Peter 2:24). In placing our sin on Christ, God ensured that all who will believe in the name of Jesus will be forgiven (Acts 10:43). Jesus' resurrection guarantees the justification of all who believe (Romans 4:25).

"The Bible specifies the content of the gospel message: "Now, brothers and sisters, I want to remind you of the gospel I preached to you, which you received and on which you have taken your stand. By this gospel you are saved, if you hold firmly to the word I preached to you. Otherwise, you have believed in vain. For what I received I passed on to you as of first importance: that Christ died for our sins according to the Scriptures, that he was buried, that he was raised on the third day according to the Scriptures, and that he appeared to Cephas, and then to the Twelve. After that, he appeared to more than five hundred of the brothers and sisters at the same time" (1 Corinthians 15:1–6). In this passage, Paul emphasizes the primacy of the gospel—it is of "first importance." The gospel message contains two historical facts, both supported by Scripture: Christ's death and His resurrection. Both those facts are bolstered by other proofs: Christ's death is proved by His burial, and His resurrection is proved by the eyewitnesses.

"The gospel of Jesus Christ is the good news that God provided the way for man to be freed from the penalty of sin (John 14:6; Romans 6:23). Everyone dies physically, but those who believe in Jesus Christ are promised a physical resurrection unto eternal life (John 11:23–26). Those who reject Christ will not only die physically but will undergo a "second death," which the Bible describes as an eternal lake of fire (Revelation 20:13–14). Jesus is the only One in whom salvation can be found (Acts 4:12).

"The gospel of Jesus Christ is the best news anyone will ever hear, and what a person does with this news will determine where he or she spends eternity. God is calling you to choose life. Call on the name of the Lord and be saved (Romans 10:13)."

From a tract, "What is the Gospel", Greg Gilbert explains in the following three paragraphs what our response should be to hearing the Gospel:

"What does God expect us to do with the information that Jesus died in our place so we can be saved from God's righteous wrath against our sins? He expects us to respond with repentance and faith.

"To repent of our sins means to turn away from our rebellion against God. Repentance doesn't mean we'll bring an immediate end to our sinning. It does mean, though, that we'll never again live at peace with our sins.

"Not only that, but we also turn to God in faith. Faith is reliance. It's a promise-founded trust in the risen Jesus to save you from your sins. If God is ever to count us righteous, he'll have to do it on the basis of someone else's record, someone who's qualified to stand in as our substitute. And that's what happens when a person is saved by Jesus: All our sins are credited to Jesus who took the punishment for them, and the perfect righteousness of Jesus is then credited to us when we place our trust in what he has done for us! That's what faith means—to rely on Jesus, to trust in him alone to stand in our place and win a righteous verdict from God!"

Because of the times, it is so very important that those of us who are true believers let our lights shine in the midst of ever-increasing darkness. We must be salt that flavors and preserves. As chaos increases, our peace, calm and joy in the middle of the storm will draw unbelievers to come to us and ask how they can have what we possess in Christ Jesus. Let the reality and sincerity of your genuine faith be evident to all in the way you live daily. Actions speak louder than words.

The purpose of knowing the Gospel of Jesus Christ is so that you are better equipped with the tools you need to explain your eternal life and hope in Jesus to others. It should also solidify your confidence in your own salvation as you take time to meditate on the Word of God, and especially on the unconditional, everlasting love of the Father towards you. The Gospel is more than most of us realize! The scriptures below are selected to show you and others the magnificence and wonder of His complete salvation available for those who truly believe, receive, and repent.

I encourage you to read this chapter often so you can use it to help and encourage others when they come to you. We are entering the times when Jesus said, "men's hearts would be failing them for fear of looking after those things coming upon the Earth." We must "work while it is day because night is coming when no man can work." Your prayers will become ever more powerful as you study and believe the Word of God. Stay submitted and surrendered daily to the Lordship of Jesus and the Leadership of the Holy Spirit.

Let me strongly encourage you to realize what an outstanding opportunity God has given you to positively impact the Kingdom during the coming days. You are God's Ambassador. You are able to minister more effectively and timely than any outside volunteer coming in to a prison on a periodic basis could ever do. Ask God for more boldness to speak the Word of God (Acts 4:27-31; 5:41-42).

I pray you will personally rededicate your life to go "all in, and all out" for Jesus. Ask the Holy Spirit to set you apart from the world, and make you ever more holy daily. Make up your mind to do the best you can to be obedient in every area of your life, and repent quickly if you fall. This is absolutely not the time to be "lukewarm", "on the fence", or "playing with God".

SOME RELEVANT SCRIPTURE PASSAGES

As true followers of Jesus Christ, we must always be prepared to respond when someone asks us about our faith in Christ Jesus – or maybe they want to know about our peace, calm and joy in the middle of the crazy, dark days our world is experiencing. Here are a number of scriptures that, when considered together, give a clear picture of the Good News of the Gospel of Jesus Christ:

1 Peter 3:15-16 "But in your hearts revere Christ as Lord. Always be prepared to give an answer to everyone who asks you to give the reason for the hope that you have. But do this with gentleness and respect, keeping a clear conscience, so that those who speak maliciously against your good behavior in Christ may be ashamed of their slander."

John 3:16-17 "For God so loved the world that he gave his one and only Son, that whoever believes in him shall not perish but have eternal life. For God did not send his Son into the world to condemn the world, but to save the world through him."

1 Corinthians 15:1-8 "Now, brothers and sisters, I want to remind you of the gospel I preached to you, which you received and on which you have taken your stand. By this gospel you are saved, if you hold firmly to the word I preached to you. Otherwise, you have believed in vain.

"For what I received I passed on to you as of first importance: that Christ died for our sins according to the Scriptures, that he was buried, that he was raised on the third day according to the Scriptures, and that he appeared to Cephas, and then to the Twelve. After that, he appeared to more than five hundred of the brothers and sisters at the same time, most of whom are still living, though some have fallen asleep. Then he appeared to James, then to all the apostles, and last of all he appeared to me also, as to one abnormally born."

Colossians 1:15-23 "The Son is the image of the invisible God, the firstborn over all creation. For in him all things were created: things in heaven and on earth, visible and invisible, whether thrones or powers or rulers or authorities; all things have been created through him and for him. He is before all things, and in him all things hold together. And he is the head of the body, the church; he is the beginning and the firstborn from among the dead, so that in everything he might have the supremacy. For God was pleased to have all his fullness dwell in him, and through him to reconcile to himself all things, whether things on earth or things in heaven, by making peace through his blood, shed on the cross. Once you were alienated from God and were enemies in your minds because of your evil behavior. But now he has reconciled you by Christ's physical body through death to present you holy in his sight, without blemish and free from accusation— if you continue in your faith, established and firm, and do not move from the hope held out in the gospel. This is the gospel that you heard and that has been proclaimed to every creature under heaven, and of which I, Paul, have become a servant."

Philippians 2:5-11 "In your relationships with one another, have the same mindset as Christ Jesus:

"Who, being in very nature God,
did not consider equality with God something to be used to his

own advantage;
rather, he made himself nothing
by taking the very nature of a servant,
being made in human likeness.
And being found in appearance as a man,
he humbled himself
by becoming obedient to death—
even death on a cross!

"Therefore God exalted him to the highest place
and gave him the name that is above every name,
that at the name of Jesus every knee should bow,
in heaven and on earth and under the earth,
and every tongue acknowledge that Jesus Christ is Lord,
to the glory of God the Father."

Acts 10:34-43 Then Peter began to speak: "I now realize how true it is that God does not show favoritism but accepts from every nation the one who fears him and does what is right. You know the message God sent to the people of Israel, announcing the good news of peace through Jesus Christ, who is Lord of all. You know what has happened throughout the province of Judea, beginning in Galilee after the baptism that John preached— how God anointed Jesus of Nazareth with the Holy Spirit and power, and how he went around doing good and healing all who were under the power of the devil, because God was with him.

"We are witnesses of everything he did in the country of the Jews and in Jerusalem. They killed him by hanging him on a cross, but God raised him from the dead on the third day and caused him to be seen. He was not seen by all the people, but by witnesses whom God had already chosen—by us who ate and drank with him after he rose from the dead. He commanded us to preach to the people and to testify that he is the one whom God appointed as judge of the living and the dead. All the prophets testify about him that everyone who believes in him receives forgiveness of sins through his name."

Acts 5:30-32 "The God of our ancestors raised Jesus from the dead—whom you killed by hanging him on a cross. God exalted him to his own right hand as Prince and Savior that he might bring Israel to repentance and forgive their sins. We are witnesses of these things, and so is the Holy Spirit, whom God has given to those who obey him."

Acts 2:22-24; 32-33 "Fellow Israelites, listen to this: Jesus of Nazareth was a man accredited by God to you by miracles, wonders and signs, which God did among you through him, as you yourselves know. This man was handed over to you by God's deliberate plan and foreknowledge; and you, with the help of wicked men, put him to death by nailing him to the cross. But God raised him from the dead, freeing him from the agony of death, because it was impossible for death to keep its hold on him... **32** God has raised this Jesus to life, and we are all witnesses of it. Exalted to the right hand of God, he has received from the Father the promised Holy Spirit and has poured out what you now see and hear."

Hebrews 1:1-3 "In the past God spoke to our ancestors through the prophets at many times and in various ways, but in these last days he has spoken to us by his Son, whom he appointed heir of all things, and through whom also he made the universe. The Son is the radiance of God's glory and the exact representation of his being, sustaining all things by his powerful word. After he had provided purification for sins, he sat down at the right hand of the Majesty in heaven."

Other important Scriptures: John 1:1-5, 9-14; Isaiah 53; Psalm 22; Acts

8:30-35; Romans 10:9-15; Acts 13:26-39; Titus 2:11-14; Colossians 1:13-14; 2 Corinthians 5:17-21.

TAKEAWAY HIGHLIGHT

The gospel of Jesus Christ is the best news anyone will ever hear, and what a person does with this news will determine where he or she spends eternity. God is calling you to choose life. Call on the name of the Lord and be saved (Romans 10:13).

PRACTICAL APPLICATION

If you have never believed the Gospel, confessed Jesus as your Savior and Lord, repented and been "born again", and you would like to do that now, please turn to pages 333-334. If you made this decision, congratulations!

From the scriptures presented above, write up your own simple summary of what is the Gospel of Jesus Christ. Think about this chapter deeply. Spend some time talking to God the Father about how your life has changed since you believed and received the "Good News". Ask the Holy Spirit to bring someone across your path who needs to know Jesus. Pray for specific people who you know are not yet believers to come to the point where they desire a personal relationship with Jesus.

WANT TO KNOW MORE?

Write to us to request the discipleship teaching on "The Gospel of Jesus Christ". Mail it to: Freedom in Jesus Prison Ministries, Attn: Teachings, P.O. Box 939, Levelland, TX 79336.

A prevalent false belief is that there are several paths to God. Do not be deceived, Jesus is the only way to our Creator, Father God. Let's examine this truth more...

Jesus is the Only Way

Do not be deceived; Jesus is the only way to God.

When four of Jesus' closest disciples went to Him privately to ask Him what would be the signs of His Second Coming and of the "end of the age", Jesus warned them several times not to be deceived. Surely, we are even now seeing all the signs come to pass before our very eyes just as He foretold. Likewise, we are already seeing signs of the great deception.

I believe the greatest part of this deception is to try to convince the world that there are more ways to God and Heaven than just through Jesus. THAT IS A LIE. DO NOT BE DECEIVED. The only way to Father God is through the finished work of Jesus Christ of Nazareth at the cross and through His resurrection.

Many are suggesting that Jesus is just one way to Heaven, not necessarily the only way. This has reportedly come from even a few influential leaders within "Christian" circles! It is heresy to espouse this view.

In this age of secular humanism where mankind says they determine their own fate and future, not God, we as Christians are susceptible to their attempts to convince everyone that truth is "relative" to what is going on in society, and so it changes with the times. We are urged to be tolerant of everyone for every reason. No-one must be "offended". We are told that everyone must be "included" and not "confronted" in any way about anything.

While we must certainly treat those who do not agree with us with respect, kindness and gentleness, we must be very careful not to compromise on Who we know is Truth–the Son of God, Jesus Christ. Jesus makes it very clear that He is the only way, the only truth and the only life. He assures us that no-one gets to the Father except through Him (see John 14:6).

Peter preached about this truth about Jesus in Acts 4:12 when he said, "Salvation is found in no one else, for there is no other name under heaven given to mankind by which we must be saved." Isaiah quotes Jehovah, Father God, in Isaiah 43:11 as saying, "I, even I, am the Lord, and apart from me there is no savior."

In a devotional entitled, "Jesus: The Only Way to Heaven", Dr. Charles Stanley writes,

"While the world has many religions, there is only one way to heaven. Jesus clearly states that 'no-one comes to the father but through me' (John 14:6). To emphasize this point, He used several picturesque descriptions, calling Himself the Living Bread, the Door, the Good Shepherd, and the Way (John 6:51; 10:9-11; 14:6)."

Dr. Stanley concludes his devotional with, "Scripture declares that there is but one way to Heaven – through faith in Jesus Christ. His gospel is a straight path from the pit of sin to the Glory of Heaven, with the promise of an abundant life in between. What we must do is go through the Door and follow the Way; then the Living Bread will sustain us."

Pastor Max Lucado wrote, "As long as Jesus is one of many options and ways to heaven, He is no option at all. As long as you can carry your own burdens, you don't need a burden bearer. As long as your situation brings you no grief, you will receive no comfort. And, as long as you can take Him or leave Him you might as well leave Him because He won't be taken half-heartedly."

I urge you to study carefully what Jesus revealed in Matthew 21, Mark 13, and Luke 21. Paul gives us further insight in 1 Thessalonians 4:13 – 5:11; 2 Thessalonians 2:1-17; 1 Timothy 4:1-2; and 2 Timothy 3:1-5. Read the visions of Daniel the prophet in Daniel chapters 7, 11 and 12. Of course, John tells us about the end of the age in Revelation. After studying these passages, I am certain you will agree that surely these times in which we are living are "the last days".

Brothers and Sisters, there is a sense of urgency in me to implore you to be careful you are not deceived – Jesus Christ of Nazareth is the only way to the Father in Heaven. Ask the Father for keen discernment through His Holy Spirit to recognize and avoid the coming great deception.

Jesus is coming back for His people (John 14:1-3). He is coming quickly, in an instant of time (Matthew 24:27). Jesus is coming soon, any day now (Revelation 22:12-13). Are you sure you're ready (Matthew 24:42-44)?

SOME RELEVANT SCRIPTURE PASSAGES

John 14:6 Jesus said, "I am the way, the truth, and the life. No one comes to the Father except through Me."

John 11:25-26 Jesus said, "I am the resurrection and the life. He who believes in me though he may die, he shall live."

Acts 4:12 "Salvation is found in no one else, for there is no other name under heaven given to mankind by which we must be saved."

John 6:44 Jesus said, "No one can come to me unless the Father who sent me draws them, and I will raise them up at the last day."

Romans 5:8-9 "But God demonstrates his own love for us in this: While we were still sinners, Christ died for us. Since we have now been justified by his blood, how much more shall we be saved from God's wrath through him!"

Romans 6:23 "For the wages of sin is death, but the gift of God is eternal life in Christ Jesus our Lord."

Romans 10:9-10 "If you declare with your mouth, 'Jesus is Lord,' and believe in your heart that God raised him from the dead, you will be saved. For it is with your heart that you believe and are justified, and it is with your mouth that you profess your faith and are saved."

Isaiah 43:11 Jehovah said, "I, even I, am the Lord, and apart from me there is no savior."

TAKEAWAY HIGHLIGHT

"As long as Jesus is one of many options and ways to heaven, He is no option at all. As long as you can carry your own burdens, you don't need a burden bearer. As long as your situation brings you no grief, you will receive no comfort. And, as long as you can take Him or leave Him you might as well leave Him because He won't be taken half-heartedly." Max Lucado

Practical Application

Prayerfully consider this: if Jesus is not the only way, why would God the Father make Him go through arguably the cruelest form of torture and death ever invented? If He is not Who He said He was, He is a liar, or a maniac or worse, and would not be worthy of any kind of following whatsoever. Also, he would not be "a good teacher" or "a prophet". For great background on why Jesus is the Only Way, check out the writings of Josh McDowell, *More than a Carpenter*, and Lee Strobel's book, *The Case for Christ.*

WANT TO KNOW MORE?

Write to us to request the discipleship teaching on "Jesus is the Only Way". Mail it to: Freedom in Jesus Prison Ministries, Attn: Teachings, P.O. Box 939, Levelland, TX 79336.

When a person believes and receives salvation in Jesus as the Only Way, the Father and the Son send their Holy Spirit to live in them for empowerment...

Holy Spirit Empowerment

Intimacy of relationship with the Father and the Son are available only through their Holy Spirit. Since the Holy Spirit is their gift to every believer to dwell inside them daily, we should learn all we can about the One Who is our Helper, Teacher, Counselor, Friend and Guide. True power to walk out the Christian life in love-motivated obedience is available only in and through the Holy Spirit.

The same power that raised Jesus from the dead dwells in you. The Father's power on Earth is administered only through His Holy Spirit. The creative power of God is the Holy Spirit. The Spirit of the Father, the Spirit of the Son, is not only around you, He lives in you! What a mystery, "Christ in you, the hope of Glory"! See Colossians 1:27.

R.B. Thieme, III wrote, "The Holy Spirit is the unseen power of God, the Person through whom divine power is conveyed."

When I was still incarcerated I saw several Christians who were released before me leave, only to return to prison within a year or so. I had also heard of others that were following Jesus in prison with me who, after their release, fell away from their relationship with Jesus Christ and returned to "the world". I don't know if they returned to a physical prison, but they returned to their emotional and spiritual prisons from which they had once been set free. I know most of them had every good and honest intention to keep walking with Him, but many were powerless to resist old habits, places, and people.

Since I have been released, however, I know personally many former offenders who were transformed in prison, and who are still walking in Christ many years later. They are strong soldiers in God's army. I have seen God working in the lives of their families. I have seen them continue to prosper and experience the abundant life Jesus came to give us (John 10:10). Many have their own effective ministries now. Broken relationships have been restored. Broken hearts have been healed.

What makes the difference in these two groups of people? What made the difference with me? It was clearly the "baptism in the Holy Spirit". I firmly believe that the extra level of empowerment brought about by being baptized (immersed) in the Holy Spirit makes all the difference in enabling and empowering us to walk out our faith effectively and genuinely in prison and then, after our release, in "the free world".

When we accept the finished work of Jesus at the Cross, and confess His resurrection as the Son of God, the Holy Spirit comes to live in us. We "possess" the Spirit, and He begins His ongoing work of sanctification to steadily make our "new man" conform to the image of Christ. However, true empowerment – God's own power – comes to us, and for us, as we totally submit to the Holy Spirit and allow Him to "possess" us–one giant step more than us merely "possessing" Him inside us. We actually are able to allow Him to "possess" us!

We are baptized (immersed) into water as an outward representation of the inward change in us. We are buried with Christ in baptism (our "old man" died); and, we are raised to walk in newness of life (our "new man" came alive). But the Book of Acts makes it clear we should also desire to be baptized (immersed) into the Holy Spirit to receive the same power that resurrected Jesus from the dead – the power to walk out this new life in the way He desires for us. He in us, and us in Him!

We know the verse that says, "Greater is He that is in me than He that is in the world" (I John 4:4). So, the Holy Spirit is in us. We possess Him. But another verse we know is "I can do all things through Him who strengthens me" (Phil. 4:13). That verse is also translated as, "I can do all things through the One who empowers me within". It is the Holy Spirit that empowers us within so that we can do everything the Father desires for us to do, and assigns us to do! But we must let Him do it. We must let Him possess us.

When Jesus finished His work on earth and returned to the Father, the Father sent the Holy Spirit to earth for each of us. Jesus' followers at that time were instructed to wait until they were endued with power from on High before they began to carry out the ministry of Jesus. We should do likewise, that is, we should seek the power of the Holy Spirit before we move out among the people in the name of Jesus. We need the power of the Holy Spirit. Within our own strength, we will burn out quickly, we will not be effective, and we can even do harm to His Kingdom.

Above all, we must remember the Holy Spirit is a person, He has a personality, and He can be grieved. His purpose in coming was to teach, lead, guide, correct, protect and comfort....the Helper who would walk alongside us as well as dwell within us. However, we must yield to Him and allow Him to do His work in us. If we refuse Him, resist Him, or grieve Him, we will restrict the work that the Father wants Him to do in our lives. He is a gift from the Father, and we need Him!

We thank the Father for His gifts. He not only gave us His Son, Jesus, but He gave us His Holy Spirit. What a marvelous Father He is. When I think about it, I realize how gullible we are to believe the enemy's lie — the lie that the Holy Spirit is not for today, that we don't need Him. If anything, the truth is we need Him even more because we are living in the last of the last days when Scripture tells us that many will be deceived. The Holy Spirit can help us to not be deceived if we will let Him lead us, and recognize that we "host" Him as the very Presence of God in us. We need Him. We need Him in His fullness.

Brothers and sisters in Christ, there are difficult times coming soon in which we will be tested. We have work He has assigned us to do. ***In our own strength we will fail Him, but by His power within us working through us - His Holy Spirit - we can endure and even excel.*** We must stand firm to the end. We must be on our guard. Read closely what Jesus teaches in Mark 13:9-13:

"You must be on your guard. You will be handed over to the local councils and flogged in the synagogues. On account of me you will stand before governors and kings as witnesses to them. And the gospel must first be preached to all nations. Whenever you are arrested and brought to trial, do not worry beforehand about what to say. Just say whatever is given you at the time, for it is not you speaking, but the Holy Spirit. Brother will betray brother to death, and a father his child. Children will rebel against their parents and have them put to death. Everyone will hate you because of me, but the one who stands firm to the end will be saved."

We will not only survive, but thrive, if we have the power and discernment of the Holy Spirit. For Jesus said, "But make up your mind not to worry beforehand how you will defend yourselves. For I will give you words and wisdom that none of your adversaries will be able to resist or contradict." (Luke 21:14-15). I urge you to learn as much as possible about your Helper!

SOME RELEVANT SCRIPTURE PASSAGES

John 14:16-17 Jesus said, "And I will ask the Father, and he will give you another advocate to help you and be with you forever— the Spirit of truth. The world cannot accept him, because it neither sees him nor knows him. But you know him, for he lives with you and will be in you."

Acts 1:8 Jesus said, "But you will receive power when the Holy Spirit comes on you; and you will be my witnesses in Jerusalem, and in all Judea and Samaria, and to the ends of the earth."

Ephesians 3:20-21 "Now to him who is able to do immeasurably more than all we ask or imagine, according to his power that is at work within us, to him be glory in the church and in Christ Jesus throughout all generations, for ever and ever! Amen."

Colossians 1:27-29 "To them God has chosen to make known among the Gentiles the glorious riches of this mystery, which is Christ in you, the hope of glory. We proclaim him, admonishing and teaching everyone with all wisdom, so that we may present everyone perfect in Christ. To this end I labor, struggling with all his energy, which so powerfully works in me."

II Thessalonians 1:11-12 "With this in mind, we constantly pray for you, that our God may count you worthy of his calling, and that by his power he may fulfill every good purpose of yours and every act prompted by your faith. We pray this so that the name of our Lord Jesus may be glorified in you, and you in him, according to the grace of our God and the Lord Jesus Christ."

Philippians 2:11-13 "... and every tongue confess that Jesus Christ is Lord, to the glory of God the Father. Therefore, my dear friends, as you have always obeyed—not only in my presence, but now much more in my absence—continue to work out your salvation with fear and trembling, for it is God who works in you to will and to act according to his good purpose."

Galatians 2:20 "I have been crucified with Christ and I no longer live, but Christ lives in me. The life I live in the body, I live by faith in the Son of God, who loved me and gave himself for me."

John 20:21-22 "Jesus said, 'Peace be with you! As the Father has sent me, I am sending you.' And with that he breathed on them and said, 'Receive the Holy Spirit.'"

Acts 1:4-5 "On one occasion, while he was eating with them, he gave them this command: 'Do not leave Jerusalem, but wait for the gift my Father promised, which you have heard me speak about. For John baptized with water, but in a few days you will be baptized with the Holy Spirit.'"

TAKEAWAY HIGHLIGHT

Intimacy of relationship with the Father and the Son are available only through their Holy Spirit. Since the Holy Spirit is their gift to every believer to dwell inside them daily, we should learn all we can about the One Who is our Helper, Teacher, Counselor, Friend and Guide. True power to walk out the Christian life in love-motivated obedience is available only in and through the Holy Spirit.

PRACTICAL APPLICATION

Have you received the Baptism of the Holy Spirit? If you would like to ask Jesus to baptize you with fire and power, please see pages 335-336.

Take a few minutes to really consider and appreciate the gift the Father and Son have given you! Ask the Father to help you learn to surrender more completely daily to the power and leadership of the Holy Spirit. Study the information in the back of this book about the Holy Spirit.

WANT TO KNOW MORE?

Write to us to request the discipleship teaching on "The Father and Son Sent us a Helper – the Holy Spirit". Mail it to: Freedom in Jesus Prison Ministries, Attn: Teachings, P.O. Box 939, Levelland, TX 79336.

True intimacy of relationship with Jesus is available through the Holy Spirit to "true disciples". Are you one? Read on...

ARE YOU SURE JESUS KNOWS YOU?

Disciples of Christ

In Matthew 28:18, the last command Jesus gave His followers was to "go and make disciples" and "teach them to obey everything I have commanded you". A disciple does their best to obey Jesus. Please understand that being "a church member" does not make you a "disciple".

Chip Brogden (*www.chipbrogden.com*) teaches in his study of the Gospel of John that the Bible gives us guidance as to the attributes of a disciple:

- Disciples are proven by their fruit (John 15:8).
- Disciples are proven by their love for one another (John 13:34-35).
- Disciples are hated by the world (John 15:18-19).
- Disciples are persecuted by those who do not know God (John 15:20-21).
- Disciples should be like their teacher (Luke 6:40).
- Disciples should obey their teacher (Luke 6:46).

Since one of the definitions of a disciple is a "disciplined learner", I believe another mark of a true disciple is someone with a growing hunger and desire to learn more about following Jesus. We are commanded to make other disciples.

In your cultivation of an intimate relationship with Jesus, are you a follower of Jesus who sincerely wants to continue to learn, and to help make other disciples?

James O. Jones, Jr. was quoted on *www.allaboutfollowingjesus.org* in these three paragraphs:

"Unfortunately, there is no foolproof method to determine whether someone is a true Christ follower, for indeed only God knows the heart of any individual. However, after many years of seeking God and the truth found in His inspired Word, I have come to the conclusion that there is one definitive desire that lies in the heart of every true believer — the desire to serve and please God with one's life.

"Notice that I did not say that the individual would necessarily be living such a life, but the desire will be there. Let me say it another way — any person claiming to be a child of God who does not have the desire in his or her heart to obey, serve, and please God has either never experienced true conversion or is in a state of spiritual infancy. If you, the reader of this article, do not have such a desire to live a life of love, obedience, and service to God, then please examine your own relationship with Him. There is no Scripture that indicates a person can be a true child of God while having no desire to please Him with one's life. It is perhaps those who only go through the motions without having a personal relationship with Christ that Jesus is addressing in this passage:

"Not everyone who says to me, 'Lord, Lord,' will enter the kingdom of heaven, but only he who does the will of my Father who is in heaven.

Many will say to me on that day, 'Lord, Lord, did we not prophesy in your name, and in your name drive out demons and perform many miracles?' Then I will tell them plainly, 'I never knew you. Away from me, you evildoers!'" (Matthew 7:21-23)."

In an article entitled "Christian Discipleship" at *www.allaboutfollowingjesus.org* we find this:

"Christian discipleship is a concept that was born when Jesus Christ hand-selected His first followers. A disciple, by definition, is a convinced adherent of a school or individual. In the case of Jesus, His disciples were those who followed Him while He was on earth, as well as those who continue to follow Him and His teachings today.

"Christian discipleship begins when you make an active choice to get to know Jesus better. By God's grace, it is then accomplished in several ways:

- You can study His Word daily and spend time alone with Him in prayer.
- You can become a member of a Bible-teaching church fellowship.
- You can seek out the companionship of other Christians who are growing with Christ.
- You can participate in ministry and meet the needs of other believers.
- You can share what you're learning about Christ with others, just like Andrew, James, John, Luke, Matthew, Peter, Paul and all the original disciples did.

"Like those first twelve, you too can be a believer who becomes a follower and messenger!"

In Luke 9:23, Jesus said, "Whoever wants to be my disciple must deny themselves and take up their cross daily and follow me." Please note that being a disciple is a daily task and decision. Jesus never promised it would be easy but we know by a number of parables that it will be rewarding both in this life and in eternity in heaven.

Chip Brogden wrote in his article "The Discipleship Test" (*www.chip-brogden.com*) this paragraph:

"The Way of the Cross is a narrow way, a difficult way, but a necessary way if we ever intend to find Life. Entering the Gate is not the end of the journey; it is the beginning of the journey. It is at the end of the Path that one finds Life (Mt. 7:14), not the beginning. Jesus never made a distinction between being saved and being a disciple. He is not "Savior" for new Christians and "Lord" for older, more deeply committed Christians. Either He is Lord of all, or He isn't Lord at all."

As true disciples and followers of Jesus Christ, I believe we all need to be sure we are representing Him well to all those around us, especially as we see the day of His return fast approaching. This is surely an exciting time in which we are living! God chose for us to be here during these last minutes of the last days. We were made for such a time as this!!!

SOME RELEVANT SCRIPTURE PASSAGES

Matthew 28:18-20 "Then Jesus came to them and said, 'All authority in heaven and on earth has been given to me. Therefore go and make disciples of all nations, baptizing them in the name of the Father and of the Son and of the Holy Spirit, and teaching them to obey everything I have commanded you. And surely I am with you always, to the very end of the age.'"

Luke 9:23 "Then he said to them all: 'Whoever wants to be my disciple must deny themselves and take up their cross daily and follow me.'"

John 15:8 Jesus said, "This is to my Father's glory, that you bear much fruit, showing yourselves to be my disciples."

John 13:34-35 Jesus said, "A new command I give you: Love one another. As I have loved you, so you must love one another. By this everyone will know that you are my disciples, if you love one another."

John 15:18-21 Jesus said, "If the world hates you, keep in mind that it hated me first. If you belonged to the world, it would love you as its own. As it is, you do not belong to the world, but I have chosen you out of the world. That is why the world hates you. Remember what I told you: 'A servant is not greater than his master.' If they persecuted me, they will persecute you also. If they obeyed my teaching, they will obey yours also. They will treat you this way because of my name, for they do not know the one who sent me."

Luke 6:40 Jesus said, "The student is not above the teacher, but everyone who is fully trained will be like their teacher."

Luke 6:46 Jesus said, "Why do you call me, 'Lord, Lord,' and do not do what I say?"

TAKEAWAY HIGHLIGHT

"The Way of the Cross is a narrow way, a difficult way, but a necessary way if we ever intend to find Life. Entering the Gate is not the end of the journey; it is the beginning of the journey. It is at the end of the Path that one finds Life (Mt. 7:14), not the beginning. Jesus never made a distinction between being saved and being a disciple. He is not "Savior" for new Christians and

"Lord" for older, more deeply committed Christians. Either He is Lord of all, or He isn't Lord at all." Chip Brogden

PRACTICAL APPLICATION

Ask yourself some questions: Would I consider myself a true disciple of Jesus Christ? If not, do I really want to be? Am I just talking the talk and not walking the walk? Am I sure I have an intimate personal relationship with Jesus if I am not making every effort to do what He has told me to do as His disciple?

WANT TO KNOW MORE?

Write to us to request the discipleship teaching on "Disciples of Christ". Mail it to: Freedom in Jesus Prison Ministries, Attn: Teachings, P.O. Box 939, Levelland, TX 79336.

Are you aware that God always has a true remnant of believers? Are you part of the remnant? Let's discover what this means...

True Remnant Believers

One of the best teaching articles I have found on this topic was written by Gilbert Owens, "Who is the Remnant?" In part, he writes in the following five paragraphs:

"A remnant is defined as a small surviving group of people. It is sometimes defined as something left over. At other times it is defined as a leftover piece of fabric remaining after the rest has been used up or sold. Throughout the course of the history of mankind, GOD HAS ALWAYS LEFT A REMNANT.

"The New Testament tells us in Romans 11:5, "Even so then, at this present time, there is a remnant according to the election of grace."

"Today the church serves as God's chosen people. And like the children of Israel, the church has become a sinful nation, comprised of believers laden with iniquity. They are a seed of evildoers, with children who are corrupter. They have forsaken the Lord and have provoked the Holy One unto anger. They have gone away backward. But despite the state of the church, God has once again left a small remnant. A remnant that is far from perfect, but a remnant that trust God.

"God's remnant are those who acknowledge God in all their ways, even when their ways sometimes do not please God. They are the ones who always confess their sins to God while believing He is always faithful and just to forgive them of their sins and to cleanse them from all unrighteousness.

"God's remnant are those who stand on God's Word and not the word of man, politicians, the media and hirelings. They believe God's Word is true today, yesterday and forever. Political correctness is not part of the character."

When "birth pains" begin for an expectant mother, they increase in both frequency and severity until the baby's arrival. I firmly believe our world has already been experiencing the "beginning of birth pains" of which Jesus spoke in Matthew 24, Mark 13 and Luke 21. Over the last few years, we have seen them only steadily increase, and with each new month there seems to be something more challenging than the month before. "Normal" as we once knew it is gone. Looking ahead, we may very well be facing even more difficult challenges.

Amidst all this uncertainty, one thing I know for sure is that God is in control. Nothing happens that He does not allow to happen or cause to happen. He alone is Sovereign. We must be certain we are true remnant believers making good choices daily. When this is true of us, unbelievers will see God's empowered "Church" effectively operating as the light in a dark world. They too, with us, can find peace, rest and a firm foundation in Christ Jesus!

Jesus could return for us any day. Are you sure you are part of the Bride, His real Church comprised of the remnant of true believers? Have you set aside every weight that might slow you down or hold you back, and turned from sins that would trip you up, in the race you are asked to run with endurance (see Hebrews 12:1-2)? Are your eyes fixed on Jesus? Are there areas of your life where you are still conformed to the world? Are you resisting the Holy Spirit's ongoing work of sanctification designed to produce in you a renewed mind and a real life transformation (see Romans 12:1-2)?

God's desire is for us to choose life in the Kingdom of God by, in, and through His Holy Spirit. He wants us to choose life, not death. Are you experiencing the abundant life Jesus came to give you (see John 10:10)? He longs for us to receive blessings available through obedience instead of reaping curses resulting from disobedience (see Deuteronomy 28).

SOME RELEVANT SCRIPTURE PASSAGES

1 Kings 19:18 Jehovah God said, "Yet I reserve seven thousand in Israel—all whose knees have not bowed down to Baal and whose mouths have not kissed him."

Isaiah 1:8-9 "Daughter Zion is left like a shelter in a vineyard, like a hut in a cucumber field, like a city under siege. Unless the Lord Almighty had left us some survivors *(a remnant)*, we would have become like Sodom, we would have been like Gomorrah."

Romans 11:5 "So too, at the present time there is a remnant chosen by grace."

Hebrews 12:1-2 "Therefore, since we are surrounded by such a great cloud of witnesses, let us throw off everything that hinders and the sin that so easily entangles. And let us run with perseverance the race marked out for us, fixing our eyes on Jesus, the pioneer and perfecter of faith. For the joy set before him he endured the cross, scorning its shame, and sat down at the right hand of the throne of God."

Romans 12:1-2 "Therefore, I urge you, brothers and sisters, in view of God's mercy, to offer your bodies as a living sacrifice, holy and pleasing to God—this is your true and proper worship. Do not conform to the pattern of this world, but be transformed by the renewing of your mind. Then you will be able to test and approve what God's will is—his good, pleasing and perfect will."

Deuteronomy 30:19-20 "This day I call the heavens and the earth as witnesses against you that I have set before you life and death, blessings and curses. Now choose life, so that you and your children may live and that you may love the Lord your God, listen to his voice, and hold fast to him. For the Lord is your life, and he will give you many years in the land he swore to give to your fathers, Abraham, Isaac and Jacob."

Joshua 24:14-15 "Now fear the Lord and serve him with all faithfulness. Throw away the gods your ancestors worshiped beyond the Euphrates River and in Egypt, and serve the Lord. But if serving the Lord seems undesirable to you, then choose for yourselves this day whom you will serve, whether the gods your ancestors served beyond the Euphrates, or the gods of the Amorites, in whose land you are living. But as for me and my household, we will serve the Lord."

John 10:10 Jesus said, "The thief comes only to steal and kill and destroy; I have come that they may have life, and have it to the full."

TAKEAWAY HIGHLIGHT

"God's remnant are those who acknowledge God in all their ways, even when their ways sometimes do not please God. They are the ones who always confess their sins to God while believing He is always faithful and just to forgive them of their sins and to cleanse them from all unrighteousness.

"God's remnant are those who stand on God's Word and not the word of man, politicians, the media and hirelings. They believe God's Word is true

today, yesterday and forever. Political correctness is not part of the character." Gilbert Owens

PRACTICAL APPLICATION

Take some time to study the scriptures above. Meditate on their meaning and see how they apply to you. Ask the Holy Spirit to show you how to make the right choices daily so that you can always be certain you are part of the remnant of true believers.

WANT TO KNOW MORE?

Write to us to request the discipleship teaching on "True Remnant Believers Choose Wisely". Mail it to: Freedom in Jesus Prison Ministries, Attn: Teachings, P.O. Box 939, Levelland, TX 79336.

The enemy will always try to tempt you to take you off track from developing intimacy of relationship with Jesus. How does a person successfully deal with temptation? Let's see...

Dealing with Temptation

No matter how long you follow Jesus, you will be tempted daily by the enemy. **There's no getting around it. Intimacy of relationship with Jesus is something the enemy hates!** The devil does not want you to positively impact others with your Christian lifestyle, nor does he want you to experience the truly abundant life Jesus came to give you. See John 10:10. Satan wants you to be led by your "flesh" and "the world", rather than be led by the Holy Spirit. Additionally, our adversary definitely does not want you to know and apply the truth of the Word.

But, there is good news! Jesus taught us by example how to resist temptation and overcome the enemy. He utilized the Word and the Holy Spirit, both of which are equally available to us today! We must learn to do what Jesus did when He was tempted.

Every day, the enemy places thoughts in my head that are designed to tempt me in the same ways my "old man" was tempted before I became a "new man" in Christ. I have learned to recognize these tricks, lures and devices of the adversary and reject them quickly. Satan cannot resurrect my "old, dead man", but he does his best daily to try to catch me off guard, and thereby convince me to act out of my old nature instead of my new one. Satan wants me to resurrect my "old man".

Whether we are incarcerated, or in the free world, we will be tempted. I know by my own experience, temptation comes quickly after you are released; and, there are many more ways the enemy tries to lure us into sin as compared to during our incarceration. For example, drugs and alcohol are available in abundance. The allure and temptation for sexual relations outside of marriage is much more prevalent. Pressures of life bear down on us. The devil uses money and accumulation of material possessions to try to entrap us. We must be alert and wise to the enemy's devices because he stalks us as a lion looking for easy prey (1 Peter 5:8-9). He gives us many kinds of thoughts.

We must learn to "take these thoughts captive to the obedience of Christ" (2 Corinthians 10:4-5), and use the spiritual weapons we have in Christ Jesus to combat the enemy (Ephesians 6:10-18). Jesus was tempted in all ways like us, yet He did not sin (Hebrews 4:15). In Him, we are overcomers!

In an article she wrote, "How to Handle Temptation", Joyce Meyer answers the question, "Why do we have to deal with temptation?"

She writes, "It strengthens our faith, our spiritual muscles. If we didn't have to stand against temptation, we'd never know our own spiritual strength. Facing temptations will either bring out the best or worst in us. Sometimes God allows us to be tested because He's preparing us for promotion. Facing temptations increases our confidence in our ability to recognize and resist the lies of the enemy."

In the same article, Joyce Meyer continues, "Sometimes Jesus allows us to face temptations so He can bring attention to areas of weakness in our lives and help us overcome them. He knows how important it is for us to know the truth about ourselves. Even though it may be painful to acknowledge that we have tendencies to be jealous, greedy or prideful, if we'll deal with it and overcome it, *that* truth will set us free. The only way you can have all that Jesus wants you to have is to be what He wants you to be. And that maturity comes in stages."

In a devotional entitled "Fighting the Battle Against Sin", Dr. Charles Stanley wrote: "The only way we can withstand the world's clamor, the devil's whispers, and our own selfish desires is by immersing ourselves in the Word of God. We must focus our attention on knowing the heavenly Father in all of His fullness, believing His promises, and obeying His commands. Only through our relationship with Jesus Christ will we be able to fight the battle against sin and stand firm. Clear your mind of any distractions, and allow the Lord to speak to you through His Word. He has much to tell you."

In an article "Dealing with Temptation", Andrew Wommack wrote: "Satan is not limitless; deception is his only weapon. All he can do is try to deceive us into thinking that God really can't or won't fulfill our lives. Every single temptation of the enemy is packaged in the form of the lust of the flesh, the lust of the eyes, or the pride of life. But they're all designed to entice us and cause us to doubt that God will meet our needs. Selfishness is always the favorite playground of the devil, and when selfishness rules in our lives, we open the door to his deceptive schemes."

In James 4:7-8 it says, "Submit yourselves, then, to God. Resist the devil, and he will flee from you. Come near to God and he will come near to you..."

Brothers and sisters in Christ, please note that the devil does not have to flee when you resist him unless you first submit to, and draw near to, God. When you respond to temptation that way, you *are* resisting the devil and he does then have to flee! He will have to find another more opportune time later (see Luke 4:13).

SOME RELEVANT SCRIPTURE PASSAGES

John 10:10 Jesus said, "The thief comes only to steal and kill and destroy; I have come that they may have life, and have it to the full."

2 Corinthians 5:17 "Therefore, if anyone is in Christ, the new creation has come: The old has gone, the new is here!"

Romans 6:8-12 "Now if we died with Christ, we believe that we will also live with him. For we know that since Christ was raised from the dead, he cannot die again; death no longer has mastery over him. The death he died, he died to sin once for all; but the life he lives, he lives to God. In the same way, count yourselves dead to sin but alive to God in Christ Jesus. Therefore do not let sin reign in your mortal body so that you obey its evil desires."

1 Peter 5:8-9 "Be alert and of sober mind. Your enemy the devil prowls around like a roaring lion looking for someone to devour. Resist him, standing firm in the faith, because you know that the family of believers throughout the world is undergoing the same kind of sufferings."

2 Corinthians 10:4-5 "The weapons we fight with are not the weapons of the world. On the contrary, they have divine power to demolish strongholds. We demolish arguments and every pretension that sets itself up against the knowledge of God, and we take captive every thought to make it obedient to Christ."

Ephesians 6:10-12 "Finally, be strong in the Lord and in his mighty power. Put on the full armor of God, so that you can take your stand against the devil's schemes. For our struggle is not against flesh and blood, but against the rulers, against the authorities, against the powers of this dark world and against the spiritual forces of evil in the heavenly realms."

Hebrews 4:15 "For we do not have a high priest who is unable to empathize with our weaknesses, but we have one who has been tempted in every way, just as we are—yet he did not sin."

TAKEAWAY HIGHLIGHT

"The only way we can withstand the world's clamor, the devil's whispers, and our own selfish desires is by immersing ourselves in the Word of God. We must focus our attention on knowing the heavenly Father in all of His fullness, believing His promises, and obeying His commands. Only through our relationship with Jesus Christ will we be able to fight the battle against sin and stand firm. Clear your mind of any distractions, and allow the Lord to speak to you through His Word. He has much to tell you." Dr. Charles Stanley

PRACTICAL APPLICATION

Think about two or three areas where you are frequently tempted. Look for one or two scriptures specific to the temptation to utilize against the enemy the next time you are tempted. Meditate on the scriptures ahead of time so that you really believe them in your heart. When the temptation comes, submit to God first by proclaiming the scripture aloud and thanking God that your old man is dead so you do not have to give in anymore. This is an effective way to resist the devil and he will, in fact, flee!

WANT TO KNOW MORE?

Write to us to request the discipleship teaching on "Dealing with Temptation". Mail it to: Freedom in Jesus Prison Ministries, Attn: Teachings, P.O. Box 939, Levelland, TX 79336.

Our intimacy of relationship with Jesus is enhanced the more we discern God's voice. Find out how to hear better...

Discerning God's Voice

In the last chapter, I shared some things I am learning about how to overcome temptation. We must realize that the specific temptation first occurs in our thoughts. The enemy cannot read our minds, but he knows us very well by observing our actions; so, he is a master of suggestion, and even makes the suggestion sound like our own voice! We must be able to discern the voices in our mind, and where they are coming from, in order to learn how to take every thought captive to the obedience of Christ (2 Corinthians 10:3-5).

Personally, I have never heard the audible voice of God, but the more I grow in Christ Jesus, the better I am about maintaining an ongoing conversation with His Holy Spirit. I sense His still small voice in my heart and mind more every day. I tell God daily that I want to be led by His Holy Spirit and not by my flesh, the world, or the devil. God really does talk to us, and He wants us to talk to Him. **Building an intimate, personal relationship with Jesus depends upon ongoing, effective communication – speaking and listening to the voice of God the Holy Spirit.**

Spiritual father Brother Lawrence once wrote, "There is not in the world a kind of life more sweet and delightful than that of a continual conversation with God."

Dr. Charles Stanley, in an article, "Knowing God's Voice", teaches us how God speaks to us through the Person of His Holy Spirit. He writes, "Knowing the voice of God through His Spirit is something we learn over time. This recognition requires that we live day to day in submission to the Lord, setting aside time to quiet our minds and still our bodies. We must also go to Him regularly throughout the day, in the midst of our tasks and obligations, joys and worries. Eventually, we will come to know His voice so well that we'll be able to hear Him even in the most difficult and busy circumstances."

We must be able to filter out all the noise and distractions in our mind so we can listen and follow the right voice. Craig Denison, in a First15 devotional entitled "The Experience of His Voice" (*www.first15.org*) writes:

"God himself dwells within us and longs to speak to our hearts. He longs for us to know the will of our heavenly Father the way Jesus did. He longs for us to follow his leading moment by moment the way the apostles did. And he longs for us to engage in conversation with him as all those who are in true relationship with one another do... In order to learn to hear his voice moment by moment whether we're in solitude or in chaos, we must make time in the secret place to seek the fullness of relationship with him. It's in seeking relationship with God that we become familiar with his voice and are able to follow him as sheep with their Shepherd."

One of the very best teachings I have found on this subject is by Gillis Triplett, "The Five-Fold Secret to Clearly Hearing God's Voice". This has very practical and detailed guidance from the Word as to how to hear God's voice clearly. This is crucial for us if we are going to be able to discern the competing voices in our head and heart. To successfully overcome temptation, we must be able to follow the right voice and reject all others.

Although the teaching is too long to include here in its entirety, Gillis Triplett teaches:

"In every decision that you are called to make and in every situation that you are faced with, there is always going to be five different voices speaking to you:

(1) The voice of God

(2) The voice of your conscience

(3) The voice of your reasoning

(4) The voice of your flesh, and

(5) The voice of the devil

"In most cases, each voice is going to lead you in the opposite direction of the voice of God. The sincere Christians who consistently miss God's voice, either: (a) don't know about all of these five voices, or (b) they have not learned how to discern which voice is speaking. Each voice has a distinct sound and is easily discernable once you know what to listen for."

He continues "...There are the seven elements that must be in place in your life, if you are going to properly discern which voice is speaking.

1. You must study the Word of God for yourself, (See 2 Timothy 2:15)
2. You must meditate on the Word of God day and night, (Joshua 1:8)
3. You must spend time praying, (Mark 1:35)
4. You must spend time communing with the Holy Spirit, (2 Corinthians 13:14)
5. You must be planted in a good church home, (Hebrews 10:24-25)

6. You must rationally consider all options, (Luke 14:28-30) and,

7. You must seek counsel from wise counselors. (See Proverbs 11:14)

"If you follow those instructions, you will come to the place, where you quickly recognize which voice is speaking to you. That is an awesome feeling to know that you know that you know–the voice of the Holy Spirit!"

In these very dark and increasingly evil days, we must let our light shine. Read Isaiah 60:1-2. Our light shines brighter the more successful we are in hearing and following the voice of our Lord and Great Shepherd, Jesus, by His Holy Spirit. It is crucial to hear and follow the Right Voice – see John 10:27. Take all the wrong thoughts captive, and cast them down!

SOME RELEVANT SCRIPTURE PASSAGES

2 Corinthians 10:3-5 "For though we live in the world, we do not wage war as the world does. The weapons we fight with are not the weapons of the world. On the contrary, they have divine power to demolish strongholds. We demolish arguments and every pretension that sets itself up against the knowledge of God, and we take captive every thought to make it obedient to Christ."

John 10:3-4 Jesus said, "The gatekeeper opens the gate for him, and the sheep listen to his voice. He calls his own sheep by name and leads them out. When he has brought out all his own, he goes on ahead of them, and his sheep follow him because they know his voice."

John 10:27 Jesus said, "My sheep listen to my voice; I know them and they follow me."

Jeremiah 33:3 Jehovah said, "Call to me and I will answer you and tell you great and unsearchable things you do not know."

John 16:12-14 Jesus said, "I have much more to say to you, more than you can now bear. But when he, the Spirit of truth, comes, he will guide you into all the truth. He will not speak on his own; he will speak only what he hears, and he will tell you what is yet to come. He will glorify me because it is from me that he will receive what he will make known to you."

Isaiah 60:1-2 "Arise, shine, for your light has come, and the glory of the Lord rises upon you. See, darkness covers the earth and thick darkness is over the peoples, but the Lord rises upon you and his glory appears over you."

TAKEAWAY HIGHLIGHT

"God himself dwells within us and longs to speak to our hearts. He longs for us to know the will of our heavenly Father the way Jesus did. He longs for us to follow his leading moment by moment the way the apostles did. And he longs for us to engage in conversation with him as all those who are in true relationship with one another do... In order to learn to hear his voice moment by moment whether we're in solitude or in chaos, we must make time in the secret place to seek the fullness of relationship with him. It's in seeking relationship with God that we become familiar with his voice and are able to follow him as sheep with their Shepherd."
Craig Denison

PRACTICAL APPLICATION

Ask yourself how much better you could resist temptation if you could more clearly distinguish the voice of the Holy Spirit from all the other competing voices and distractions. Tell the Holy Spirit you want to learn to hear Him better. Decide to set aside time daily just to talk to God and listen for His response. Throughout the day, get in the habit of communicating with the Holy Spirit - He is your Helper, Friend and Guide - talk with Him.

WANT TO KNOW MORE?

Write to us to request the discipleship teaching on "Discerning God's Voice" which includes the entire teaching mentioned above by Gillis Triplett. Mail it to: Freedom in Jesus Prison Ministries, Attn: Teachings, P.O. Box 939, Levelland, TX 79336.

Discerning the voice of the Holy Spirit is crucial to cooperating with Him as He works into us the realization of God's desire of sanctification and holiness...

Sanctification and Holiness

I am very concerned for many in the Church who believe they are "saved" yet continue to live pretty much the same as before. Real repentance must accompany faith and grace to be truly saved. Repentance includes turning from our old way of life, like a U-turn on a highway, and being determined to keep following Jesus. Then there will be evidence in our daily lives that we are truly born again and have actually become a new creation.

We might occasionally fall, but we are quick to repent, get to our feet and keep going the right direction. We do not let the enemy convince us to fall back into our old lifestyle. When we are truly saved, we are not "sinless", but we will definitely **sin less**!

Yet, some preachers today seem to be presenting a message that allows an ongoing lifestyle of sin even after one comes to Christ, saying that grace covers it all anyway. Some refer to this teaching as "hyper-grace", or even "greasy grace". This is a dangerous teaching which is leading many astray.

These false teachers may quote Romans 5:20, "But where sin increased, grace increased all the more". However, they do not quote the rest of the passage continuing in Romans 5:21 – 6:2, explaining "so that, just as sin reigned in death, so also grace might reign through righteousness to bring eternal life...", and then Paul exclaims, "What shall we say, then? Shall we go on sinning so that grace may increase? By no means! We died to sin; how can we live in it any longer?"

When we begin an intimate personal relationship with Jesus, the Holy Spirit is given to us to begin the process of making us more like Jesus every day (see Romans 8:29). This is the ongoing process of "sanctification". Sanctification is the act or process of acquiring sanctity, of being made or becoming holy...to sanctify is to literally "set apart for particular use in a special purpose or work and to make holy or sacred." Sanctify also means "to free from sin: purify."

Titus 2:11-14 "For the grace of God has appeared that offers salvation to all people. It teaches us to say 'No' to ungodliness and worldly passions, and to live self-controlled, upright and godly lives in this present age, while we wait for the blessed hope—the appearing of the glory of our great God and Savior, Jesus Christ, who gave himself for us to redeem us from all wickedness and to purify for himself a people that are his very own, eager to do what is good."

Jesus paid the ultimate price with His Blood so that God the Father could expect from his born-again children a life of holiness and sanctification. Is this possible on our own efforts? No. But it is absolutely available to us when we fully surrender to the Holy Spirit's leadership by submitting to His ongoing mission to sanctify us, set us apart for His service, and produce holiness in our character and lifestyle. We cannot achieve this, but He can!

In a daily devotional entitled "A Call to Holiness" by Dr. Charles Stanley, I found these three paragraphs which Dr. Stanley wrote based on 1 Peter 1:13 – 2:3:

"Believers are called to be sanctified people who live holy lives. Holiness means being set apart by God for His purposes. This process of sanctification begins when we receive Jesus Christ as our personal Savior, and it continues for the rest of our lives.

"The Holy Spirit draws our will and longings to align with His. As we submit to Him, we will begin to desire what He desires. With His leading, we will choose to consecrate our conduct, our conversation, and ultimately our character to God alone. He teaches us how to make holiness a way of life rather than see it as some lofty place of enlightenment we can never reach. God has placed us where we live and work, not to be "pious" or to isolate ourselves as if in incubators, but to reflect who Christ is as we walk among other people. If we are in the process of being conformed to Jesus' likeness, then the longer we live and mature spiritually, the more others should be able to recognize the Savior in us. Our hearts should grow softer, and our willingness to love and serve should increase.

"If we are Christ's ambassadors, then our lives must be holy; otherwise, we are misrepresenting Him. If we are the body of Christ, then our hands are His hands, our eyes are His eyes, and our feet are His feet. When we allow Jesus to speak, love, and serve through us, others will be compelled to ask why we live such vibrant lives. All followers of Christ are called to be holy. To answer this call daily is to embrace the Great Commission."

A "First15 Devotional" (*www.first15.org*) by Craig Denison entitled "Sanctification and Holiness" contained these two paragraphs:

"God knows that sanctification doesn't come about through our efforts. I can in no way sanctify myself, because in and of myself I have no holiness. The truth God has for us today is simply this: Sanctification comes about by true relationship with our heavenly Father alone. Holiness is the direct result of openly and continually encountering the nature of a perfect, loving and available God.

"If we are going to experience the fruit of righteousness we must learn to trust God in his plan for our sanctification. We must learn to trust that in encountering him we will experience freedom from our sin and healing for the wounds that drive us to the things of the world."

Someone who is truly saved responds to the overwhelming love of the Father by living a life that aims to please Him. Someone who is born-again no longer desires to live their old lifestyle. It hurts them inside when they succumb to temptation and they want to quickly repent to stay in right relationship with the Father. They do not continue practicing a lifestyle of sin. In 1 John 3:9, John tells us, "No one who is born of God will continue to sin, because God's seed remains in him; he cannot go on sinning, because he has been born of God."

In *The Jesus Bible* an article states, "A relationship with Jesus brings overflowing joy and lasting satisfaction (John 17:3). Following Him in discipleship leads to an abundant life (John 10:10). Every day Jesus' presence, provision and plan for a believer are sufficient. He is enough. Holiness for Christians is evidence that satisfaction in life does not require the fleeting and empty pleasures of sin."

The best way to witness to others is for them to see the power of your truly transformed life. Often no words are even needed. Others will want what they see in you – real evidence of the Holy Spirit's righteousness, love, peace, joy, patience, goodness, gentleness, faithfulness and self-control.

SOME RELEVANT SCRIPTURE PASSAGES

1 Peter 1:13-2:3 "Therefore, with minds that are alert and fully sober, set your hope on the grace to be brought to you when Jesus Christ is revealed at his coming. As obedient children, do not conform to the evil desires you had when you lived in ignorance. But just as he who called you is holy, so be holy in all you do; for it is written: 'Be holy, because I am holy.'

17 Since you call on a Father who judges each person's work impartially, live out your time as foreigners here in reverent fear. For you know that it was not with perishable things such as silver or gold that you were redeemed from the empty way of life handed down to you from your ancestors, but with the precious blood of Christ, a lamb without blemish or defect. He was chosen before the creation of the world, but was revealed in these last times for your sake. Through him you believe in God, who raised him from the dead and glorified him, and so your faith and hope are in God.

22 Now that you have purified yourselves by obeying the truth so that you have sincere love for each other, love one another deeply, from the heart. For you have been born again, not of perishable seed, but of imperishable, through the living and enduring word of God. For, 'All people are like grass, and all their glory is like the flowers of the field; the grass withers and the flowers fall, but the word of the Lord endures forever.' And this is the word that was preached to you.

2:1 Therefore, rid yourselves of all malice and all deceit, hypocrisy, envy, and slander of every kind. Like newborn babies, crave pure spiritual milk, so that by it you may grow up in your salvation, now that you have tasted that the Lord is good."

Romans 8:29 "For those God foreknew he also predestined to be conformed to the image of his Son, that he might be the firstborn among many brothers and sisters."

Titus 2:11-14 "For the grace of God has appeared that offers salvation to all people. It teaches us to say 'No' to ungodliness and worldly passions, and to live self-controlled, upright and godly lives in this present age, while we wait for the blessed hope—the appearing of the glory of our great God and Savior, Jesus Christ, who gave himself for us to redeem us from all wickedness and to purify for himself a people that are his very own, eager to do what is good."

John 17:3 Jesus said, "Now this is eternal life: that they know you, the only true God, and Jesus Christ, whom you have sent".

John 10:10 Jesus said, "The thief comes only to steal and kill and destroy; I have come that they may have life, and have it to the full."

1 John 3:1-3 "See what great love the Father has lavished on us, that we should be called children of God! And that is what we are! The reason the world does not know us is that it did not know him. Dear friends, now we are children of God, and what we will be has not yet been made known. But we know that when Christ appears, we shall be like him, for we shall see him as he is. All who have this hope in him purify themselves, just as he is pure."

1 John 2:29 "If you know that he is righteous, you know that everyone who does what is right has been born of him."

1 John 1:6-7 "If we claim to have fellowship with him and yet walk in the darkness, we lie and do not live out the truth. But if we walk in the

light, as he is in the light, we have fellowship with one another, and the blood of Jesus, his Son, purifies us from all sin."

1 John 3:5-6 "But you know that he appeared so that he might take away our sins. And in him is no sin. No one who lives in him keeps on sinning. No one who continues to sin has either seen him or known him."

1 John 3:9-10 "No one who is born of God will continue to sin, because God's seed remains in them; they cannot go on sinning, because they have been born of God. This is how we know who the children of God are and who the children of the devil are: Anyone who does not do what is right is not God's child, nor is anyone who does not love their brother and sister.

Ephesians 1:3-4 Praise be to the God and Father of our Lord Jesus Christ, who has blessed us in the heavenly realms with every spiritual blessing in Christ. For he chose us in him before the creation of the world to be holy and blameless in his sight."

2 Peter 3:10-12 "But the day of the Lord will come like a thief. The heavens will disappear with a roar; the elements will be destroyed by fire, and the earth and everything done in it will be laid bare. Since everything will be destroyed in this way, what kind of people ought you to be? You ought to live holy and godly lives as you look forward to the day of God and speed its coming..."

TAKEAWAY HIGHLIGHT

Someone who is truly saved responds to the overwhelming love of the Father by living a life that aims to please Him. Someone who is born-again no longer desires to live their old lifestyle. It hurts them inside when they succumb to temptation and they want to quickly repent to stay in right relationship with the Father. They do not continue practicing a lifestyle of sin. In 1 John 3:9, John tells us, "No one who is born of God will continue to sin, because God's seed remains in him; he cannot go on sinning, because he has been born of God."

PRACTICAL APPLICATION

Have you been burdened and discouraged thinking that it was up solely to you and your efforts to live a Godly life? Receive this truth: The Holy Spirit will do this in and through you progressively more daily in direct relation to your daily re-commitment to surrendering to the Holy Spirit's Leadership, and continuously submitting to the Lordship of Jesus. Hard to believe? Yes, but it is true. Re-read this truth several times. Think deeply about it. What will you do about this revelation?

WANT TO KNOW MORE?

Write to us to request the discipleship teaching on "Sanctification and Holiness". Mail it to: Freedom in Jesus Prison Ministries, Attn: Teachings, P.O. Box 939, Levelland, TX 79336.

Since the Holy Spirit is so crucial to intimacy of relationship with Jesus we need to understand more about Him. Let's learn...

Understanding the Holy Spirit

God is Spirit, so for us to have an intimate relationship with Him it must be through the Holy Spirit in our spirit Who connects us to the Father and Son, Jesus. **Our relationship will grow stronger daily the more we understand about the One living in us after we are saved, that is, the Person of the Holy Spirit.**

Derek Prince, in *Declaring God's Word*, wrote about access to God through the Spirit in an article entitled, "Access by the Spirit". Here are two paragraphs of what he wrote:

"We cannot leave out the Holy Spirit and still have access. Many Christians focus on the fact that we have access to God through His Son, Jesus. That is perfectly true but it is not the whole truth. It is through the Son, by the Spirit, to the Father. Likewise, the Father indwells us when we are in the Son, through His Spirit. In each direction, whether we are going to God or whether God is coming to us, the Spirit is an essential part of the equation. We have access in the Son through the Spirit to the Father. The Father indwells us when we are in the Son through the Spirit.

"If we leave the Holy Spirit out of that equation, we have no access to God, and God has no access to us. We are totally dependent on the Holy Spirit."

My friend and ministry partner, Carol Breeden, was the author of Peace in Him. She graduated to Heaven in 2020 but was known by all her friends as someone who was so filled with peace that we knew she had a real understanding of the Holy Spirit. In 2016, she wrote the following five paragraphs:

"The Holy Spirit is part of the God-head. The God-head (or Trinity) is made up of God the Father (Abba Father), God the Son (Jesus) and God the Holy Spirit. The Holy Spirit has always been with the Father. He is one with the Father just as Jesus is one with the Father. They are three in one, and one in three.

"For us there was a beginning of "time", but the Father, Son and Holy Spirit have never been part of the increments of time. They have always been and will always be. They have always worked together in unity and harmony. There is nothing that the Father has done that His Son and Holy Spirit have not played an important part, even the creation of earth.

"When Jesus finished His work on earth and returned to the Father, the Father sent the Holy Spirit to earth for each of us. Jesus' followers at that time were instructed to wait until they were endued with power from on High before they began to carry out the ministry of Jesus. We should do likewise, that is, we should seek the power of the Holy Spirit before we move out among the people in the name of Jesus. We need the power of the Holy Spirit. Within our own strength, we will burn out quickly, we will not be effective, and we can even do harm to His Kingdom.

"Above all, remember, the Holy Spirit is a person, He has a personality, and He can be grieved. His purpose in coming was to teach, lead, guide, correct, protect and comfort–the Helper who would walk alongside us as well as dwell within us. However, we must yield to Him and allow

Him to do His work in us. If we refuse Him, resist Him, or grieve Him, we will restrict the work that the Father wants Him to do in our lives. He is a gift from the Father, and we need Him!

"We thank the Father for His gifts. He not only gave us His Son, Jesus, but He gave us His Holy Spirit. What a marvelous Father He is. When I think about it, I realize how gullible we are to believe the enemy's lie — the lie that the Holy Spirit is not for today, that we don't need Him. If anything, the truth is we need Him even more because we are living in the last of the last days when Scripture tells us that many will be deceived. The Holy Spirit can help us to not be deceived if we will let Him lead us, and recognize that we "host" Him as the very Presence of God in us. We need Him. We need Him in His fullness."

In a teaching entitled "Our Constant Companion", Dr. Charles Stanley wrote, "Despite His constant presence, many believers have never given the Holy Spirit a serious thought, but a deeper understanding of His role in our lives can transform us. He's ready and able to help us become the people God wants us to be. Furthermore, we need His powerful anointing to accomplish whatever the Lord has called us to do. We can't even understand the Bible without His guiding interpretation. Whether we realize it or not, the Holy Spirit is a vital part of our lives."

On August 30, 2011, Albert Lee wrote the daily devotional for Our Daily Bread which was entitled "Christ Living in Us". These are his two concluding paragraphs:

"As we strive to live a God-pleasing life, we realize that in spite of our best intentions and determination, we often stumble and fall short. By our strength alone, it is impossible. Oh, how we need the Lord's help. And it has been provided. Paul declares it with these delightful words, 'It is no longer I who live, but Christ lives in me; and the life which I now live in the flesh I live by faith in the Son of God" (Galatians 2:20).

"We cannot finish the Christian race on our own. We have to do so by depending on Jesus living in us."

How does Jesus live in us? By His Holy Spirit indwelling us. Brothers and sisters in Christ let us choose to learn as much about the Holy Spirit as possible. You will be so glad you did.

SOME RELEVANT SCRIPTURE PASSAGES

Matthew 3:16-17 "As soon as Jesus was baptized, he went up out of the water. At that moment heaven was opened, and he saw the Spirit of God descending like a dove and alighting on him. And a voice from heaven said, "This is my Son, whom I love; with him I am well pleased." *(Please note that the Father, Son and Holy Spirit – the Trinity – are all present.)*

2 Corinthians 13:14 "May the grace of the Lord Jesus Christ, and the love of God, and the fellowship of the Holy Spirit be with you all."

Luke 24:48-49 Jesus said, "You are witnesses of these things. I am going to send you what my Father has promised; but stay in the city until you have been clothed with power from on high."

Acts 1:4-8 Jesus said, "On one occasion, while he was eating with them, he gave them this command: 'Do not leave Jerusalem, but wait for the gift my Father promised, which you have heard me speak about. For John baptized with water, but in a few days you will be baptized with the Holy Spirit.' Then they gathered around him and asked him, 'Lord, are you at this time going to restore the kingdom to Israel?' He said to them: 'It is not for you to know the times or dates the Father has set by his own authority. But you will receive power when the Holy Spirit comes on you; and you will be my witnesses in Jerusalem, and in all Judea and Samaria, and to the ends of the earth.'"

John 14:15-18 Jesus said, "If you love me, keep my commands. And I will ask the Father, and he will give you another advocate to help you and be with you forever— the Spirit of truth. The world cannot accept him, because it neither sees him nor knows him. But you know him, for he lives with you and will be in you. I will not leave you as orphans; I will come to you."

John 14:25-27 "All this I have spoken while still with you. But the Advocate, the Holy Spirit, whom the Father will send in my name, will teach you all things and will remind you of everything I have said to you. Peace I leave with you; my peace I give you. I do not give to you as the world gives. Do not let your hearts be troubled and do not be afraid."

John 15:26-27 Jesus said, "When the Advocate comes, whom I will send to you from the Father—the Spirit of truth who goes out from the Father—he will testify about me. And you also must testify, for you have been with me from the beginning."

John 16:7-11 Jesus said, "But very truly I tell you, it is for your good that I am going away. Unless I go away, the Advocate will not come to you; but if I go, I will send him to you. When he comes, he will prove the world to be in the wrong about sin and righteousness and judgment: about sin, because people do not believe in me; about righteousness, because I am going to the Father, where you can see me no longer; and about judgment, because the prince of this world now stands condemned."

John 16:12-15 Jesus said, "I have much more to say to you, more than you can now bear. But when he, the Spirit of truth, comes, he will guide you into all truth. He will not speak on his own; he will speak only what he hears, and he will tell you what is yet to come. He will glorify me because it is from me that he will receive what he will make known to you. All that belongs to the Father is mine. That is why I said the Spirit will receive from me what he will make known to you."

Joel 2:28-29 "And afterward, I will pour out my Spirit on all people. Your sons and daughters will prophesy, your old men will dream dreams, your young men will see visions. Even on my servants, both men and women, I will pour out my Spirit in those days."

TAKEAWAY HIGHLIGHT

"Despite His constant presence, many believers have never given the Holy Spirit a serious thought, but a deeper understanding of His role in our lives can transform us. He's ready and able to help us become the people God wants us to be. Furthermore, we need His powerful anointing to accomplish whatever the Lord has called us to do. We can't even understand the Bible without His guiding interpretation. Whether we realize it or not, the Holy Spirit is a vital part of our lives." Dr. Charles Stanley

PRACTICAL APPLICATION

Mentally envision water. In what three ways does water present itself? Liquid, solid (ice), and gas (steam). These are three presentations of the same thing; but they are all still, chemically speaking, water. Similarly, envision the sun. It produces flame, light, and heat all at once; still it is the one thing of the sun. This helps us better understand the Trinity of God: Father, Son and Holy Spirit; but they are all still God. God has described Himself to us in the Bible as three persons, or aspects of the One person of God. Although the word "trinity" is not in the Bible, it is the word assigned to the true concept of the three Persons of the One God.

WANT TO KNOW MORE?

Write to us to request the discipleship teaching on "Understanding the Holy Spirit". Mail it to: Freedom in Jesus Prison Ministries, Attn: Teachings, P.O. Box 939, Levelland, TX 79336.

Seeing how important the Holy Spirit is to experiencing intimacy of relationship with Jesus, let's look at some of the roles the Holy Spirit fulfills in the life of a committed follower of Jesus...

Roles of the Holy Spirit in Our Lives

The Holy Spirit is the unseen power of God, the person through whom divine power is conveyed. It is clear that man's power or might is inadequate to accomplish God's purposes. This can be done *only* by His Spirit. **Our progression in intimacy of relationship with God is determined in large part by how much we allow the Spirit of God to work in and through us to benefit the Kingdom.**

The Kingdom of God - God's domain - is not a physical, material thing, observable with our eyes nor is it discernible by physical senses. Rather, it is the domain wherein we surrender to God the Holy Spirit within us. Then He can work through us to positively impact the world around us.

Jesus laid aside His deity and came to earth as man. Before He began His ministry at the age of 30, He was baptized in the Holy Spirit. What Jesus did, everything He accomplished, was made possible because of the power of God within Him, and that power was the Holy Spirit. Also, it was the power of the Holy Spirit that resurrected Jesus from the dead! We need this power in us just as much as did Jesus....maybe even more because we were born with the sinful nature that came from the first Adam, and Jesus was not.

The miracles, signs and wonders performed by Jesus' followers, such as Peter and later Paul, were possible *only* by the power of the Holy Spirit who dwelt in them. It is the same for us today. The Holy Spirit within us is God's gift to us. The Holy Spirit in us produces spiritual fruit (love, joy, peace, etc.). It is also the power of the Holy Spirit working through us that enables us to do the works of Jesus…and greater works (John 14:12-14).

It is possible to have a powerless "form of godliness" that comes from self-focus and self-will (or selfishness). It is only as we deny and surrender self that we can acknowledge and receive power from the Holy Spirit. When we are immersed in the Holy Spirit, and He in us, He leads us, guides us, protects us, strengthens us and empowers us. Without the Holy Spirit, we cannot successfully walk the Christian walk. It is the power of the Holy Spirit working through us that does the work of Jesus. Also, it is by the power of the Holy Spirit that people are drawn to Jesus.

We thank the Father for the gift of the Holy Spirit—our Comforter, Teacher, Guide, Helper, and Friend. It is the Holy Spirit who convicts us when we begin to go in the wrong direction. It is the Holy Spirit who whispers to us and tells us the direction we should go and the words we should say, just like it was the Holy Spirit who directed Jesus. If we are not being directed and led by the Holy Spirit, then we are trying to do something in our own power. We can never be successful or effective in our own power. That is why Jesus and the Father sent the Holy Spirit to us.

In a devotional entitled "A Helper for all Occasions", Dr. Charles Stanley included these three paragraphs:

"Our Helper has a distinct role within the Trinity. The Father reigns over all, while the Son sits at His right hand, interceding for believers. Meanwhile, the Holy Spirit enables Christians to accomplish the work God has designed for each one to do.

"The Father knew we couldn't follow Him without help—that was why Jesus told the disciples to remain in Jerusalem until after the arrival of the Holy Spirit. Whatever we are called to do in daily obedience or in lifelong vocation, our Helper offers direction. And when we are beset by tough times or temptations, God's Spirit provides strength and encouragement.

"The Holy Spirit is intimately involved in our life. He is more a part of us than our bones and blood. We are privileged to have a divine Helper guiding us on the path of God's will."

Does every true believer have access to the same Holy Spirit power? How can we be sure we are in a position to receive what He wants to do in and through us? Dr. Charles Stanley addressed these questions in the following two paragraphs from a devotional entitled "Clothed with Power":

"We often think that the power of the Holy Spirit is available only to pastors and missionaries. However, the truth is that this power is offered to every person who is willing to serve God and meet the requirements given in Scripture. First, we must be convicted of our inadequacy. This means acknowledging we cannot work for God without the aid of His Spirit. Next, recognizing and admitting our inadequacy grows out of a pure life. Confessing sin and repenting are necessary to maintain fellowship with God. When we allow deliberate sin to enter our life, we short-circuit the power of the Holy

Spirit. Finally, every person who appropriates divine energy has an active prayer life.

"When we trust in God to provide the stamina for the work He calls us to do, we are clothed in power. Is your confidence in yourself or in Him?"

Our continued growth in intimacy of relationship with Jesus depends in large part on our ability to surrender to the Holy Spirit's leading us moment by moment. Our listening to and following Him empowers our love-motivated obedience.

SOME RELEVANT SCRIPTURE PASSAGES

Luke 24:49 "I am going to send you what my Father has promised; but stay in the city until you have been clothed with power from on high."

Acts 1:8 "But you will receive power when the Holy Spirit comes on you; and you will be my witnesses in Jerusalem, and in all Judea and Samaria, and to the ends of the earth."

Galatians 2:20 "I have been crucified with Christ and I no longer live, but Christ lives in me. The life I now live in the body, I live by faith in the Son of God, who loved me and gave himself for me."

John 14:15-17 "If you love me, keep my commands. And I will ask the Father, and he will give you another advocate to help you and be with you forever— the Spirit of truth. The world cannot accept him, because it neither sees him nor knows him. But you know him, for he lives with you and will be in you."

John 15:26 "When the Advocate comes, whom I will send to you from the Father—the Spirit of truth who goes out from the Father—he will testify about me."

John 16:12-15 "I have much more to say to you, more than you can now bear. But when he, the Spirit of truth, comes, he will guide you into all the truth. He will not speak on his own; he will speak only what he hears, and he will tell you what is yet to come. He will glorify me because it is from me that he will receive what he will make known to you. All that belongs to the Father is mine. That is why I said the Spirit will receive from me what he will make known to you."

TAKEAWAY HIGHLIGHT

The Holy Spirit is the unseen power of God, the person through whom divine power is conveyed. It is clear that man's power or might is inadequate to accomplish God's purposes. This can be done only by His Spirit. Our progression in intimacy of relationship with God is determined in large part by how much we allow the Spirit of God to work in and through us to benefit the Kingdom. Our listening to and following Him empowers our love-motivated obedience.

PRACTICAL APPLICATION

What roles do you see the Holy Spirit playing in your life? Are you increasingly comprehending His Power available to you? Dr. Charles Stanley has used this example:

"The Spirit of God indwells all believers. But there is a considerable distinction between having the Holy Spirit within us and the Holy Spirit releasing His power in our life. Consider the difference between a sedan and a race car. Both vehicles run, but what is under the hood of the race car makes it far more powerful than the sedan. When God's Spirit enables you, your performance will be like that of a race car."

WANT TO KNOW MORE?

Write to us to request the discipleship teaching on "Roles of the Holy

Spirit". Mail it to: Freedom in Jesus Prison Ministries, Attn: Teachings, P.O. Box 939, Levelland, TX 79336.

The more we surrender to the work and power of the Holy Spirit, He brings forth fruit we can never consistently produce on our own. Let's see what kind...

Fruit of the Holy Spirit

As relationships develop among people it is not at all uncommon that they begin to share common traits and characteristics. **Similarly, in our pursuit of intimacy of relationship with Jesus, the Holy Spirit begins to develop in us more of the character qualities of Christ.** Paul writes in Romans that we are to be conformed to the image of Christ. Spiritual fruit in our lives is one way the Holy Spirit makes this happen for us.

"But the fruit of the Spirit is love, joy, peace, patience, kindness, goodness, faithfulness, gentleness and self-control. Against such things there is no law." (Galatians 5:22-23).

Dr. O. S. Hawkins wrote about this verse in *The Joshua Code*:

"At first glance, there appears to be a grammatical error in this verse. Note carefully: 'The fruit of the Spirit is love, joy, peace...' The truth is that the fruit of the Spirit is love. Love, period. The nine fruits listed here are a cluster describing the evidence of the life of Christ within us. The fruit is singular here because it is the outcropping of one's life within. The fruit represents what we are rather than what we do. Here we are reintroduced to the principle of being before doing. What we do is determined by who, or whose, we really are!"

Dr. Charles Stanley, in an article entitled "Fruitful Living", writes "Nothing makes the kingdom of God more compelling to unbelievers than Christians who demonstrate the Spirit's life within them. Jesus said it this way: 'Let your light shine before men in such a way that they may see your good works, and glorify your Father who is in heaven.' (Matt. 5:16) A life characterized by the fruit of the Spirit cannot help but be noticed. It stands out like a candle in a dark room. It makes some people uncomfortable and others downright mad. But there will always be a handful who say, 'There's something different about you. What is it?'"

As an example, Joyce Meyer says, "All the fruit of the Spirit were planted inside you in seed form. Through the Spirit you can experience joy and peace in every circumstance, no matter how difficult or painful."

The world needs to see the evident work of the Spirit's fruitfulness in our lives. It is the fragrance that comes from this fruit that invites nonbelievers to become members of the body. We can only give off that fragrance when we are completely filled, fully submitted, and truly led by the Holy Spirit. On our own, without the Holy Spirit and without the fruit, we cannot be effective witnesses. The world will see right through us.

Dr. David Jeremiah, in an article entitled "Out on a Limb", wrote "The word 'fruit' describes the demonstrative results of Christian maturity. If we're growing in Christ, there should be evidence of it. People should see the signs of our Christian faith. The Father is glorified when we bear much fruit. Are you fruitful?"

We cannot produce this fruit on our own any more than a branch of a tree can produce leaves or fruit on its own. It must be attached (a part of) the trunk and roots of the tree. Likewise, we must be attached to (in) Jesus and filled with the Holy Spirit in order to produce fruit. Our part is to fully submit to God, the Holy Spirit. When we yield to the Holy Spirit Who is in us, the Holy Spirit will produce fruit from within us.

Submitting is not the easiest thing to do. It takes a conscious and deliberate act of our will. It is giving up our will and yielding our spirit to His Spirit. When we have accomplished this, then we are walking in the Spirit. The more we walk in the Spirit, the more characteristics of the fruit will be produced within us. This is what I mean when I encourage you to "go all in" for Jesus.

We are to live and move and have our being in Him. The fruit that is produced in us changes our heart. When our heart is changed, our whole being is changed. As we participate with the Holy Spirit and allow this to happen in our lives, we will become progressively more like Jesus daily and our intimacy of relationship with Him will grow.

SOME RELEVANT SCRIPTURE PASSAGES

1 John 3:2 "Dear friends, now we are children of God, and what we will be has not yet been made known. But we know that when Christ appears, we shall be like him, for we shall see him as he is."

Romans 8:29 "For those God foreknew he also predestined to be conformed to the image of his Son, that he might be the firstborn among many brothers and sisters."

Galatians 5:22-23 "But the fruit of the Spirit is love, joy, peace, forbearance, kindness, goodness, faithfulness, gentleness and self-control. Against such things there is no law."

John 15:1-5 "I am the true vine, and my Father is the gardener. He cuts off every branch in me that bears no fruit, while every branch that does bear fruit he prunes so that it will be even more fruitful. You are already clean because of the word I have spoken to you. Remain in me, as I also remain in you. No branch can bear fruit by itself; it must remain in the vine. Neither can you bear fruit unless you remain in me. I am the vine; you are the branches. If you remain in me and I in you, you will bear much fruit; apart from me you can do nothing."

Matthew 7:16-20 "By their fruit you will recognize them. Do people pick grapes from thornbushes, or figs from thistles? Likewise, every good tree bears good fruit, but a bad tree bears bad fruit. A good tree cannot bear bad fruit, and a bad tree cannot bear good fruit. Every tree that does not bear good fruit is cut down and thrown into the fire. Thus, by their fruit you will recognize them."

Matthew 3:8 "Produce fruit in keeping with repentance."

TAKEAWAY HIGHLIGHT

The world needs to see the evident work of the Spirit's fruitfulness in our lives. It is the fragrance that comes from this fruit that invites nonbelievers to become members of the body. We can only give off that fragrance when we are completely filled, fully submitted, and truly led by the Holy Spirit. On our own, without the Holy Spirit and without the fruit, we cannot be effective witnesses. The world will see right through us.

PRACTICAL APPLICATION

Imagine yourself working as a "fruit inspector". By honestly examining the fruit coming forth in your life, would you say you are participating more daily with the Holy Spirit to bring forth good fruit in keeping with Jesus, or are you primarily still influenced by the enemy to display bad fruit? Think about this seriously. Identify specific character qualities in you of both types.

WANT TO KNOW MORE?

Write to us to request the discipleship teaching on "Fruit of the Holy Spirit". Mail it to: Freedom in Jesus Prison Ministries, Attn: Teachings, P.O. Box 939, Levelland, TX 79336.

Are you thinking something like, "I can't do this" or "This is too hard for me" or "I don't have the power to make this happen"? You're right, but the good news is that the Holy Spirit can and will do it all if you let Him. We must access His Power...

Baptism in the Holy Spirit

When we accept the finished work of Jesus at the Cross, and confess His resurrection as the Son of God, the Holy Spirit comes to live in us. We "possess" the Spirit. He begins His ongoing work of sanctification to steadily make our "new man" conform to the image of Christ. However, true empowerment - God's own power - comes to us, and for us, as we totally submit to the Holy Spirit and allow Him to "possess" us–one giant step more than us merely "possessing" Him inside us.

This distinction is very real and life-impacting for our Christian walk. **It also increases our hunger and thirst for more of God which has a direct, positive benefit to our increasingly intimate relationship with Jesus.**

We are baptized (immersed) into water as an outward representation of the inward change in us. We are buried with Christ in baptism (our "old man" died); and, we are raised to walk in newness of life (our "new man" came alive). But the Book of Acts makes it clear we should also desire to be baptized (immersed) into the Holy Spirit to receive the same power that resurrected Jesus from the dead - the power to walk out this new life in the way He desires for us. **He in us, and us in Him!**

When I was still incarcerated I saw several Christians who were released before me leave, only to return to prison within a year or so. I had also heard of others that were following Jesus in prison with me who, after their release, fell away from their relationship with Jesus Christ and returned to "the world". I don't know if they returned to a physical prison, but they returned to their emotional and spiritual prisons from which they had once been set free. I know most of them had every good and honest intention to keep walking with Him, but many were powerless to resist old habits, places, and people.

Since I have been released, however, I know personally many former offenders who were transformed in prison, and who are still walking in Christ many years later. They are strong soldiers in God's army. I have seen God working in the lives of their families. I have seen them continue to prosper and experience the abundant life Jesus came to give us (John 10:10). Many have their own effective ministries now. Broken relationships have been restored. Broken hearts have been healed.

What made the difference in these two groups of people? What made the difference with me? It was clearly the "Baptism in the Holy Spirit". I firmly believe that the extra level of empowerment brought about by being baptized (immersed) in the Holy Spirit makes all the difference in enabling and empowering us to walk out our faith effectively and genuinely in prison and then, after our release, in "the free world".

The Apostle Paul understood and taught the extra level of empowerment resulting from the Holy Spirit. He had several prayers stressing this concept that he often prayed for believers, including this one:

Ephesians 3:16-21 "I pray that out of his glorious riches ***he may strengthen you with power through his Spirit in your inner being***, so that Christ may dwell in your hearts through faith. And I pray that you, being rooted and established in love, ***may have power***, together with all the saints, ***to grasp*** how wide and long and high and deep is the love of

Christ, and ***to know*** this love that surpasses knowledge—***that you may be filled to the measure of all the fullness of God***. Now to him who is able to do immeasurably more than all we ask or imagine, ***according to his power that is at work within us***, to him be glory in the church and in Christ Jesus throughout all generations, for ever and ever! Amen."

From this passage we can see that we are strengthened with God's power through the Holy Spirit in us. It is only by that power that we intimately experience the love of Christ and His fullness. God's ability to do for us far more than we can ask or imagine is according to the power of the Spirit we allow to work within us!

In another scripture, Paul recognized this:

I Corinthians 2:3-5 "I came to you in weakness and fear, and with much trembling. My message and my preaching were not with wise and persuasive words, but with ***a demonstration of the Spirit's power***, so that your faith might not rest on men's wisdom, ***but on God's power***."

As Paul realized his own natural inability to perform his assigned work, the supernatural ability and power of the Spirit flowed through him to others, building their faith!

We need the Holy Spirit in order to carry out our assignments with excellence, effectiveness, and power. As an example, let's think of some megastars in the Sports world. Some people come to mind immediately like LeBron James, Stephen Curry, Tom Brady, Payton Manning, Patrick Mahomes, just to name a few. When one of these stars is on the bench, the opponent's defense plays what might be their normal schemes and alignments. But when one of our stars re-joins the game the defense has to drastically change what they do. In this sense, these stars could surely be called "game changers"!

In similar fashion, but multiplied many times, the Holy Spirit is "The Game Changer" for the Christian walk, and also for our intense pursuit of intimacy of relationship with God!

SOME RELEVANT SCRIPTURE PASSAGES

Acts 10:37-38 "You know what has happened throughout Judea, beginning in Galilee after the baptism that John preached— how God anointed Jesus of Nazareth with the Holy Spirit and power, and how he went around doing good and healing all who were under the power of the devil, because God was with him."

Zechariah 4:6 "So he said to me, This is the word of the LORD to Zerubbabel: `Not by might nor by power, but by my Spirit,' says the LORD Almighty."

Acts 4:31-33 "After they prayed, the place where they were meeting was shaken. And they were all filled with the Holy Spirit and spoke the word of God boldly. All the believers were one in heart and mind. No one claimed that any of his possessions was his own, but they shared everything they had. With great power the apostles continued to testify to the resurrection of the Lord Jesus, and much grace was upon them all."

Acts 19:1-7 "While Apollos was at Corinth, Paul took the road through the interior and arrived at Ephesus. There he found some disciples and asked them, 'Did you receive the Holy Spirit when you believed?' They answered, 'No, we have not even heard that there is a Holy Spirit.' So Paul asked, 'Then what baptism did you receive?' 'John's baptism,' they replied. Paul said, 'John's baptism was a baptism of repentance. He told the people to believe in the one coming after him, that is, in Jesus.' On hearing this, they were baptized in the name of the Lord

Jesus. When Paul placed his hands on them, the Holy Spirit came on them, and they spoke in tongues and prophesied. There were about twelve men in all."

Acts 10:44-48 "While Peter was still speaking these words, the Holy Spirit came on all who heard the message. The circumcised believers who had come with Peter were astonished that the gift of the Holy Spirit had been poured out even on Gentiles. For they heard them speaking in tongues and praising God. Then Peter said, 'Surely no one can stand in the way of their being baptized with water. They have received the Holy Spirit just as we have.' So he ordered that they be baptized in the name of Jesus Christ. Then they asked Peter to stay with them for a few days."

Luke 11:11-13 "Which of you fathers, if your son asks for a fish, will give him a snake instead? Or if he asks for an egg, will give him a scorpion? If you then, though you are evil, know how to give good gifts to your children, how much more will your Father in heaven give the Holy Spirit to those who ask him!"

Matthew 3:11 John the Baptist said, "I baptize you with water for repentance. But after me comes one who is more powerful than I, whose sandals I am not worthy to carry. He will baptize you with the Holy Spirit and fire."

TAKEAWAY HIGHLIGHT

When we accept the finished work of Jesus at the Cross, and confess His resurrection as the Son of God, the Holy Spirit comes to live in us. We "possess" the Spirit. He begins His ongoing work of sanctification to steadily make our "new man" conform to the image of Christ. However, true empowerment – God's own power – comes to us, and for us, as we totally submit to the Holy Spirit and allow Him to "possess" us–one giant step more than us merely "possessing" Him inside us.

This distinction is very real and life-impacting for our Christian walk. It also increases our hunger and thirst for more of God which has a direct, positive benefit to our increasingly intimate relationship with Jesus.

PRACTICAL APPLICATION

Scripture is our most powerful witness to and explanation of truth. Carefully study the scriptures above, and those concerning the Holy Spirit listed in the back of this book, to gain a more thorough understanding of the Holy Spirit Baptism of fire and power. Have you asked Jesus to baptize you in the Holy Spirit? If not, what are you waiting for?

WANT TO KNOW MORE?

Write to us to request the discipleship teaching on "Baptism in the Holy Spirit". Mail it to: Freedom in Jesus Prison Ministries, Attn: Teachings, P.O. Box 939, Levelland, TX 79336.

Pursuing intimacy of relationship with Jesus is greatly enhanced by possessing a proper fear of God. Although this sounds contradictory, it's true. Read on...

The Fear of the Lord

A healthy fear of the Lord is important to our desire and ability to pursue a deeper intimacy of relationship with Him. Too little emphasis has been placed on this in recent years.

"The fear of the Lord" is not being taught in most churches across our country. Most believers cannot properly define it, and very few possess it. Yet, it is a major theme running through the entire Bible. There are over 150 distinct and explicit references to the fear of the Lord in Scripture.

"The fear of God is the very soul of godliness. If you separate the soul of man from his body, in a few days all you have is a stinking, decaying corpse. Similar results occur when the fear of God is separated from godliness. To be devoid of the fear of God is to be devoid of Biblical religion in one's experience with God. The measure of growth in any individual or church is in the measure of one increasing in the fear of God. To be ignorant of the fear of God is to be without a very important element in any believer's growth and development." (Albert N. Martin)

What is the fear of the Lord? Derek Prince taught, "Fear of the Lord is having a deep awe, reverence, and respect for Him; and a healthy fear of doing anything that would displease Him. It is honoring God as God because of His great glory, holiness, majesty and power. It is the result of a deep appreciation of our own nothingness and of the infinite greatness and majesty of God. It stands opposed to pride and self-confidence.

"For believers, it is not a fear that God will ever judge them for their sin (John 5:24; Romans 8:1). However, all God's children should possess a holy fear that trembles at the Word of God and causes them to turn away from evil."

The world is full of the fear of evil, but there is very little fear of God. A true fear of God enables one to receive more of God's perfect love, which casts out fear (1 John 4:18). As believers, if we have an ever-increasing revelation and possession of the fear of God, we will never need to worry about the fear of evil, or fear any other circumstance.

In *Our Daily Bread*, they wrote, "To 'fear' the Lord God is to give Him the highest respect. For the believer, it is not a matter of feeling intimidated by Him or His character. But out of respect for His Person and authority, we walk in all His ways and keep His commandments. Out of 'love', we serve Him with all our heart and with all our soul – rather than merely out of duty. Love flows out of our deep gratitude for His love for us, rather than our likes and dislikes. 'We love Him because He first loved us' (I John 4:19)"

Dr. David Jeremiah, in a devotional entitled "Life's Starting Point" wrote, "Since the Bible says there is 'no condemnation to those who are in Christ Jesus' (Romans 8:1), we've been delivered from the fear of God's wrath. Yet Paul told the Philippian believers to "work out [their] own salvation with fear and trembling" (Philippians 2:12). For believers, the fear of God is the astonished reverence we feel as we gaze upon His majesty, contemplate His immensity, and recognize His infinite power. That's a missing ingredient in much of Christianity."

In an article entitled "Fostering Fear of God" R.C. Sproul wrote, "Martin Luther made an important distinction concerning the fear of God. He distinguished between servile fear and filial fear. He described servile fear as that kind of fear a prisoner has for his torturer. Filial fear is the fear of a son who loves his father and does not want to offend him or let him down. It is a fear born of respect. When the Bible calls us to fear God, it is issuing a call to a fear born of reverence, awe, and adoration. It is a respect of the highest magnitude."

Along with awe, reverence and respect for God, we will have a humble, submissive attitude as an expression of having the fear of the Lord in our lives. When we are arrogant, conceited, self-sufficient and self-proclaiming there is no evidence of the true fear of the Lord in us, and it will not be possible to fully develop an intimacy of relationship with God.

SOME RELEVANT SCRIPTURE PASSAGES

Deuteronomy 6:1-2 "These are the commands, decrees and laws the Lord your God directed me to teach you to observe in the land that you are crossing the Jordan to possess, so that you, your children and their children after them may fear the Lord your God as long as you live by keeping all his decrees and commands that I give you, and so that you may enjoy long life."

Deuteronomy 5:29 "Oh, that their hearts would be inclined to fear me and keep all my commands always, so that it might go well with them and their children forever!"

Deuteronomy 10:12-13 "And now, O Israel, what does the Lord your God ask of you but to fear the Lord your God, to walk in all his ways, to love him, to serve the Lord your God with all your heart and with all your soul, and to observe the Lord's commands and decrees that I am giving you today for your own good?"

1 Chronicles 16:25-26 "For great is the Lord and most worthy of praise; he is to be feared above all gods. For all the gods of the nations are idols, but the Lord made the heavens."

Psalm 34:7-11 "The angel of the Lord encamps around those who fear him, and he delivers them. Taste and see that the Lord is good; blessed is the man who takes refuge in him. Fear the Lord, you his saints, for those who fear him lack nothing. The lions may grow weak and hungry, but those who seek the Lord lack no good thing. Come, my children, listen to me; I will teach you the fear of the Lord."

Proverbs 2:1-5 "My son, if you accept my words and store up my commands within you, turning your ear to wisdom and applying your heart to understanding, and if you call out for insight and cry aloud for understanding, and if you look for it as for silver and search for it as for hidden treasure, then you will understand the fear of the Lord and find the knowledge of God."

Proverbs 9:10 "The fear of the Lord is the beginning of wisdom, and knowledge of the Holy One is understanding."

Acts 9:31 "Then the church throughout Judea, Galilee and Samaria enjoyed a time of peace. It was strengthened; and encouraged by the Holy Spirit, it grew in numbers, living in the fear of the Lord."

Acts 10:34-35 "Then Peter began to speak: 'I now realize how true it is that God does not show favoritism but accepts men from every nation who fear him and do what is right.'"

TAKEAWAY HIGHLIGHT

Along with awe, reverence and respect for God, we will have a humble, submissive attitude as an expression of having the fear of the Lord in our lives. When we are arrogant, conceited, self-sufficient and self-proclaiming there is no evidence of the true fear of the Lord in us, and it will not be possible to fully develop an intimacy of relationship with God.

PRACTICAL APPLICATION

Ask the Holy Spirit to show you whether you have a proper fear of the Lord. Do you want to always do your best to please Him, or are you generally more concerned with pleasing man? Study the scriptures above and write down all the benefits of a healthy fear of God.

WANT TO KNOW MORE?

Write to us to request the discipleship teaching on "The Fear of the Lord". Mail it to: Freedom in Jesus Prison Ministries, Attn: Teachings, P.O. Box 939, Levelland, TX 79336.

As distinguished from the positive benefits of the fear of the Lord, our relationship with God is hindered when we fear man or anything else. And, today the world is filled with fear...

Do Not Fear

The fear of man, fear of the world, and fear of impending events, are all stumbling blocks in our path of increasing intimacy of relationship with God. **This kind of fear is the opposite of trusting God. Instead, we must choose to exercise faith in His Faithfulness, His Promises and His Word.**

In recent years, our world has been subjected to many events, illnesses, wars, economic crises, geologic changes, global pandemics, famine, drought, floods, and lawlessness. The powers that be *"declare"* their own narratives about these events in such a way that objective truth is becoming hard to find and discern. Who or what are we to believe?

As committed followers and lovers of Jesus, we *declare* that all these things are given names that have to submit to the Name above all names, Jesus Christ!!! We will believe God and His Word. We are *declaring* Psalm 91 over our lives daily, and I recommend you do that as well. In fact, I invite you to stop reading right now, turn to Psalm 91, and meditate on what the Lord your God *declares* in His Word. Go ahead, I'll wait...

In March, 2020, as COVID broke out, our ministry Founder, Don Castleberry, wrote these following three paragraphs:

"Fear is the natural feeling of alarm that can be used by God to warn us of imminent danger, pain or disaster. We have Holy Spirit... you **do** know He is your counselor and guide, right? We must stay in constant contact with Him. He will tell you which way to go, when to do it, and how to do it. We are not to be afraid of what we have no control over, and we have no control of the coronavirus and the pain, horror and death that it is causing everywhere. We have Father God, Jesus, and Holy Spirit as our heavenly advisors–get close to them, know them, worship and praise them with reckless abandon.

"The time is far past when we should have already been expressing our faith in God to everyone that would listen, including the fact that the spirit of fear is our enemy, and we have power... God's power... over this spirit. Be advised... God is well aware of what is happening and He wants us, His people, to show other people His power which is already available to us.

"Fear surrounds you where you live, through rumors, half-truths, and out and out lies. Yet I know prisoners with such faith in God, such Holy Spirit power, that the devil knows better than to test them because he will be defeated by the Word of God. With all the fear on the media, some people have literally been sucked so far down that they don't know what to believe. BELIEVE THE WORD! Proverbs 29:25 says, "The fear of man brings a snare." God is stronger than any man. Just fear God!"

Dr. David Jeremiah wrote, in a devotional entitled, "Do Not Be Afraid – The Opposite of Fear":

"When we think of faith, we think of belief. And when we think of the opposite of belief, we naturally think of unbelief. Therefore, we conclude that the opposite of faith is unbelief. And from a dictionary perspective, that is true. But the Bible usually sets something besides unbelief in opposition to faith — and that is fear. From a grammatical point of view, the opposite of believing may be *not* believing. But from the perspective of life, the opposite of faith is fear."

Jim Denison, *www.denisonministries.org*, wrote the following two paragraphs in an article entitled, "Hoping in Hope, or Hoping in God":

"The psalmist announces, 'God is our refuge and strength, a very present help in trouble' (Psalm 46:1). I told our church that a "refuge" is a place where we go to escape, to be sheltered and safe. But we must choose to go there. If we think we can face the storm unaided, a refuge cannot help us.

"So go to God every time fear finds you. The Hebrew word for *refuge* is literally translated, 'a place to which we flee.' Don't walk—run. Flee to your Father's help, power, love, and grace. Seek and trust the strength he offers."

What an exciting time to be alive and to know who we are IN Christ Jesus! **God has appointed us to be living at this exact moment in history, near the end of days, because He knows we will properly represent Him through the challenging days ahead.**

We must stand strong, be filled with courage, and boldly proclaim His message of hope, salvation and deliverance to all around us, wherever we are. Now more than ever, we must be the light in the darkness. Let the Holy Spirit fill you so full of peace and joy that you are over-flowing! As you are consistently maintaining calmness in the midst of very trying and worrisome circumstances, unbelievers around you will be compelled to come to you to ask, *"What must I do to be saved? I want what you have!"*

We believe strongly that we are entering the "beginning of birth pains" of Matthew 24:8. The Earth will be facing many problems with each passing year. Like birth pains, tragic events will increase steadily in severity and frequency. The Bible says there will be signs in the heavens and men's hearts will be failing them for fear for looking after those things that are coming upon the Earth (Luke 21:10-11, 25-28). Devastating earthquakes and powerfully eruptive volcanos will become more frequent. Wars are increasing all around the world. Recent locust swarms that devastated eastern Africa, the Middle East, Pakistan and China were the worst in recent history reminding everyone of the locust plagues of Egypt. Droughts are getting much worse in some areas, while floods of Biblical proportions are increasing in severity and frequency in other parts of the world. Supply chains are significantly disrupted, and will soon begin to result in massive shortages, especially food. Meteors striking the Earth will be more frequent and will be causing significant fires.

None of this surprises God. In fact, His Word foretells it. Do not fear. God is Faithful, Able and True. He will never leave us or forsake us. Make a choice daily to represent Him well to all those around you.

Brothers and sisters in Christ, be strong and very courageous (Joshua 1:9). During these challenging and exciting times we will see a great, last days' soul harvest bringing hundreds of millions into the Kingdom of God. Pray diligently for your family, for the lost souls around you, for our incarcerated family around the world, all the prison Chaplains and Volunteers, the prisons' correctional officers, our leaders, our country, and for all the Body of Christ.

Do not fear. God the Father, Jesus, and the Holy Spirit are firmly in control!

SOME RELEVANT SCRIPTURE PASSAGES

Matthew 14:27 "But Jesus immediately said to them: 'Take courage! It is I. Don't be afraid.'"

John 14:1, 27 "Jesus said, 'Do not let your hearts be troubled. You believe in God; believe also in me... Peace I leave with you; my peace I give you. I do not give to you as the world gives. Do not let your hearts be troubled and do not be afraid.'"

Isaiah 44:8 "Do not tremble, do not be afraid. Did I not proclaim this and foretell it long ago? You are my witnesses. Is there any God besides me? No, there is no other Rock; I know not one."

Joshua 1:8-9 "Keep this Book of the Law always on your lips; meditate on it day and night, so that you may be careful to do everything written in it. Then you will be prosperous and successful. Have I not commanded you? Be strong and courageous. Do not be afraid; do not be discouraged, for the Lord your God will be with you wherever you go."

Mark 5:36 "Overhearing what they said, Jesus told him, 'Don't be afraid; just believe.'"

Acts 18:9 "One night the Lord spoke to Paul in a vision: 'Do not be afraid; keep on speaking, do not be silent.'"

2 Chronicles 20:15 "He said: 'Listen, King Jehoshaphat and all who live in Judah and Jerusalem! This is what the Lord says to you: 'Do not be afraid or discouraged because of this vast army. For the battle is not yours, but God's.'"

Psalm 91:5-7 "You will not fear the terror of night, nor the arrow that flies by day, nor the pestilence that stalks in the darkness, nor the plague that destroys at midday. A thousand may fall at your side, ten thousand at your right hand, but it will not come near you."

Luke 12:4 Jesus said, "I tell you, my friends, do not be afraid of those who kill the body and after that can do no more."

1 Peter 3:14 "But even if you should suffer for what is right, you are blessed. 'Do not fear their threats; do not be frightened.'"

TAKEAWAY HIGHLIGHT

We must stand strong, be filled with courage, and boldly proclaim His message of hope, salvation and deliverance to all around us, wherever we are. Now more than ever, we must be the light in the darkness. Let the Holy Spirit fill you so full of peace and joy that you are over-flowing! As you are consistently maintaining calmness in the midst of very trying and worrisome circumstances, unbelievers around you will be compelled to come to you to ask, "What must I do to be saved? I want what you have!"

PRACTICAL APPLICATION

Ask the Holy Spirit to bring to your mind the events troubling your soul which are causing anxiety and robbing your peace. One by one, turn them over to God and choose to trust Him to protect, comfort, encourage and guide you. Remind the devil he's under your feet!

WANT TO KNOW MORE?

Write to us to request the discipleship teaching on "Do Not Fear". Mail it to: Freedom in Jesus Prison Ministries, Attn: Teachings, P.O. Box 939, Levelland, TX 79336.

Fear is often used as a system of control and deception. Jesus repeatedly warned us not to be deceived, yet it is so very prevalent in the world. Do not be deceived ...

Do Not Be Deceived

When the Disciples asked Jesus about the signs of the days immediately prior to His Return, He emphasized the possibility of overwhelming deception. Jesus used phrases such as "do not be deceived"; "be careful that no one deceives you"; and, "if possible, even the elect would be deceived".

As believers we have the Holy Spirit living inside us, guiding us daily to a deeper relationship with Jesus, and giving us the gift of discernment to help us not to be deceived. Our challenge is to learn to better hear His voice and be willing to be obedient.

Shonda Whitworth, *www.fortressofhopeministries.com*, wrote in an article, "Can A Believer Be Deceived", the following four paragraphs:

"Adam and Eve walked with God every day and knew Him on a very personal level. Due to this intimacy, they knew God's heart. But then the serpent showed up. How did he get Eve to take the forbidden fruit? He did not force it down her throat, but he cunningly tricked her by asking, 'Did God really say ...?'

"Ever since Genesis, the enemy has twisted the truth, lied, schemed, and fooled believers. No one is exempt from this wicked tactic. So, we must train ourselves by the Word of God to recognize it.

"Galatians 6:7 says, ***'Do not be deceived, God is not mocked; for whatever a man sows, that he will also reap' (NKJV).*** Sowing and reaping are farming terms. We wouldn't plant potatoes then at harvest time look for carrots. That's just ridiculous, right? The same principle applies in the Spirit realm.

"According to this passage, we can be duped and not realize it. The definition for "deceive" from the Greek means "to lead astray, cause to wander; to roam." Deception sneaks up on us. How do we know if we've been living in deception? We look at the fruit of our lives."

Sinclair Ferguson, in an article entitled "Can Satan Deceive God's Elect?" wrote, "If we think Christians cannot be deceived, the deception has already begun."

Deception is believing what is not true. More than ever, it seems people are intentionally misleading others. In 2 Timothy 3:13, Paul writes, "evildoers and impostors will go from bad to worse, deceiving and being deceived."

Tom Ascol, in an article entitled "Self-deception" teaches about the very real problem of people deceiving themselves. Here are two paragraphs:

"If deception is dangerous, self-deception is disastrous. When you have been deceived by another, that person shares the blame for your condition, but when your deception is self-imposed, you alone are accountable. Further, self-deception is perniciously destructive. It is hard to detect and harder to eliminate.

"Think about it. Have you ever met a person who admitted to being self-deceived? The very nature of self-deception is that there is no conscious awareness of believing lies. Self-deception emerges from living on a self-referential basis. Such people measure themselves by themselves and compare themselves to themselves and, Paul says, 'are not wise' (2 Corinthians 10:12)."

The Holy Spirit will always guide us in ways that line up with the Word and the character of Jesus. The more studied we are in the Word the easier it is to discern the leading of the Holy Spirit. Jesus warned about false prophets. We must be very careful to whom we listen, and everything we hear should be carefully tested by the Word.

Adrian Rogers, Love Worth Finding Ministries, in an article entitled "False Prophets: Their Method, Manner and Motive", included these two paragraphs:

"In these last days, Scripture warns that false prophets will arise and deceive many. Believers who are not well-grounded make easy targets for doctrines that may sound good but are filled with error.

"Some doctrines are deadly: those that alter the Deity of Christ, redefine the Trinity — or even deny the Trinity. Sometimes a charmer will lead the susceptible off into error that results in physical death — Jonestown and Waco come to mind. We must sharpen our awareness and be alert — not just for ourselves but for our loved ones who might otherwise be drawn to a false prophet."

Here are some deceptions already prevalent in our world about which I want to warn you:

1. **Deception**: Some believe there are more ways to God than through Jesus.

   Truth: Jesus is the ONLY Way!

2. **Deception**: After I am saved, I can keep sinning because of grace.

   Truth: Grace is not permission to sin, but the power to resist sin. If a person does not turn from their old way of life, they have not repented. Without true repentance, they are not saved.

3. **Deception**: The Bible was written by fallible men, so the Bible has errors.

   Truth: God's Word is without error. God means what He says, and says what He means. All Scripture is Divinely inspired, and men were led to write by the Holy Spirit.

4. **Deception**: God does not do things today the way He did in Jesus' day.

   Truth: God does not change. Jesus Christ is the same yesterday, today and forever. God still does what He always did.

5. **Deception**: We do not need to be led by the Holy Spirit daily like the early Christians because now we have the Bible to guide us.

   Truth: The Holy Spirit is our Helper, Teacher, Friend and Guide. He will lead us and never contradict the Word.

6. **Deception**: God is not three persons in One Divine Being (the Trinity); rather, God is just an impersonal universal force.

   Truth: The Father is God, the Son is God, and the Holy Spirit is God–all uncreated, co-equal and co-eternal, all of Whom want a personal relationship with us.

7. **Deception**: There is no eternal "Hell", and a loving God would not send someone there.

Truth: God does not send anyone to Hell. He is so loving that He will not make someone be with Him in Heaven who did not choose Him on Earth. Man chooses.

8. **Deception**: If a person's good works outweigh their bad, they will go to Heaven.

   Truth: A person gets to Heaven by grace alone through faith alone in Jesus alone. All "work" was done by Him and finished at Calvary.

9. **Deception**: As Christians, we do not need the Old Testament.

   Truth: All Scripture is divinely inspired and given to us as encouragement and examples. Jesus said, "Scripture cannot be broken".

10. **Deception**: A person can "be a god" or "become a god".

    Truth: There is Only One God, and He is uncreated. A created being cannot become uncreated. God is the uncreated First Cause of everything.

11. **Deception**: Aliens from other worlds seeded our planet and created us. They are coming back to save us.

    Truth: Fallen Angels, that is, demons, are once again trying to insert themselves into this world from another dimension, the spiritual realm, not another planet. God is our Creator and Jesus is our only Savior!

Do not be deceived. Your ongoing pursuit of deeper relationship with God will help you guard against the lies and deception of the enemy.

SOME RELEVANT SCRIPTURE PASSAGES

Matthew 24:4-5 Jesus answered: "Watch out that no one deceives you. For many will come in my name, claiming, 'I am the Messiah,' and will deceive many."

Matthew 24:10-11 "At that time many will turn away from the faith and will betray and hate each other, and many false prophets will appear and deceive many people."

Matthew 24:23-24 "At that time if anyone says to you, 'Look, here is the Messiah!' or, 'There he is!' do not believe it. For false messiahs and false prophets will appear and perform great signs and wonders to deceive, if possible, even the elect."

John 8:44 Jesus said, "You belong to your father, the devil, and you want to carry out your father's desires. He was a murderer from the beginning, not holding to the truth, for there is no truth in him. When he lies, he speaks his native language, for he is a liar and the father of lies."

Jeremiah 9:6 "You live in the midst of deception; in their deceit they refuse to acknowledge me, declares the Lord."

Proverbs 14:8 "The wisdom of the prudent is to give thought to their ways, but the folly of fools is deception."

Jeremiah 23:25-26 "I have heard what the prophets say who prophesy lies in my name. They say, 'I had a dream! I had a dream!' How long will this continue in the hearts of these lying prophets, who prophesy the delusions of their own minds?"

1 Timothy 4:1-2 "The Spirit clearly says that in later times some will abandon the faith and follow deceiving spirits and things taught by demons. Such teachings come through hypocritical liars, whose consciences have been seared as with a hot iron."

2 Thessalonians 2:9-12 "The coming of the lawless one will be in accordance with how Satan works. He will use all sorts of displays of power through signs and wonders that serve the lie, and all the ways

that wickedness deceives those who are perishing. They perish because they refused to love the truth and so be saved. For this reason God sends them a powerful delusion so that they will believe the lie and so that all will be condemned who have not believed the truth but have delighted in wickedness."

TAKEAWAY HIGHLIGHT

The Holy Spirit will always guide us in ways that line up with the Word and the character of Jesus. The more studied we are in the Word the easier it is to discern the leading of the Holy Spirit. Jesus warned about false prophets. We must be very careful to whom we listen, and everything we hear should be carefully tested by the Word.

Do not be deceived. Your ongoing pursuit of deeper relationship with God will help you guard against the lies and deception of the enemy.

PRACTICAL APPLICATION

In reviewing the preceding examples of Deception and Truth, think about which ones you've heard before. Perhaps you have even believed some of them or know someone who does. Find scriptures that support each Truth listed. Talk to the Holy Spirit for more insight and discernment in your life.

WANT TO KNOW MORE?

Write to us to request the discipleship teaching on "Do Not Be Deceived". Mail it to: Freedom in Jesus Prison Ministries, Attn: Teachings, P.O. Box 939, Levelland, TX 79336.

One of the biggest deceptions for believers can be holding on to un-forgiveness towards ourselves thinking that we deserve whatever we get. We must forgive ourselves...

Forgiving Ourselves

Growing in relationship with God first requires we receive His love and forgiveness. Once we believe that He really does forgive us, then we must choose to forgive ourselves. We must be free of our past so that we will be unburdened of guilt, shame, regret, remorse and embarrassment. Then it becomes easier to follow the Holy Spirit daily and trust God with our future.

Unforgiveness toward self holds back many Christians from enjoying everything of the abundant life Jesus came to give us. Until we really stop to evaluate this in our own lives we will be leaving a door open for the enemy to torment us, and our relationship with God is hindered.

Perhaps you are feeling like I did after I had been in prison long enough to be free of all the physical effects of my addictions. I realized I hated myself for what I had done to ruin my life. I never blamed anyone else – only me – for the mistakes I made, one after another, that eventually led me to prison. In fact, I was so disappointed with myself as the cause of a wasted life that I spent many years hopelessly deep in depression, leading to several suicide attempts.

I had pushed away and broken relationship with all my friends and family. Prior to going to prison I was homeless for three years. I had no material possessions other than what was in the prison's property room. I was convinced there was no hope of anything ever getting better. I thought my future could be no better than my past.

I will never forget the first glimmer of hope I experienced as I began to accept God's forgiveness of me and the removal of all my sin – past, present and future. I had never experienced the peace, emotional freedom and mental release I felt when God showed me I must forgive myself, so I could trust Him and move forward as the "new creature" he made me when I was "born again". I had to decide to "let the past be the past". I accepted the truth of His Word that he no longer held my past against me. He showed me I too had to stop holding my past against me. I needed to accept His forgiveness, forgive myself, and move on.

Ancient tyrants had a custom of binding a dead body to a captive as punishment, and making the captive drag the cumbersome and offensive burden with him wherever he went. Most often disease resulted, and death followed.

Similarly, the Romans had a practice of taking a convicted murderer into the desert, staking him down, and then laying the corpse of his victim on top of him. It wasn't long before the convict died of disease, exposure, starvation and/or smothering under the stench and decay of rotting flesh.

Why am I telling you this? Just as the corruption from that corpse would fall upon the guilty man until he eventually died, so does the burden of our own un-forgiveness towards ourselves eat away at us – bringing destruction, corruption and death.

Robert Moment, in an article entitled "How to Forgive Yourself" wrote this:

"Have you thought about giving *yourself* the gift of forgiveness this year? Are you ready to be free and ready to move ahead into a life of graciousness and love in the future? If you are, you must forgive yourself for the mistakes you've made – and that can be a difficult thing to do! It's easy to try and hide our mistakes and not think about them, but what we hide has power over us; it can sit there in the back of our minds and fester, eating away at our self-assurance and our sense of God's love for us, making us wonder if we are truly worthy. We have to let go of our mistakes and forgive ourselves just as God forgives us. And He *does* forgive us, completely and with no reservations! (Nehemiah 9:17; Luke 6:37)"

Jesus prayed to the Father, "Forgive us our debts, as we also have forgiven our debtors" (Matthew 6:12). We can forgive ourselves as a "debtor" because our "old man" is dead. We died in Christ when He died. Dead men no longer owe anything. Their debts are forgiven. You are not to hold your former self accountable for what a dead man did. No matter how serious a criminal's offenses may have been, he is no longer subject to prosecution and punishment after he dies.

In Mark 11:25, Jesus said, "And when you stand praying, if you hold anything against anyone, forgive him, so that your Father in heaven may forgive you your sins." You are included in the category as "anyone". You are not to "hold anything" against yourself.

Os Hillman, in an article entitled "Forgiving Ourselves" gave this example of the effect of holding on to our past:

"The murderer was condemned to life in prison. Then one day something amazing happened. The guard came and opened the jail cell. 'You are free to go. Someone else is taking your place,' said the guard. 'How can this be? I am still guilty!' said the prisoner. 'Your debt has been paid. You are free to leave,' said the guard once more. The prisoner decided not to leave. 'I cannot allow another to pay my debt,' said the prisoner. Because of his pride he chose to remain in bondage."

Craig Denison, "First15 Devotional", closed his article on this topic with this paragraph:

"Your heavenly Father is beckoning you to forgive yourself today. He's waiting to fill you with his mercy and grace to overflowing. He's ready to lead you into a lifestyle of loving yourself as he has loved you. **Run out to meet him today.** Allow him to clothe you with love, honor and grace. Allow him to show you the depths of his compassion for you. And live today in light of the glorious grace of Jesus."

"Bury your past or it will bury you." (Dwight Thompson)

SOME RELEVANT SCRIPTURE PASSAGES

Isaiah 43:18-19 "Forget the former things; do not dwell on the past. See, I am doing a new thing! Now it springs up; do you not perceive it? I am making a way in the desert and streams in the wasteland."

Philippians 3:13 "...But one thing I do: Forgetting what is behind and straining toward what is ahead, I press on toward the goal to win the prize for which God has called me heavenward in Christ Jesus."

Ephesians 4:31-32 "Get rid of all bitterness, rage and anger, brawling and slander, along with every form of malice. Be kind and compassionate to one another, forgiving each other, just as in Christ God forgave you."

Luke 6:37 "Do not judge, and you will not be judged. Do not condemn, and you will not be condemned. Forgive, and you will be forgiven."

Isaiah 1:18 "Come now, let us reason together, says the Lord. Though your sins are like scarlet, they shall be as white as snow; though they are as red as crimson, they shall be like wool."

I John 1:9 "If we confess our sins, he is faithful and just and will forgive us our sins and purify us from all unrighteousness."

TAKEAWAY HIGHLIGHT

Growing in relationship with God first requires we receive His love and forgiveness. Once we believe that He really does forgive us, then we must choose to forgive ourselves. We must be free of our past so that we will be unburdened of guilt, shame, regret, remorse and embarrassment. Then it becomes easier to follow the Holy Spirit daily and trust God with our future.

PRACTICAL APPLICATION

Ask the Holy Spirit to help you make a private list of the things in your past you are ashamed of, still feel guilty for, you're embarrassed about, or sins for which you don't feel forgiven.

Meditate on the complete love and forgiveness you already have from the Father because of the finished work of Jesus. Talk to God one last time about these things, then destroy the list. From now on, do not let the devil continue to accuse you over your past. It is forgiven. Move on.

WANT TO KNOW MORE?

Write to us to request the discipleship teaching on "Forgiving Self". Mail it to: Freedom in Jesus Prison Ministries, Attn: Teachings, P.O. Box 939, Levelland, TX 79336.

As we begin to realize how much we have been forgiven, and how much God loves us, we will want to extend that love and forgiveness to others. Let's examine why this is important...

Forgiving Others

Our continued growth into increasing intimacy of relationship with Jesus is severely hindered if we have un-forgiveness in our heart towards anyone for anything.

Mark 11:25 Jesus said, "And when you stand praying, if you hold anything against anyone, forgive him, so that your Father in heaven may forgive you your sins."

A number of other scriptures make it clear that holding on to un-forgiveness is an act of stubborn disobedience and rebellion towards God. Jesus forgave us; we must forgive others.

One of the primary reasons Jesus came was so we could have forgiveness through His blood. One of the last things Jesus did was to pray to God, asking His Father to forgive those who had spit upon Him, ridiculed Him, beat Him, mocked Him, and nailed Him to that cross. We must also be willing to love and pray for those who have harmed us. We must be willing to forgive them.

In an article entitled, "I Choose Forgiveness", Dr. James McDonald writes, "Jesus leaves no doubt that there is never an acceptable reason for un-forgiveness. He taught that forgiveness is limitless. It's every time, all the time, forgive!" What is forgiveness? James McDonald continues, "First of all, you must understand what forgiveness is not. Forgiveness is not a feeling. You will never **feel** like forgiving. Forgiveness is a choice; it is an act of the will. Forgiveness is the decision to release a person from the obligation that results when they injure you. It is treating them as though it never happened. It is *not pretending* it never happened. It is treating them *as though* it never happened. There's a big difference."

When we hold un-forgiveness towards someone, it causes a root of bitterness in us – a stronghold for the enemy. We are turned over to "the tormenters" of anger, resentment, hatred, temper, and control – all of which can lead to retaliation, violence and even murder. A seed of un-forgiveness planted in a ground of hurt gives us a harvest of pain. It grieves our spirit, torments our mind, and distresses us emotionally. All these, combined with a desire for vengeance or retaliation, hurts *us*–not the person who offended us. Often times they may not even realize their offense. This has been likened to drinking poison ourselves, thinking it will kill the other person.

We need to come to God and *choose to forgive* the person who has hurt us. James McDonald writes, "It is not 'I need to forgive', not 'I should forgive', not 'I'm going to forgive someday', but 'I do forgive this person'... After we have forgiven someone we will not bring it up again to the person we've forgiven; we won't bring it up to other people; and, we will not bring it up to our self." We may never really "forget", but we will deliberately choose not to remember – and not continue to hold it against someone–any longer. We refuse to let the enemy win when he tries to bring it up to us in our mind in the future. Instead we will "take every thought captive", and remind ourselves and the enemy that the person has been forgiven and released!

There are many emotional hurts, wounds and offenses caused by un-forgiveness and bitterness. We must learn how to be healed from this "soul pain" once and for all.

In her article, "Forgive", by Joyce Meyer, she explains, "We have to talk about forgiveness because the number of lives that are ruined through anger and un-forgiveness is astonishing. Some people don't know any better, but there are many Christians who do know better yet they are unwilling to make the right choice. They live according to their feelings, rather than moving beyond them to do the better thing... It's time to get a new perspective and realize that when you refuse to forgive, the person you're really hurting the most is you!"

Dr. Charles Stanley, in an article entitled "Genuine Forgiveness", writes, "Do you have an emotional wound that has never healed? Maybe someone wronged you or a loved one years ago, and the injury remains. From time to time, similar situations bring the painful emotions right back to the surface. Close friends and family members may have lost patience with your inability to move on. You, too, wonder how much longer the suffering will last. My friend, freedom from hurt and anger comes only through complete forgiveness.

"You can experience liberty from old wounds that now hold you in bondage. When the Holy Spirit reminds you of those who need your forgiveness, don't ignore His still small voice (I Kings 19:12). Find the courage and strength to face the past, and willingly release others from the emotional debts you might feel they owe you. Only then will you know genuine freedom from bitterness, resentment, and un-forgiveness."

Pastor Gary Delay, in his book, *Transformation*, explains, "Forgiveness is the foundational truth of Christianity...Dealing with forgiveness issues introduces the very real need to ask God to heal the hurts, wounds and offenses caused by the offender. It is when we deal with our emotional hurts and wounds that we will experience the freedom that God has for each of us. We will no longer feel the hurts that are associated with the event or person that we have forgiven...When we are hurt, wounded, or offended, forgiveness must be an immediate response. It must become our lifestyle.

"Refusing to forgive a person creates an invisible cord that binds us to that person. It binds us to every person in our lives who has hurt, wounded, or offended us whom we refuse to forgive. This prolongs the pain and deepens the wound. Until we choose to forgive these people, we will be imprisoned with and bound to them. To forgive them is to be set free to be what God wants us to be. By pardoning them we will be set free, unbound, and pardoned ourselves by God."

Brothers and sisters in Christ, your progress in pursuing intimate relationship with Jesus is hindered when we hold on to un-forgiveness. Make a decision to forgive today.

SOME RELEVANT SCRIPTURE PASSAGES

Matthew 6:14-15 "For if you forgive men when they sin against you, your heavenly Father will also forgive you. But if you do not forgive men their sins, your Father will not forgive your sins."

Matthew 5:23-24 "Therefore, if you are offering your gift at the altar and there remember that your brother has something against you, leave your gift there in front of the altar. First go and be reconciled to your brother; then come and offer your gift."

Mark 11:25 "And when you stand praying, if you hold anything against anyone, forgive him, so that your Father in heaven may forgive you your sins."

Ephesians 4:31-32 "Get rid of all bitterness, rage and anger, brawling and slander, along with every form of malice. Be kind and compassionate to one another, forgiving each other, just as in Christ God forgave you."

Hebrews 12:15 "See to it that no one misses the grace of God and that no bitter root grows up to cause trouble and defile many."

1 John 2:9-11 "Anyone who claims to be in the light but hates his brother is still in the darkness. Whoever loves his brother lives in the light, and there is nothing in him to make him stumble. But whoever hates his brother is in the darkness and walks around in the darkness; he does not know where he is going, because the darkness has blinded him."

James 4:17 "Anyone, then, who knows the good he ought to do and doesn't do it, sins."

TAKEAWAY HIGHLIGHT

One of the primary reasons Jesus came was so we could have forgiveness through His blood. One of the last things Jesus did was to pray to God, asking His Father to forgive those who had spit upon Him, ridiculed Him, beat Him, mocked Him, and nailed Him to that cross. We must also be willing to love and pray for those who have harmed us. We must be willing to forgive them.

Our continued growth into increasing intimacy of relationship with Jesus is severely hindered if we have un-forgiveness in our heart towards anyone for anything.

PRACTICAL APPLICATION

The decision to forgive those who have hurt us–even though we do not presently "feel like it" – is so very, very important! Ask the Holy Spirit to show you every event and person who has hurt you. Make a list. Then pray a separate prayer of forgiveness over each one on the list. After you have prayed through them all one at a time, destroy this list.

Over the next few days and weeks the Spirit will bring other events and people to your remembrance. Deal with them quickly and fully in the same manner. You will have a new sense of freedom and lightness of being. Express it gratefully and joyously to Jesus!

WANT TO KNOW MORE?

Write to us to request the discipleship teaching on "Forgiving Others – Parts 1 & 2". Mail it to: Freedom in Jesus Prison Ministries, Attn: Teachings, P.O. Box 939, Levelland, TX 79336.

Asking others to forgive us for how we have hurt or offended them requires humility, kindness and wisdom. It's challenging, but let's learn about it...

Asking Forgiveness from Others

When we have offended or hurt others, we must ask God to forgive us so that we do not hamper our progression in relationship with Him. Also, whenever wisdom and practicality allow us, we should ask forgiveness from those whom we have offended. Asking others to forgive us is sometimes a difficult thing for us to do because of pride. It requires humility to admit we were wrong, and to ask someone to forgive us.

Most people never attempt to heal broken relationships because they refuse to take responsibility for their own actions, and it forces them to come face to face with their own pride. It is hard to admit you have done something wrong and put yourself at the mercy of others. We have all seen people try to squirm their way out of a difficult confrontation about something painful they have done. The most insecure people use denial or blaming others to escape from having to wake up to their own failure. **Being humble is the key to experiencing forgiveness and healing. Humble yourself; it is the first step toward being forgiven.**

Many people carry around a significant amount of guilt as a result of actions they have taken that have been hurtful to others. Many times this guilt can have significant consequences for the person carrying it, and will limit their ability to enjoy the abundant life Jesus died to give them. When we have hurt someone and we want to repent for our action we need to ask forgiveness from both God and, when it is possible, the person we have wronged.

No one likes rejection. God, we know, accepts us and will forgive us when we humbly repent. A person we have hurt may not. These people are sometimes hurt so badly that they don't even want to hear from you to give you the chance to apologize. Someone cannot be forced to forgive you. All you can do is show remorse, ask for forgiveness, and pray for them.

If someone chooses not to forgive you that is their choice, not yours. You cannot control them, you can only control yourself. By apologizing and seeking forgiveness, you have done all that you can control. God may have to work with them awhile before they choose to forgive. Ask God the Father to bless them and reveal Himself more fully to them.

You cannot let someone else's inability or unwillingness to forgive you bind you to the point where you are unable to let go of the feelings of guilt. Even if the offended party cannot forgive you, you need to take comfort in the fact that God has forgiven you. Once you have done your part, then it will be time to release yourself from any guilt that may be harboring within you and holding you back from realizing the full potential God has planned for your life.

In my sin, I had in one way or another offended all my family and friends. I had pushed or driven everyone away. As I began to learn about forgiveness, I sensed that I needed to get past my pride so that I could humble myself to ask forgiveness from the ones I had offended who I could go ahead and contact from inside prison. At first, it was my two brothers and my younger sister. I felt a burden begin to lift off me as I wrote and mailed those first letters asking for forgiveness.

It was a great experience to hear my name called at "mail call" for the first time in the ten months that I had then been incarcerated. My two brothers quickly answered me, and let me know they were not holding anything against me. They both expressed their regret for where I was and why I was there, but they also both asked if they could do anything to help me. God showed me that it might just be possible to receive forgiveness from others if I would just humbly ask.

With my sister, however, it took until after I had been released and walking out my Christian life for a time, before she forgave me. I had offended her the most. But, praise God, our relationship has been restored, and we are closer than we have been in a long time.

My son was the same way. In spite of the many letters I wrote him, he never responded while I was incarcerated. But in early 2013, two years after my release, God arranged a wonderful reunion meeting of reconciliation. What a blessing! I still pray regularly for that relationship to be fully restored.

God the Father commands us to humble ourselves and seek forgiveness from those we have offended (Matthew 5:23-24). In order to do so, we must first admit to ourselves that we hurt someone by our actions or words. As painful as it may be, we must come to the point where we admit we are guilty and not make any excuses for our behavior. We need to understand the amount of pain we have caused and accept responsibility.

First, we must ask the Father to forgive us for what we have done, and ask the Holy Spirit to give us strength to communicate with the person we have hurt. In prison, I was only able to write to those for whom I had their addresses. However, I promised God that I would contact the others at the first opportunity. For those I could not reach even after my release, I told the Father I would immediately ask them for forgiveness whenever He chose to bring them across my path. I prayed for them, and asked God to bless them and heal them from the hurt I caused them.

Sometimes we may not legally be allowed to contact the person if they were victim of our crime, or if there are legal restraining orders in place. Also, each situation is unique and we should always ask the Holy Spirit for wisdom as to when and whether we should contact them. If they do not know about the offense, get right with God and ask for His guidance and discernment whether to contact them.

For those with whom we make contact, either verbally or in writing, we must be honest and humble. We don't "apologize" just to make a bad situation go away. We need to clearly explain what we are "sorry" or remorseful for, without any excuses.

Pastor Gary Delay, in his book *Transformation*, teaches, "Just saying 'I'm sorry' and 'I apologize' are not adequate in asking someone's forgiveness. These are words that recognize the problem only. They do not suggest a solution or take action to resolve an offense. Both of these phrases are grossly inadequate in regards to forgiveness. We must specifically ask, 'Will you forgive me?'

"The word 'apology' expresses regret; it does not forgive. It makes us sorry and sorry leaves us guilty. Saying 'I'm sorry' or making an apology does not get the work of forgiveness done because forgiveness is not about guilt, defense, excuses, pity or substitutes. Forgiveness is about reconciliation and healing."

For example, we may say something like, "I'm sorry. I was wrong for (be specific). I sinned. Would you please forgive me? How can I make this right?" We move from a specific admission of our guilt to an attempt at a conversation about reconciliation.

Once we have asked them to forgive us, we need to let the other person respond without getting defensive. We should not expect them to immediately jump up with joy (or forgiveness) the moment we humbly ask. We may need to give the person time to sort out their feelings. They may need time to be able to deliberately "choose" to forgive in spite of their "feelings", and what may be their lingering pain, consequences or circumstances.

Even if the other person refuses to forgive us right then, we will have done what God expects us to do to try to make things right and clear our consciences. We have accepted responsibility and demonstrated that we want to change. The best way for us to respond going forward is to show ourselves continually trustworthy, and not slip back into the wrongful behavior.

In an article entitled "Do I really need to ask for forgiveness?" on *www.iblp.org* are included these two paragraphs:

"Sometimes when God asks us to do something, instead of obeying, **we try to rationalize away the need to take action**. With seeking forgiveness, our pride can get in the way, because asking for forgiveness requires us to humble ourselves before those we have offended.

"In Matthew 5:23–24, **Jesus commanded us to be reconciled** with those we have offended. This is an amazing command! God wants us to be reconciled to those we have offended, even if it means interrupting our time of worship in order to pursue that reconciliation. If you have put off asking for forgiveness, don't delay any longer, but go in humility, ask for forgiveness, and seek to be reconciled."

Remember, the Bible shows us the Father's own Son died, so we could be reconciled to God; and we are, now, a minister of that reconciliation. We've been forgiven by the Father. We must both humbly seek, and freely give, forgiveness.

SOME RELEVANT SCRIPTURE PASSAGES

Matthew 5:23-24 Jesus said, "Therefore, if you are offering your gift at the altar and there remember that your brother or sister has something against you, leave your gift there in front of the altar. First go and be reconciled to them; then come and offer your gift".

Hebrews 12:15 "See to it that no one misses the grace of God and that no bitter root grows up to cause trouble and defile many."

1 John 1:6-7 "If we claim to have fellowship with him yet walk in the darkness, we lie and do not live by the truth. But if we walk in the light, as he is in the light, we have fellowship with one another, and the blood of Jesus, his Son, purifies us from all sin."

1 John 1:9 "If we confess our sins, he is faithful and just and will forgive us our sins and purify us from all unrighteousness."

James 4:17 "Anyone, then, who knows the good he ought to do and doesn't do it, sins."

TAKEAWAY HIGHLIGHT

When we have offended or hurt others, we must ask God to forgive us so that we do not hamper our progression in relationship with Him. Also, whenever wisdom and practicality allow us, we should ask forgiveness from those whom we have offended. Asking others to forgive us is sometimes a difficult thing for us to do because of pride. It requires humility to admit we were wrong, and to ask someone to forgive us. Being humble is the key to experiencing forgiveness and healing. Humble yourself; it is the first step toward being forgiven.

PRACTICAL APPLICATION

Ask the Holy Spirit to show you some of the people you have hurt and offended. Talk to the Father to admit you were wrong and tell Him you do not want to do things like that again. Thank Him for His forgiveness, and ask Him for wisdom, timing and discernment as to the people you might be able to contact to ask their forgiveness.

WANT TO KNOW MORE?

Write to us to request the discipleship teaching on "Asking Forgiveness from Others". Mail it to: Freedom in Jesus Prison Ministries, Attn: Teachings, P.O. Box 939, Levelland, TX 79336.

The enemy does not want us to grow in relationship with Jesus so we need to understand some key concepts about spiritual warfare. Are you ready to learn?

Spiritual Warfare

One way the enemy tries to keep us from continuing to develop an intimate personal relationship with Jesus is to distract us, tempt us, and destroy us. We are in a real battle, and we need to be wise, courageous and persistent in combatting the devil's schemes.

In his article, "Fight from Victory, Not for Victory", Joseph Prince says, "God does not need you to defeat the devil today. Jesus has already done it and given you the victory. (Colossians 2:15, Romans 8:37) Your part is to enforce the victory by simply standing your ground, which is victory ground. In other words, you "fight" **from** victory ground by standing. You don't fight **for** victory."

Jesus told a parable in Mark 3:27, "In fact, no one can enter a strong man's house and carry off his possessions unless he first ties up the strong man. Then he can rob his house."

In the internet article, "Binding the Strongman", (author unattributed) we are told, "It is time that we take back what is ours, and to proclaim the victory that Jesus has already won for us on the cross. Satan has already been defeated—he knows what his outcome is—he knows already where he is going, but it is his intention to take as many of us with him that he possibly can. He creeps in, in such subtle ways, that we don't even realize it—we see more and more divorces, more and more immorality, more and more people caught up in pornography, more and more abortions, more and more babies being born out of wedlock, more and more bankruptcies—the list goes on and on." We must take control over our lives, and those of our families, by binding Satan and his forces and loosing the power of God through His Holy Spirit.

The article continues, "Now, the enemy has always been here to taunt and tempt and tear up people's lives, but there has never been a battle such as there is raging now, in these last days. There is only one War—the one between God and Satan, but there are many, many battles in that war, just as in any war that we see fought out here on this earth between the natural man and his enemies. God, in His Word, teaches us through the Scriptures in the Bible how to defend ourselves, and He is constantly showing us in the Word just how the enemy (Satan) attacks and what he uses to pull us away from God and His Promises."

We are soldiers in the Army of God! As Christian soldiers we must wage war against all evil, not in our own power but in the power of the Spirit with spiritual weapons.

We are not called to sit passively as the enemy tries to steal, kill and destroy us and our loved ones. When we are born again, we are enlisted into the Army of God. By knowing Jesus and the power of His resurrection and the fellowship of His suffering (Phil. 3:10), we can confront and break the power that demons exert over us and others. We can actively recruit others too! As true disciples in God's Kingdom we are called to wage intense spiritual warfare through the power of the Holy Spirit (see Luke 4:14-19). In this way we can set others free from the power of darkness.

In the Life in the Spirit Study Bible, by Zondervan, Editor Donald Stamps explains:

"At the present time we are involved in a spiritual warfare that we wage by the power of the Holy Spirit (Rom. 8:13-14):

1. Against the sinful desires within ourselves (I Pet. 2:11);
2. Against the ungodly pleasures of the world and temptations of every sort (Matt. 13:22, Gal. 1:4, James 1:14-15, I John 2:16); and,
3. Against Satan and his forces (II Cor. 10:3-5, Eph. 6:10-12).

"In our warfare of faith (I Timothy 1:18-19), we are called to:

1. Endure hardships like good soldiers of Christ (II Tim. 2:3);
2. Suffer for the gospel (Matt. 5:10-12, Rom. 8:17, II Cor. 11:23, II Tim. 1:8);
3. Fight the good fight of the faith (I Tim. 6:12, II Tim. 4:7);
4. Wage war (II Cor. 10:3);
5. Persevere (Eph. 6:18);
6. Conquer (Rom. 8:37);
7. Be victorious (I Cor. 15:57);
8. Triumph (II Cor. 2:14);
9. Defend the gospel (Phil. 1:16);
10. Contend for the faith (Phil. 1:27, Jude 3);
11. Not be frightened by opponents (Phil. 1:28);

12. Put on the full armor of God and stand firm (Eph. 6:13-14);

13. Destroy Satan's strongholds (II Cor. 10:4);

14. Take captive every thought (II Cor. 10:5); and,

15. Become powerful in battle (Heb. 11:34)."

Derek Prince, in his book, *Pulling Down Strongholds*, wrote, "Those who are citizens of God's Kingdom are already involved in spiritual warfare. It is not optional for them. The only decision we can make is whether or not we will be a part of the Kingdom of God by faith in Jesus Christ and submission to His Lordship. If you are already a part of His Kingdom, then you are at war with the kingdom of Satan. You simply need to recognize this reality, become spiritually equipped, and learn how to fight against Satan's kingdom – because, if you don't, you are going to be a casualty of spiritual warfare."

Our adversary, Satan, who is the Devil and the prince of this world, goes around like a roaring lion seeking whom he may devour (I Pet. 5:8). He is also the slanderer of God's people, tempting them and accusing them day and night. We must also be aware that he sometimes disguises himself as an angel of light (II Cor. 11:14) seeking if possible to deceive the very elect.

In the articles and notes of the *Life in the Spirit Study Bible*, they teach that we must know for Whom we are fighting:

"We represent the Kingdom of Heaven (or Kingdom of God). We are citizens of this Kingdom (Phil. 3:20; Eph. 2:19; Heb. 11:16; John 14:2-3). First and foremost our citizenship as Christians is in Heaven, not of this world; we have become strangers and aliens on earth (Rom. 8:22-24; Gal. 4:26; Heb. 11:13; Heb. 13:14; I Pet. 1:17; I Pet. 2:11).

"In regard to our life's walk, values and direction, Heaven is now our Fatherland. We have been born from above (John 3:3), our names are written on Heaven's register (Phil. 4:3), our lives are guided by Heavenly standards, and our rights and inheritance are reserved in Heaven (I Pet. 1:4).

"It is to Heaven that our prayers ascend (II Chron. 6:21; II Chron. 30:27) and our hope is directed (Heb. 6:19-20). Many of our friends and family members are already there, and we will be there soon. Jesus is there also, preparing a place for us, and He has promised to return and take us to Himself (John 14:1-4; Rom. 8:17; Eph. 2:6; Col. 3:1-3; Heb. 12:22-24). God has prepared for us the eternal city (Heb. 11:16).

"In Matt. 11:12, Jesus indicates that the Kingdom of Heaven is taken hold of only by forceful people who are committed to breaking away from the sinful practices of the human race and who turn to Christ, his Word and His righteous ways. No matter what the cost may be, such people vigorously seek the Kingdom and all its power. In other words, experiencing the Kingdom of Heaven with all its blessings requires earnest endeavor and diligent faith–spiritual warfare that includes the will to resist Satan, sin and an often-corrupt society.

"We have on our side the Commander of the Army of the Lord (Josh. 5:14). There are spiritual forces fighting on our behalf (Heb. 1:14; II Kings 6:15-17). We are not alone in our struggles on this earth (Acts 12:5-11; Acts 18:9-10; Acts 23:11; Acts 27:23). The Holy Spirit remains constantly at our side as our Helper and Defender (John 14:16-23). God Himself trains us (Ps. 144:1-2) and He is our strength. If God be for us, who can be against us (Rom. 8:31)?"

As prisoners some of you may think you are "employed" by the state prison system, but you are "deployed" there in the darkness to bring the Kingdom of Light!

True, committed believers in prison may be considered as being behind enemy lines! They are God's special forces often operating secretly in small numbers to spoil the enemy's plans and organize resistance to his evil schemes. Like the Navy SEALS, or the Army's Airborne Rangers, Christian prisoners are at the very tip of the spear, the leading edge of our attack on Satan and his forces. Be ready. Be vigilant. Be strong and very courageous (Joshua 1:5-9). Be strong in the Lord and in His mighty power (Eph. 6:10).

There is no one more important to prison ministry than believers still behind razor wire. They are in the best position to see what needs to be done, and who needs help, in the ongoing battle to bind the strongman and carry off his possessions!

"To remain passive in the face of battle is to be defeated before we begin. As Christians, we have to learn how to fight in a way that honors and depends upon God." Dr. Charles Stanley

SOME RELEVANT SCRIPTURE PASSAGES

2 Corinthians 10:3-5 "For though we live in the world, we do not wage war as the world does. The weapons we fight with are not the weapons of the world. On the contrary, they have divine power to demolish strongholds. We demolish arguments and every pretension that sets itself up against the knowledge of God, and we take captive every thought to make it obedient to Christ."

Ephesians 6:10-18 "Finally, be strong in the Lord and in his mighty power. Put on the full armor of God, so that you can take your stand against the devil's schemes. For our struggle is not against flesh and blood, but against the rulers, against the authorities, against the powers of this dark world and against the spiritual forces of evil in the heavenly realms. Therefore put on the full armor of God, so that when the day of evil comes, you may be able to stand your ground, and after you have done everything, to stand. Stand firm then, with the belt of truth buckled around your waist, with the breastplate of righteousness in place, and with your feet fitted with the readiness that comes from the gospel of peace. In addition to all this, take up the shield of faith, with which you can extinguish all the flaming arrows of the evil one. Take the helmet of salvation and the sword of the Spirit, which is the word of God. And pray in the Spirit on all occasions with all kinds of prayers and requests. With this in mind, be alert and always keep on praying for all the Lord's people."

Matthew 11:12 (NKJV) "And from the days of John the Baptist until now the kingdom of heaven suffers violence, and the violent take it by force."

1 Peter 5:8 "Be sober, be vigilant; because your adversary the devil walks about like a roaring lion, seeking whom he may devour."

2 Corinthians 11:12-15 "For such *are* false apostles, deceitful workers, transforming themselves into apostles of Christ. And no wonder! For Satan himself transforms himself into an angel of light. Therefore *it is* no great thing if his ministers also transform themselves into ministers of righteousness, whose end will be according to their works."

2 Thessalonians 3:3-5 "But the Lord is faithful, who will establish you and guard *you* from the evil one. And we have confidence in the Lord concerning you, both that you do and will do the things we command you. Now may the Lord direct your hearts into the love of God and into the patience of Christ."

TAKEAWAY HIGHLIGHT

"Those who are citizens of God's Kingdom are already involved in spiritual warfare. It is not optional for them. The only decision we can make is

whether or not we will be a part of the Kingdom of God by faith in Jesus Christ and submission to His Lordship. If you are already a part of His Kingdom, then you are at war with the kingdom of Satan. You simply need to recognize this reality, become spiritually equipped, and learn how to fight against Satan's kingdom – because, if you don't, you are going to be a casualty of spiritual warfare." Derek Prince

PRACTICAL APPLICATION

Think about the ways the enemy attacks, tempts or distracts you in his attempt to get you off track from pursuing intimacy of relationship with Jesus. How do you normally react? What ways have you found to resist him? Find specific scriptures to use against him when he comes to try to steal, kill and destroy. Ask the Holy Spirit to teach you to wage war His way!

WANT TO KNOW MORE?

Write to us to request the discipleship teaching on "Spiritual Warfare – Parts 1-3". Mail it to: Freedom in Jesus Prison Ministries, Attn: Teachings, P.O. Box 939, Levelland, TX 79336.

Our continued growth as Christians can be aided through successfully handling tests and trials. Find out the keys to maturity. Read on...

Tests and Trials

The growth and maturity of our relationship with Jesus is very definitely impacted by how we as Christians handle the many tests and trials that come our way.

We all face them. Christians are surely not exempt! For example, see John 16:33; James 1:2-4; and, Romans 5:3-5. How can we trust God in the midst of them? Why do they come? What should our response be? Surely, we can all be overcomers, and end up stronger in our faith; but, we certainly can be challenged by and through the process. Amen?

"There is nothing that can touch a believer's life unless it comes through the permissive will of God. That means He has complete control, even when it feels as if Satan has been allowed to run rampant through our personal life." Dr. Charles Stanley

In an article, "Deep Things", by Os Hillman, he writes:

"There is a process God uses to draw us into greater levels of intimacy. The first phase involves a depth of soul experience that causes great pain in our lives. We seek God for deliverance from the incredible emotional pain this causes. Our primary motivation for seeking God is to get out of our pain.

"During this time, God meets us in the depths of darkness. We discover that He never left us but is in the midst of the darkness. We develop a new relationship with God. Gradually our motivation turns from removal of pain to love and intimacy with God. This is the place our Heavenly Father desires us to be."

In the midst of tests and trials we must choose to continue to trust God, lean into Him, and seek His will and plan for our lives. Dr. Charles Stanley says, "The Lord's purpose in using trials to test us is not to see what we will do (He already knows that), but to strengthen our faith through the experience. He wants us to understand that every hardship or pain is an opportunity for spiritual growth and ever increasing trust in Him.

"Our spiritual lives are full of highs and lows, valleys and mountaintops. But some people panic, or grow bitter and angry, when they face a disappointing situation. They ask, *Where is God? Why hasn't He answered my prayer? Why is He silent while I'm hurting?* Many believers become disillusioned and hopeless. And instead of seeing a valley, they see an endless tunnel with no light at the end.

"Now I ask you to look deep within your heart and be completely honest with yourself and with the Father. Do you have doubts? Are you finding it difficult to believe in the Lord because of the troubles you're experiencing? Is it challenging to trust that your situation can ever be better or that something good can come from it?

"You may feel as if your situation is impossible to overcome. It may appear unending, and you may be weary and disheartened. But don't give up hope. Cling to the promise that God acts on behalf of those who wait for Him. Keep seeking Him, and He will deliver you from the trials you're enduring."

Sometimes you may feel like giving up because you are stressed out and overwhelmed by the situation you are facing. The devil wants us to spend our days in anxiety, frustration, fear, disbelief and feeling distanced from God. The enemy wants us to focus on our circumstances, but that never helps. Instead, we must stop thinking about what is wrong and fix our eyes on God. He is in control. His timing is perfect. He is always with us. He is ready, willing and able to help us in every situation no matter how bad.

Dr. Charles Stanley writes, "Through the power of the Holy Spirit, believers have the ability to endure difficulty and accomplish whatever the Lord calls them to do. By claiming the adequacy of Christ, we can face every circumstance with a sense of confidence—not in ourselves but in God, who is capable."

Going through trying times is never easy. In an article I read by Sheila Walsh, "The Sacred Ache: No Tear Forgotten", she wrote, "In the midst of our pain and grief - and especially at the front end - we may imagine God has abandoned us, forgotten us, dismissed us, or simply ignored us. We're not the first occupants of this broken planet to feel this way, nor will we be the last...Sometimes we feel alone in our heartache and wonder if God hears us or even cares. But even while we are doubting His goodness, God is listening and planning to bring beauty and restoration to our situation."

Joyce Meyer, in her article, "Don't Panic! This is Only a Test", writes "Sometimes God allows or even arranges for us to go through difficulties in this life because it's during those times that we grow in our faith and develop more of the character of Christ. Trials reveal what we really believe, and what's really inside our hearts. They test us. And until we're in a situation where we have no choice but to face an issue we need to deal with, we don't really know what we would do."

Derek Prince, in his article, "The Purpose of Testing", says "Collins English Dictionary gives an interesting definition of the verb **test**: *to ascertain the worth of a person...by subjection to certain examinations.* God does not test us because He is angry with us or wants to put us down. On the contrary, testing is a mark of God's favor. He tests us because He wants to establish our value. A jeweler will subject gold or silver to certain tests. He does this because they are valuable. He does not bother to test base metals such as iron or tin."

Tests and trials come to build us up for what God has for us tomorrow; to get our attention so we will learn something God is trying to teach us; and, for us to learn more about God and to know more about ourselves. Dr. Charles Stanley says, "Often, there are lessons that can only be learned through hardship. Therefore, God will allow difficulties to enter into our lives for His purposes."

God has plans for us that will use what we are learning in our pain and tears. His Word says, "You keep track of all my sorrows. You have collected all my tears in Your bottle. You have recorded each one in Your book." (Psalm 56:8) Can you imagine? He collects all our tears! He sees our pain. In the place of our anguish, anxiety and tears He will fill us with His love and presence.

In his devotional, "Seeing Adversity from God's Viewpoint", Dr. Charles Stanley shared:

"When adversity hits you like a ton of bricks, it could easily throw you into a pit of discouragement and despair. Although you may regard difficulties as setbacks, the Lord sees them as times for great advancement. His purpose in allowing them is not to destroy you but to stimulate your spiritual growth. In His great wisdom, the Lord knows how to take an awful situation and use it to transform you into the image of Christ and equip you to carry out His will.

"Every adversity that comes into your life is sifted through God's permissive will. That doesn't mean the difficulty itself is His perfect will, but He's allowed the trial to touch you so that He can use it to accomplish His wonderful purposes for your life. Although some of the suffering we see and experience seems senseless or blatantly evil, we must recognize that we have a very limited perspective and cannot always understand what the Lord is doing."

Keep trusting in God. Recall situations He has brought you through before. Ask Him what you should be learning. Lean on Him! A primary purpose behind God's tests is to produce trust for Him in us.

"Faith that can't be tested can't be trusted." Dr. Adrian Rogers

SOME RELEVANT SCRIPTURE PASSAGES

John 16:33 Jesus said, "I have told you these things, so that in me you may have peace. In this world you will have trouble. But take heart! I have overcome the world."

James 1:2-4 "Consider it pure joy, my brothers and sisters, whenever you face trials of many kinds, because you know that the testing of your faith produces perseverance. Let perseverance finish its work so that you may be mature and complete, not lacking anything."

Romans 5:3-5 "Not only so, but we also glory in our sufferings, because we know that suffering produces perseverance; perseverance, character; and character, hope. And hope does not put us to shame, because

God's love has been poured out into our hearts through the Holy Spirit, who has been given to us."

2 Corinthians 11:23-28 "Are they servants of Christ? (I am out of my mind to talk like this.) I am more. I have worked much harder, been in prison more frequently, been flogged more severely, and been exposed to death again and again. Five times I received from the Jews the forty lashes minus one. Three times I was beaten with rods, once I was pelted with stones, three times I was shipwrecked, I spent a night and a day in the open sea, I have been constantly on the move. I have been in danger from rivers, in danger from bandits, in danger from my fellow Jews, in danger from Gentiles; in danger in the city, in danger in the country, in danger at sea; and in danger from false believers. I have labored and toiled and have often gone without sleep; I have known hunger and thirst and have often gone without food; I have been cold and naked. Besides everything else, I face daily the pressure of my concern for all the churches."

Mark 15:34 "And at three in the afternoon Jesus cried out in a loud voice, *'Eloi, Eloi, lema sabachthani?'* (which means 'My God, my God, why have you forsaken me?')."

2 Corinthians 12:7-10 "...Therefore, in order to keep me from becoming conceited, I was given a thorn in my flesh, a messenger of Satan, to torment me. Three times I pleaded with the Lord to take it away from me. But he said to me, 'My grace is sufficient for you, for my power is made perfect in weakness.' Therefore I will boast all the more gladly about my weaknesses, so that Christ's power may rest on me. That is why, for Christ's sake, I delight in weaknesses, in insults, in hardships, in persecutions, in difficulties. For when I am weak, then I am strong."

Galatians 6:7 "Do not be deceived: God cannot be mocked. A man reaps what he sows."

Hebrews 13:5 "Keep your lives free from the love of money and be content with what you have, because God has said, 'Never will I leave you; never will I forsake you.'"

Romans 15:13 "May the God of hope fill you with all joy and peace as you trust in Him, so that you may overflow with hope by the power of the Holy Spirit."

2 Corinthians 1:3-4 "Praise be to the God and Father of our Lord Jesus Christ, the Father of compassion and the God of all comfort, who comforts us in all our troubles, so that we can comfort those in any trouble with the comfort we ourselves receive from God."

TAKEAWAY HIGHLIGHT

Sometimes you may feel like giving up because you are stressed out and overwhelmed by the situation you are facing. The devil wants us to spend our days in anxiety, frustration, fear, disbelief and feeling distanced from God. The enemy wants us to focus on our circumstances, but that never helps. Instead, we must stop thinking about what is wrong and fix our eyes on God. He is in control. His timing is perfect. He is always with us. He is ready, willing and able to help us in every situation no matter how bad.

"Through the power of the Holy Spirit, believers have the ability to endure difficulty and accomplish whatever the Lord calls them to do. By claiming the adequacy of Christ, we can face every circumstance with a sense of confidence—not in ourselves but in God, who is capable." Dr. Charles Stanley

PRACTICAL APPLICATION

Give some thought to how some previous trials and tests worked out for you in the past, and think about what you were able to learn from them. What challenges are you going through today? In light of what you read above, are you trusting God in the midst of your tests now?

WANT TO KNOW MORE?

Write to us to request the discipleship teaching on "Tests and Trials–Trusting God and His Purposes". Mail it to: Freedom in Jesus Prison Ministries, Attn: Teachings, P.O. Box 939, Levelland, TX 79336.

Regarding our continued growth in relationship with Jesus, the way we respond to tests and trials is crucial. Find out the proper response...

Tests and Trials – Proper Response

Our relationship with Jesus can either grow or be hindered through tests and trials; it is our response to them during and afterwards that makes the difference.

In the last chapter we began discussing Tests and Trails. We learned that we all face them. Christians are not exempt! We learned how to trust God in the midst of them. We then discovered some answers to "Why do trials and tests come?" This particular chapter follows up to talk primarily about how we should respond to tests and trials.

Beginning with my salvation in prison in 2009, I have been learning by specific experience that responding appropriately to life's tests and trials is not always easy. Realizing, and repeatedly confessing, that God really is in control, and that His timing is perfect, has been one of the most important ways for me to get through these challenges. I have chosen (in spite of my feelings) to believe and verbally confess continually these scriptures–Job 13:15; Genesis 50:20; Romans 8:28; and, James 1:2-4. I know they will help you too! Look them up. Meditate on their truth. Memorize them.

In his article, "Growing in Our Adversity", Dr. Charles Stanley writes, "Adversity is the universal experience of mankind, and it can either hinder or accelerate our spiritual growth – it all depends on how we respond."

He tells us, "Adversity is a condition of suffering and hardship involving anguish, pressure, trials, heartaches, or disappointments. It may be physical or emotional in nature, and either long or short in duration, but it is always painful."

One of the most important responses we must have to successfully handle tests and trials is to "endure" or "persevere" through them (Romans 5:1-5; James 1:2-4). Derek Prince, in his article, "Enduring Under Trials", teaches us that "endurance produces character that has stood the test. In essence, we are talking about the formation of our character. We can rejoice (boast, glory and exult) in tribulation because only tribulation produces endurance. Endurance, in turn, produces proven character."

Derek Prince continues, in reference to James 1:2-4, that "James is saying that if we go through the test and hold out, it will shape every area of our character and personality. It will make us complete, fully-rounded Christians."

God knows the end from the very beginning. He may be using our test and trial to turn us away from a direction and path that He knows holds greater adversity, pain or disappointment in the future. We must choose to trust Him.

"There are two ways of getting out of a trial. One is to do your best in an attempt to get rid of it, and then be thankful when it is over. The other is to recognize it as a challenge from God to claim a greater blessing than you have ever known, and to face it with full commitment to the Lord as an opportunity to obtain a larger measure of divine grace." (J. Allen Blair)

In a devotional by Dr. Charles Stanley, "Trials and Joy", covering James 1:2-4, 12, we learn:

"First of all, we need to understand that these verses are not telling us to be happy in our pain, but rather to rejoice in the blessings that accompany suffering. The word *consider* is an accounting term that means "to evaluate." When we look at hardships from God's perspective and place the proper value on them, we can rejoice in the beneficial outcome, even while experiencing pain. Humanly speaking, trials hurt; but from the Lord's point of view, they help.

"The only way to rejoice during trials is to understand what God wants them to accomplish. Regardless of the difficulty's source, we can know that the Lord wants to use it to test our faith and thereby produce endurance and spiritual maturity. In every trial, He has hidden a precious character gem, but whether we receive it depends upon our response. Those who want to be transformed into the image of Christ can rejoice in the many benefits that accompany suffering."

In these very challenging last days, tests and trials seem to be coming more often. God's refining fire is wanting to purge us, remove the impurities, and make us stronger for His Kingdom work. It all begins in us individually; and, the results He is obtaining in us must be clearly evident and impactful to our families and all those around us.

"We do not have to seek weaknesses, infirmities, tribulations, temptations, or trials. We already have them. The key is how do we respond to them? We can fight them, or we can embrace them." (Chip Brogden)

Dr. Charles Stanley has written, "Our human tendency is to plot a course through a situation toward the easiest solution. But believers who strike out on their own do not mature in their faith. Moreover, they miss out on the blessings of following the Lord's plan. Stopping to praise can keep us from taking the easy way out and direct us to the right path—namely, *the way of God's will... Praise is not the obvious reaction to hardship, but it is the wisest response."*

He also teaches that, "The Scriptures are filled with examples of people who faced adversity, and on the other side of the experience, discovered how God worked through their situations to bring about good. Without exception, they all CHOSE, in spite of their feelings, to respond to adversity in the proper fashion."

Our response to very real tests and trials reveals a lot about where we are in our journey. Certainly, our Father knows what we need, and He desires for us to continue to grow and mature spiritually. He expects us to be strengthened by testing, and purified in the fire. When tested, we want to be sure to respond joyfully, wisely and patiently. James 1:2-5 has been such a strong confession of mine in the midst of tests and trials. I recommend you memorize it and confess it regularly. It will help you!

"Our response to what happens is more important than what happens. Here is a mystery: one man's experience drives him to curse God, while another man's identical experience drives him to bless God. Your response to what happens is more important than what happens." Chip Brogden

Dr. Charles Stanley, in his article, "When We Don't Understand Why", writes that, "Trials, difficulties, and suffering bring out a variety of attitudes and responses. Some people become angry with God for allowing the situation while others are able to rejoice in Him knowing that He's doing something good in their lives through the hardship. But one of the most common responses is to want to know why this happened. What is the purpose? Why me, my child, or my family? Yet so many times, we don't understand, and God doesn't reveal the reason to us. How should we respond then?"

In his article, "Encouraging Ourselves", Dr. Charles Stanley teaches that, "All believers need encouragement in difficult seasons of our lives." Many times there is really nobody who fully understands your situation, or perhaps you are isolated away from those who really love you and could offer comfort and encouragement. "That's why it's important that you and I know how to encourage ourselves spiritually. Although we need fellowship, the foundation of the Christian life is a personal relationship with God. Every believer should know how to find encouragement directly from the Lord."

"Since we cannot avoid having tribulation in this world, we might as well make the best possible use of every circumstance we find ourselves in. Begin to see all your temptations, tests, and trials as opportunities for growing, maturing, and learning how to live as an Overcomer. Then your problem will become your greatest opportunity for knowing God – for the depth of your revelation is measured by the depth of your suffering." (Chip Brogden)

In his book, *Lord of All*, Chip Brogden wrote these two paragraphs:

"The Lord does not test us with the intent of making us stumble. That is the way the adversary works. No, the Lord indeed tests us and proves us, but His Way is to strengthen us in the testing, whereas the devil wants to weaken us in the testing. It has been said that our circumstances will either leave us better or they will leave us bitter. Ultimately, the decision is ours. We should steadfastly resist the temptation of satan, but we should also learn to distinguish between the assault of the enemy and the proving of the Lord.

"Jesus already knows what He is going to do. In His mind it is as good as done. But He waits, and He proves us. Not because He does not know us, but because we do not know ourselves."

Brothers and sisters in Christ, I urge you to try to view each test and trial as an opportunity to grow and mature in our relationship with God. We all have trials. We must be very careful to respond to them in the right way.

"Are you in a crisis today? If so, the Lord wants to turn it into an awesome opportunity for you to develop new skills, strengthen your character, and draw you closer to Him. If you obey God and leave all the consequences to Him, He will conform you to the image of His Son and use all situations for your ultimate blessing." (Dr. Charles Stanley)

SOME RELEVANT SCRIPTURE PASSAGES

Romans 8:28 "And we know that in all things God works for the good of those who love him, who have been called according to his purpose."

Genesis 50:20 "You intended to harm me, but God intended it for good to accomplish what is now being done, the saving of many lives."

Job 13:15 "Though He slay me, yet will I trust Him..."

James 1:2-4 "Consider it pure joy, my brothers and sisters, whenever you face trials of many kinds, because you know that the testing of your faith produces perseverance. Let perseverance finish its work so that you may be mature and complete, not lacking anything."

Romans 5:1-4 "Therefore, since we have been justified through faith, we have peace with God through our Lord Jesus Christ, through whom we have gained access by faith into this grace in which we now stand. And we boast in the hope of the glory of God. Not only so, but we also glory in our sufferings, because we know that suffering produces perseverance; perseverance, character; and character, hope."

TAKEAWAY HIGHLIGHT

In these very challenging last days, tests and trials seem to be coming more often. God's refining fire is wanting to purge us, remove the impurities, and make us stronger for His Kingdom work. It all begins in us individually; and, the results He is obtaining in us must be clearly evident and impactful to our families and all those around us.

"We do not have to seek weaknesses, infirmities, tribulations, temptations, or trials. We already have them. The key is how do we respond to them? We can fight them, or we can embrace them." (Chip Brogden)

PRACTICAL APPLICATION

Are you going through a test or trial right now? How are you responding? Be honest; in light of what you've read above, how should you be responding?

Here is an example of how you might want to talk to God about your current trial:

Prayer in the Midst of a Trial

Father God, I praise You! I thank You! I love You!! You alone are worthy of all praise, honor, glory, and power!!!

Thank You for Your Son, Jesus. Thank you for giving me Your Holy Spirit as my Helper, Teacher, Guide, Friend and Encourager! I need Him to help me through this time of trial and testing.

Please help me see this test and my circumstances from Your perspective. I want to rise above all this and see it all through Your eyes.

Father, You have my full attention. I want to learn well the lessons You have for me as I face this difficulty. I want to grow closer to You. I trust You. I know Your timing is perfect, and that You are in control. Help me discern by Your Holy Spirit the source and cause of this trial. I want to be stronger and more mature spiritually as a result of going through this test while trusting solely in You. You are my strength!

Thank You for loving me enough to trust me with this test. I want to please You. In the Name of Jesus I pray. Amen.

WANT TO KNOW MORE?

Write to us to request the discipleship teaching on "Tests and Trials – Proper Response". Mail it to: Freedom in Jesus Prison Ministries, Attn: Teachings, P.O. Box 939, Levelland, TX 79336.

When God does not answer as soon as we think He should, our faith may be tested. What is faith? How do we get it? How does it increase? Read on...

Faith

One of the most important factors in our ability to continue to grow in our intimate relationship with God is our faith.

How do we get faith? Faith comes! The Bible says that faith comes by hearing, and hearing by the Word of God. See Romans 10:17. Reading the Word out-loud, hearing the Word proclaimed by others, confessing the Word over our situations, and praying the Word back to God–all these allow us to hear the Word of God, and will thereby increase our faith! **Faith comes.**

Abraham's faith was accounted to him as righteousness (see Romans 4:9,11,13). We are saved through faith (Ephesians 2:8). We walk by faith, live by faith, pray in faith, believe by faith, see through faith, and confess our faith! Without faith it is impossible to please God. **Faith pleases God.**

"And without faith it is impossible to please God, because anyone who comes to him must believe that he exists and that he rewards those who earnestly seek him." Hebrews 11:6

Of this verse, Derek Prince commented, "First of all, we must believe that God exists. Most of us, I suppose, in our hearts, really are aware of that. But beyond that, we have to believe that God rewards those who earnestly seek Him. You see, faith is, ultimately, faith in the goodness of God – in His reliability, in His dependability – and without that faith in God's goodness we cannot please Him. It begins with believing in God and in His goodness. That is the root and the source of all true success and the life that pleases God."

The Life in the Spirit Study Bible by Zondervan has an article on Faith that includes the following:

"Our salvation comes as a gift of God's grace and is appropriated by the response of faith (Romans 5:20b-21).

"Faith in Jesus Christ is God's requirement for receiving his free gift of salvation. Faith is what we believe about Christ and our heart's response of trust that causes us to follow him as Lord and Savior (cf. Matthew 4:19; 16:24; Luke 9:23-25; John 10:4,27; 12:26; Revelation 14:4).

1. The New Testament (NT) conception of faith includes four main elements:

    a. Faith means firmly believing and trusting in the crucified and risen Christ as our personal Lord and Savior. It involves believing with all our hearts (Romans 6:17; Ephesians 6:6; Hebrews 10:22), yielding up our wills and committing our total selves to Jesus Christ as he is revealed in the NT.

    b. Faith involves repentance, i.e., in true sorrow turning from sin (Acts 17:30; 2 Corinthians 7:10) and turning to God through Christ. Saving faith is always a repentant faith (Acts 2:37-38).

    c. Faith includes obedience to Jesus Christ and his Word as a way of life inspired by our faith, by our gratitude to God and by the regenerating work of the Spirit (John 3:3-6; 14:15,21-24; Hebrews 5:8-9). It is an obedience that "comes from faith" (Romans 1:5). Therefore, faith and obedience belong inseparably together (cf. Romans 16:26). Saving faith without the commitment to sanctification is impossible.

d. Faith includes a heartfelt personal devotion and attachment to Jesus Christ that expresses itself in trust, love, gratitude and loyalty. Faith in an ultimate sense cannot properly be distinguished from love. It is a personal activity of trust and loving self-giving directed toward Christ (cf. Matthew 22:37; John 21:15-17; Acts 8:37; Romans 6:17; Galatians 2:20; Ephesians 6:6; 1 Peter 1:8).

2. Faith in Jesus as Lord and Savior is both the act of a single moment and a continuing attitude that must grow and be strengthened. Because we have faith in a specific person who died for us (Romans 4:25; 8:32; 1 Thessalonians 5:9-10), our faith should become greater (Romans 4:20; 2 Thessalonians 1:3; 1 Peter 1:3-9). Trust and obedience develop into loyalty and devotion (Romans 14:8; 2 Corinthians 5:15); loyalty and devotion develop into an intense feeling of personal attachment to and love for the Lord Jesus Christ (Philippians 1:21; 3:8-10). This faith in Christ brings us into a new relationship with God and exempts us from his wrath (Romans 1:8; 8:1); through that new relationship we become dead to sin (Romans 6:1-18) and indwelt by the Holy Spirit (Galatians 3:5; 4:6)."

From the *Life in the Spirit Study Bible* comments on Hebrews 11:1 we learn that:

"Hebrews chapter 11 demonstrates that faith is trust in God in all circumstances, which enables the believer to persevere and remain steadfastly loyal to God and his Word at all times. It is a faith that believes in spiritual realities (v. 1), leads to righteousness (v.4), seeks God (v.6), believes in his goodness (v.6), has confidence in his Word (vv.7,11), obeys his commands (v.8), regulates life on his promises (vv. 13,39), rejects the spirit of this present evil age (v. 13), seeks a heavenly home (vv.14-16; cf 13:13-14), perseveres in testing (vv.17-19), blesses the next generation (v. 21), refuses sin's pleasures (v. 25), endures persecution (v. 27), performs mighty acts of righteousness (vv. 33-35), suffers for God (vv.25,35-38), and does not return to "the country they had left", i.e. the world (vv.15-16)."

Joyce Meyer wrote in a devotional article entitled "From Faith to Faith" the following:

"After many years of being doubtful and fearful, I have definitely decided faith is much better. Faith enables us to enjoy our lives and to do amazing things. Living by faith is not a feeling we have; it is a conscious decision we must make.

"Faith is simply the conscious, deliberate choice to put our trust in God. It's at the heart of everything great we'll ever do. It becomes more natural and we get better at it the more we do it.

"If you will begin by exercising faith for simple things, eventually you will have no difficulty trusting God for great things. I remember going to a garage sale and trusting God to help me find a pair of tennis shoes for one of my children for two dollars because that was all I had. I saw God's faithfulness, and eventually I was able to trust God to cover the needs we have for an international ministry."

Dr. Charles Stanley, in a devotional entitled "Preparation for Greater Service" said,

"In Luke 17:5, the apostles asked Christ to increase their faith. The Lord told them that if they had faith as small as a mustard seed, they could do great things. God does not enlarge our faith instantly. He begins with what little we have and proceeds to grow it... The Lord will provide occasions for you to believe Him and respond in obedience. These situations are what we call 'problems.' Begin to look at each difficulty as an opportunity designed by God specifically for the purpose of increasing your faith so He can do great things in and through you."

In another devotional article, "Acquiring Great Faith", Dr. Stanley elaborates on this concept in light of Hebrews 11:17-19 in order to teach us:

"I've had people tell me, 'I wish I had great faith.' While most of us would like God to just drop that kind of confidence into our laps, it's not the way He operates. Faith increases as a result of our obedience in little things. We all marvel at Abraham's willingness to offer up Isaac at the Lord's command. But have you ever stopped to consider all of his smaller steps of submission that prepared the way for this enormous test?

"Throughout his lifetime, Abraham obeyed God. At the Lord's command, he left his country (Gen. 12:1-4), was circumcised (17:10, 26), conceived Isaac when he and his wife were old (21:1-3), and sent his son Ishmael away (vv. 9-14). By the time he was asked to offer Isaac as a sacrifice, he already knew that God would always be faithful to His promises. Abraham's previous experiences had taught him to trust the Lord.

"In the same way, each small step of obedience solidifies *our* confidence in God. Then, when He challenges us with a more difficult assignment, a firm foundation of assurance enables us to trust and obey. Great acts of faith flow from our past interactions with the Lord. By neglecting His simple commands, we miss priceless opportunities to witness His faithfulness.

"Having trouble trusting the Lord for something big? Maybe it's because you've ignored those 'small' and 'insignificant' promptings of the Holy Spirit. God considers each of His commands important and promises to reward every act of obedience, regardless of size. Great faith begins with little steps."

Sometimes we discover that our timing and God's timing don't seem to "line up". We wonder if God has even heard our prayers. When the enemy tries to get me to start doubting and acting in unbelief due to my impatience, I have found it best to confess repeatedly that "God is in control, and His timing is perfect!" By this confession from my heart, I am exercising and stating my faith aloud, submitting to God, and drawing near to God. Guess what? The devil has to flee! See James 4:7-8.

Teresa Jenkins, in her article "Help Me Believe" wrote along these lines regarding our doubt:

"Thankfully, God never gives up on us, but I'm sure He still gets a little exasperated at our unbelief. Anything that we face can be fixed, healed, changed, or made new with faith. But we continue to doubt. Why? Because it's what we are used to. Because we are impatient. We forget so easily that time really means nothing to God. What seems to take too long to us is just the beginning for God."

Never give up. God is Faithful. I challenge you to learn more about faith. Choose to trust God all day every day. Keep your eyes on Jesus instead of the storm!

SOME RELEVANT SCRIPTURE PASSAGES

Hebrews 11:1-2 "Now faith is confidence in what we hope for and assurance about what we do not see. This is what the ancients were commended for."

Romans 1:17 "For in the gospel the righteousness of God is revealed—a righteousness that is by faith from first to last, just as it is written: 'The righteous will live by faith.'"

Romans 1:17 AMPC "For in the Gospel a righteousness which God ascribes is revealed, both springing from faith and leading to faith [disclosed through the way of faith that arouses to more faith]. As it is written, 'The man who through faith is just *and* upright shall live *and* shall live by faith.'"

Romans 10:17 "Consequently, faith comes from hearing the message, and the message is heard through the word about Christ."

Ephesians 2:8-9 "For it is by grace you have been saved, through faith—and this is not from yourselves, it is the gift of God—not by works, so that no one can boast."

Hebrews 11:6 "And without faith it is impossible to please God, because anyone who comes to him must believe that he exists and that he rewards those who earnestly seek him."

Mark 11:23-24 "Truly I tell you, if anyone says to this mountain, 'Go, throw yourself into the sea,' and does not doubt in their heart but believes that what they say will happen, it will be done for them. Therefore I tell you, whatever you ask for in prayer, believe that you have received it, and it will be yours."

Hebrews 11:17-19 "By faith Abraham, when God tested him, offered Isaac as a sacrifice. He who had embraced the promises was about to sacrifice his one and only son, even though God had said to him, 'It is through Isaac that your offspring will be reckoned.' Abraham reasoned that God could even raise the dead, and so in a manner of speaking he did receive Isaac back from death."

Romans 4:9, 13 "Is this blessedness only for the circumcised, or also for the uncircumcised? We have been saying that Abraham's faith was credited to him as righteousness… It was not through the law that Abraham and his offspring received the promise that he would be heir of the world, but through the righteousness that comes by faith."

Luke 17:5 "The apostles said to the Lord, 'Increase our faith!'"

Mark 9:21-24 "Jesus asked the boy's father, 'How long has he been like this?' 'From childhood,' he answered. 'It has often thrown him into fire or water to kill him. But if you can do anything, take pity on us and help us.' 'If you can'? said Jesus. 'Everything is possible for one who believes.' Immediately the boy's father exclaimed, 'I do believe; help me overcome my unbelief!'"

TAKEAWAY HIGHLIGHT

"First of all, we must believe that God exists. Most of us, I suppose, in our hearts, really are aware of that. But beyond that, we have to believe that God rewards those who earnestly seek Him. You see, faith is, ultimately, faith in the goodness of God – in His reliability, in His dependability – and without that faith in God's goodness we cannot please Him. It begins with believing in God and in His goodness. That is the root and the source of all true success and the life that pleases God." Derek Prince

PRACTICAL APPLICATION

Think about challenging situations in your past where God came through for you. Although it might not have been when you wanted, it ended up being right on time. Remembering God's faithfulness, help and provision in the past increases our faith for the present. What is an area of your life for which you are currently trusting God? Be patient. Believe. Wait on God.

WANT TO KNOW MORE?

Write to us to request the discipleship teaching on "Faith". Mail it to: Freedom in Jesus Prison Ministries, Attn: Teachings, P.O. Box 939, Levelland, TX 79336.

Although our faith is tested by circumstances which can cause impatience, our relationship with God is strengthened when we wait on Him. What does this look like? Read on...

Waiting on God

How does waiting on God affect our relationship with Him? Learning to trust Him in all things, and relying on His timing rather than our own, develops patience in us that He promises to reward.

Waiting "came with the territory" when I was in prison. I remember waiting on chow, waiting on medical, waiting on mail, waiting on parole, and waiting for count to clear. Most often, it was a frustrating – and generally disappointing–process.

But God tells us repeatedly that we will be blessed when we wait hopefully, but patiently, on Him! The Amplified version of Psalm 27:14 says, *"Wait and hope for and expect the Lord; be brave and of good courage and let your heart be stout and enduring. Yes, wait for and hope for and expect the Lord."*

Dr. Charles Stanley said, "Waiting on God can be a tricky business, full of both temptations and blessings. What we need are eyes to see and ears to hear how the Lord is leading us, as we trust Him for the future. Life gives us no choice but to wait. Yet, patience is becoming a rare quality in today's world. How often do we complain when something doesn't happen on the schedule we have in mind, or when some unforeseen obstacle prevents us from moving forward?"

In his article, "Willing to Wait", Dr. Stanley writes, "For those of us who call upon the name of Jesus, patience is a characteristic we should cultivate. No one is born with it – just look at a new-born baby! Rather, patience is a spiritual fruit, which is developed over time (Gal. 5:22-23). Without it, we'll never become the people God desires us to be or achieve what He's planned for us to do."

It is in "waiting on God" that we discover His will and purpose for us (Lamentations 3:25). He tells us we will receive supernatural strength and energy (Isaiah 40:31). We will see the fulfillment of our faith (Isaiah 49:23). We will see the Father working on our behalf (Isaiah 64:4). We learn to look for Him in every situation and circumstance of life.

Isaiah 40:31 (NKJV) "But those who wait on the Lord Shall renew their strength; They shall mount up with wings like eagles, They shall run and not be weary, They shall walk and not faint."

In the Dr. David Jeremiah devotional, "Soaring through Life", on Isaiah 40:31, he states,

"Isaiah thought the eagle was the perfect metaphor for the person who gained strength from God. The person who waits on (depends on, trusts in) the Lord will find the strength to 'mount up with wings like eagles.' By definition, soaring means to be far above the problems of life; it means seeing what's happening on earth from God's perspective. With soaring comes understanding; with understanding comes patience and contentment.

"If you are flying by your own strength today, wait on the Lord. Rise up with His power and gain His perspective on your circumstances."

Dr. Foley Beach, in an article entitled, "Waiting on the Lord", includes these two paragraphs:

"Those who wait on the Lord shall renew their strength. Isn't it amazing how exhausted we can get doing God's work? However, as we wait for his leadership and direction, and his coming, our strength is renewed. Too often, rather than waiting patiently, quietly, expectantly, and in his word, we are fretting and anxious and non-trusting– and our strength is zapped. Those who wait on the Lord will renew their strength.

"Those who wait on the Lord will soar on wings as eagles. It is an interesting thing about eagles – They soar they don't fly. They wait for the correct wind, and then they ride that wind – soaring to the heights. Isn't that a great picture for us as we wait on the Lord? When the wind of the Spirit moves and blows, we ride with wings as eagles to where he wants us to go."

Dr. Charles Stanley, in a devotional entitled, "The Consequence of Impatience", shares this:

"We send a strong, negative message by exhibiting impatience toward God. When we demonstrate an inability to tolerate delay, we are telling the Lord, 'I do not trust Your timing; mine is better.'

"At times, we all stand at a fork in the road of life and must decide whether we're willing to wait for God's prompting. It's critical that we obey Him and be patient with His schedule and plan."

By understanding more about what it means to "wait on God", I pray you will be encouraged to wait patiently on the Lord. You are not alone, and your loving heavenly Father has not given up on you. Allocate time every day to grow stronger in the Word. Learn to pray more for others. Ask the Holy Spirit to show you how to build a firm foundation so that you will be rock-solid spiritually. Use your "time of waiting" to your spiritual advantage. Allow the Holy Spirit and the Word to mold you into the vessel God wants you to be.

"The Holy Spirit never leaves a surrendered vessel unfilled or unused." (Dr. *Adrian Rogers)*

SOME RELEVANT SCRIPTURE PASSAGES

Psalm 40:1-4a "I waited patiently for the LORD; he turned to me and heard my cry. He lifted me out of the slimy pit, out of the mud and mire; he set my feet on a rock and gave me a firm place to stand. He put a new song in my mouth, a hymn of praise to our God. Many will see and fear and put their trust in the LORD. Blessed is the man who makes the LORD his trust..."

Psalm 27:14, AMP "Wait and hope for and expect the Lord; be brave and of good courage and let your heart be stout and enduring. Yes, wait for and hope for and expect the Lord."

Psalm 130:5 "I wait for the LORD, my soul waits, and in his word I put my hope."

Isaiah 30:18 "Yet the LORD longs to be gracious to you; he rises to show you compassion. For the LORD is a God of justice. Blessed are all who wait for him!"

I Thessalonians 1:9b-10 "They tell how you turned to God from idols to serve the living and true God, and to wait for his Son from heaven, whom he raised from the dead—Jesus, who rescues us from the coming wrath."

Titus 2:11-14 "For the grace of God that brings salvation has appeared to all men. It teaches us to say 'No' to ungodliness and worldly passions, and to live self-controlled, upright and godly lives in this present age, while we wait for the blessed hope—the glorious appearing of our great God and Savior, Jesus Christ, who gave himself for us to redeem us from all wickedness and to purify for himself a people that are his very own, eager to do what is good."

Isaiah 40:31 (NKJV) "But those who wait on the Lord Shall renew *their* strength; They shall mount up with wings like eagles, They shall run and not be weary, They shall walk and not faint."

TAKEAWAY HIGHLIGHT

By understanding more about what it means to "wait on God", I pray you will be encouraged to wait patiently on the Lord. You are not alone, and your loving heavenly Father has not given up on you. Allocate time every day to grow stronger in the Word. Learn to pray more for others. Ask the Holy Spirit to show you how to build a firm foundation so that you will be rock-solid spiritually. Use your "time of waiting" to your spiritual advantage. Allow the Holy Spirit and the Word to mold you into the vessel God wants you to be.

PRACTICAL APPLICATION

Think about an area of your life right now where you might be getting impatient for God to act. After meditating on the above scriptures ask the Holy Spirit to help you trust God's timing. Be intentional about learning to wait expectantly, hopefully and patiently for God's perfect will and plan for your life. He will never let you down!

WANT TO KNOW MORE?

Write to us to request the discipleship teaching on "Waiting on God". Mail it to: Freedom in Jesus Prison Ministries, Attn: Teachings, P.O. Box 939, Levelland, TX 79336.

Building a good relationship depends on communication. Prayer can be one of the most intimate parts of our relationship with God. Let's learn more about talking to Him...

SPENDING TIME WITH HIM

Effective Prayer

In order to develop a relationship with someone there must be good, two-way communication. Certainly this applies to pursuing an intimacy of relationship with Jesus. Prayer is a primary way God has given us to communicate with Him.

As believers, prayer is our right and privilege. We are commanded to pray; but prayer should be thought of as more than a command. It is a means of getting closer to God!

"The greatest problem we face is not unanswered prayer but unoffered prayer." Dr. Adrian Rogers

It is a joy, an honor and a privilege to share the gospel with you, and to teach you what the Spirit is revealing about living the abundant life Jesus came to bring us (John 10:10b). It is a "much more" kind of life; a "pressed down, shaken together" type of life; an "open the windows of heaven and pour out more than you can contain" type of fulfilled existence in Christ!

One of the key requirements to experiencing this kind of abundant life in Christ is to be in constant communication with God through prayer.

We are called not just into a "relationship", but even deeper into a true "union", a "oneness", an "intimacy" in Christ. Our prayer life is critical.

True remnant believers are empowered to pray by and through the Holy Spirit. The fervent prayers of a righteous man or woman are powerfully effective. As born again believers we are new creations in Christ and partake of His Righteousness. Therefore, according to James 5:13-16, we know our prayers are important to the Body of Christ, and that our Father is moved by them to respond.

A great man of prayer, Dr. J. Allen Blair wrote, "The fact that the eternal and sovereign Creator of the universe has made Himself accessible to humans overwhelms me. Just to think that we can call on Him at any time with the confidence that He listens and responds is absolutely awesome!" He continues, "...there is unlimited power in prayer. We can be assured that prayer changes things. God gives us a never-ending invitation in Jeremiah 33:3 saying, *'Call to me and I will answer you and tell you great and unsearchable things you do not know.'* Prayer brings heaven down to man and man up to heaven."

The best way to get to know someone is to talk frequently with that person. The secret to a successful Christian life is an intimate relationship with the Lord Jesus. An effective prayer life is imperative if we want to achieve this relationship.

Jesus Himself set the example for us in Mark 1:35, "Very early in the morning, while it was still dark, Jesus got up, left the house and went off to a solitary place, where he prayed." The best possible way to begin the day is with prayer and a time of Bible reading. Jesus also taught the necessity of prayer in Luke 18:1, by saying that men "should always pray and not give up." Nothing is too small for God to be concerned about, or too big for God to be able to handle (Philippians 4:6; Jeremiah 32:27). He says that we are to come boldly to Him to ask for what we need (Hebrews 4:16).

In response to the disciples' request in Luke 11:1, Jesus taught them to pray by teaching them what is called "the Lord's Prayer." Also, the Bible teaches in I Thessalonians 5:16-18, "Be joyful always; pray continually; give thanks in all circumstances, for **this is God's will for you** in Christ Jesus." It is God's will that we pray. If we have any intentions of pleasing God, or of having His blessing upon our life, we must do those things He wants us to do.

After more than 70 years on this planet, I assure you there has never been a more important time to pray. God has put us here on purpose, with a purpose, in what I believe are the final moments before the return of King Jesus! Wherever we find ourselves daily, we must be the light in the darkness, and well represent Jesus to the world. Prayer and the Word of God are the most powerful weapons we have in the spiritual warfare raging around us (see Ephesians 6:10-18). Praying God's Word is crucial for true disciples (see John 15:7-8).

There are so many around us who are not yet born again, including some members of our family and closest friends. Now, more than ever, we must pray for their salvation. Also, we see so many people facing serious illness, or grieving for loved ones who have passed on into eternity. Many are in bondage to the demonic spirit of fear, living in suicidal depression, or enslaved to addictions of every kind. Brothers and sisters in Christ, we must PRAY, PRAY, PRAY.

While I was incarcerated, I began to study and learn many things from the Bible about how to pray effectively. I began to pray specifically for certain people and situations; and, witnessed so many answers to my prayers! I made a list of many of my prayers, and kept track of how and when they were answered. WOW, this was faith-building for me in wonderful, lasting ways!

What elements constitute "effective praying"? *The Life in the Spirit Study Bible*, by Zondervan, answers this way:

1. "To pray effectively, we must genuinely praise and adore God. (Psalm 150; Acts 2:47; Romans 15:11)
2. Like praise and adoration, we are to pray with genuine thanksgiving to God. (Psalm 100:4; Matthew 11:25-26; Philippians 4:6)
3. Sincere confession of known sins is essential to a faithful prayer. (James 5:15-16; Psalm 51; Luke 18:13; I John 1:9; II Chronicles 7:14)
4. God also instructs us to ask according to our "needs" (not necessarily our "wants"). As James writes, "we do not receive because we do not ask, or we ask with the wrong motives". (James 4:2-3; Psalm 27:7-12; Matthew 7:7-11)
5. We must pray faithfully and fervently for others. (Numbers 14:13-19; Psalm 122:6-9; Luke 22:31-32; Luke 23:34; John 17:9, 20)"

Prayer is not simply asking God for things. I used to think that was the main purpose and method of prayer. Rather, it is foremost a time to praise and thank Him. The Psalmist wrote in Psalm 107:8-9, *"Let them give thanks to the Lord for His unfailing love and His wonderful deeds for men, for He satisfies the thirsty and fills the hungry with good things."* There is nothing that gets the heart and mind in a spirit of prayer more than an attitude of joyful praise to the Lord. Praise lifts our thoughts off of ourselves and centers them on God instead.

We need to learn to give praise to God in prayer. If we do, we will find prayer time not only enjoyable but exceedingly fruitful and profitable.

Take advantage of this remarkable privilege God has given. Be grateful. Be humble. Spend time talking to God frequently throughout the day. Your prayers do not need to be long and "poetic". God knows your heart. He knows your weaknesses, needs and sins already. He just wants you to acknowledge them to Him. Also, don't do all the talking. Be quiet and listen to what He is saying to you!

Be consistent in prayer. Don't use it as an emergency measure only when trouble strikes.

"He who does not pray when the sun shines,
does not know how to pray when the clouds come."
Dr. J. Allen Blair

Let's learn to be powerful, effective prayer warriors! Our families need us to do it, and so do the rest of those around us.

SOME RELEVANT SCRIPTURE PASSAGES

Jeremiah 33:3 "Call to Me, and I will answer you, and show you great and mighty things, which you do not know."

Mark 1:35 "Now in the morning, having risen a long while before daylight, He went out and departed to a solitary place; and there He prayed."

Luke 18:1 "Then He spoke a parable to them, that men always ought to pray and not lose heart."

Philippians 4:6-7 "Be anxious for nothing, but in everything by prayer and supplication, with thanksgiving, let your requests be made known to God; and the peace of God, which surpasses all understanding, will guard your hearts and minds through Christ Jesus."

Jeremiah 32:27 "I am the Lord, the God of all mankind. Is anything too hard for me?"

Hebrews 4:16 "Let us then approach God's throne of grace with confidence, so that we may receive mercy and find grace to help us in our time of need."

1 Thessalonians 5:16-19 "Rejoice always, pray continually, give thanks in all circumstances; for this is God's will for you in Christ Jesus. Do not quench the Spirit."

John 15:7-8 "If you remain in me and my words remain in you, ask whatever you wish, and it will be done for you. This is to my Father's glory, that you bear much fruit, showing yourselves to be my disciples."

Psalm 100:4 "Enter his gates with thanksgiving and his courts with praise; give thanks to him and praise his name."

Psalm 107:8 "Let them give thanks to the Lord for his unfailing love and his wonderful deeds for mankind."

2 Chronicles 7:13-14 "When I shut up the heavens so that there is no rain, or command locusts to devour the land or send a plague among my people, if my people, who are called by my name, will humble themselves and pray and seek my face and turn from their wicked ways, then I will hear from heaven, and I will forgive their sin and will heal their land."

TAKEAWAY HIGHLIGHT

In order to develop a relationship with someone there must be good, two-way communication. Certainly this applies to pursuing an intimacy of relationship with Jesus. Prayer is a primary way God has given us to communicate with Him.

As believers, prayer is our right and privilege. We are commanded to pray; but prayer should be thought of as more than a command. It is a means of getting closer to God!

PRACTICAL APPLICATION

Based on your study of the material and scriptures above, ask the Holy Spirit to show you how your prayers may be more effective. Practice a time of listening as part of your private prayer time with God. He likes talking to you.

WANT TO KNOW MORE?

Write to us to request the discipleship teaching on "Effective Prayer". Mail it to: Freedom in Jesus Prison Ministries, Attn: Teachings, P.O. Box 939, Levelland, TX 79336.

Do you want to know more about the pattern and purpose of prayer? Read on...

The Pattern and Purpose of Prayer

Cultivating and maintaining an intimate relationship with God requires constant communication.

Over the last several years, as I have attempted to make some sort of sense of everything going on in these last days, I have come to believe increasingly more in the power and necessity of prayer.

I am sure you too have a real burden in your heart to pray for your family, the lost, our country, and world events. Now more than ever we must learn how to pray powerfully, and commit to spending more time daily in God's Presence talking to Him and listening for His answers.

Dr. Adrian Rogers said, **"Tragically, many of our prayers are so vague that if God were to answer them we wouldn't even know it."** Be bold and specific. Pray the scriptures and His promises. There is nothing you cannot talk to God about. Open your heart to Him and pour out your concerns. Dr. Rogers also said, **"If it's big enough to concern you, it's big enough to concern God."**

Learning to feel comfortable talking to God in prayer is important for our continued growth in Christ. It is also absolutely crucial for prevailing in spiritual warfare!

In his devotional, “The Strength to Stand”, Dr. Charles Stanley teaches:

“To stand firm in this life, we need the power of our living Lord operating within us. To have God’s divine power released in us requires serious, sustained prayer (Ephesians 3:18). When we communicate with the Father, His Holy Spirit will give us discernment so that we can recognize truths about spiritual warfare and gain insight into the adversary’s tactics (1 Corinthians 2:14). Starting each morning with the Lord lets Him strengthen us to stand steadfastly for Christ, no matter what is in store for us that day.

“Prayer is an essential element in our protection against the devil. If we are prayerless—that is, if we fail to seek God’s guidance and neglect to put on His armor by faith every day—then we will be defeated. Our understanding and vision apart from the Lord are too limited and the enemy is too powerful for us to stand alone. However, Romans 8:37 tells us that with God, we will be more than conquerors. He will make us ready if we draw close to Him through prayer, listen to His instructions, and follow through with obedience.”

Surely you sense the activity of principalities and powers all around you, and see all the evidence of the spiritual forces of wickedness running rampant in this dark world. But Satan is a defeated foe, and we are on the winning side! The devil is scared of a Christian who knows his delegated authority in Christ Jesus, and effectively wields the Word and prayer as his weapons. I am asking the Holy Spirit to give us all a burning desire to learn to pray more powerfully.

Dr. Charles Stanley writes in his article, “The Pattern of Powerful Prayer”, “So often we hear requests to bless, protect, and provide for a person. While these are fine to ask of the Lord, there is another, more powerful way to pray: When we use Scripture to speak to the heavenly Father, our conversation contains His own divine authority." He says that praying effectively isn't something we naturally know how to do, but we can learn!

"When we pray, it is not just saying words that are going up in the atmosphere and maybe the Lord is hearing them and maybe He's not. Prayer is entering into God's Presence face to face, with our requests and petitions."
Perry Stone

The Rock of Ages Prison Ministry teaching on prayer describes an acrostic to help us pray:

A Adoration
C Confession
T Thanksgiving
S Supplication and Petitions

"**Adoration** is praise focusing on who God is. **Confession** is acknowledging your sins before God in order to receive forgiveness. **Thanksgiving** is expressing gratitude to God for specific acts and provisions. Always give God thanks for people in your life and all His many spiritual, physical and material blessings. **Supplication and Petitions** – Supplication is making requests and expressing desires to God. Petition is asking God for our needs."

Our prayers should be more about others than about ourselves. The Bible gives us many examples and instructions to pray for other people. Some of the Scripture references include: 2 Corinthians 1:11; Romans 1:9-10; Ephesians 1:16; Philippians 1:3-4; Colossians 1:3; 1 Thessalonians 1:2; John 17:6-26. Praying for others is not just a command or responsibility, it is a privilege. Seeing God answer your prayers for the lives and circumstances of others builds your own faith and lifts you up higher in your own expectations of prayer.

How are we to pray for others? Paul has provided us four great examples of how to pray effectively to God on behalf of others. Read and meditate on Paul's prayers for others in Ephesians 1:16-19; Ephesians 3:14-21; Philippians 1:9-11; Colossians1:9-11. You will be blessed also if you will "personalize" these prayers and pray them for yourself daily. They are included in the supplementary material with this book.

Based on the four prayers Paul prayed mentioned above, our prayers for our Christian brothers and sisters (and ourselves) should include asking God that they may:

1. Understand God's will, and gain spiritual wisdom,
2. Live holy lives pleasing to the Lord,
3. Bear fruit for Christ,
4. Be strengthened spiritually by the Holy Spirit,
5. Persevere in faith and righteousness,
6. Give thanks to the Father,
7. Continue in the hope and assurance of heaven,
8. Experience the nearness of Christ,
9. Be filled with the revelation of the complete love of Christ,
10. Be filled in every way with the fullness of God,
11. Show love and kindness to others,
12. Discern evil,
13. Be sincere and blameless, and
14. Eagerly await the Lord's return.

There has never been a more important time to pray. We must seriously and diligently petition God daily; and, seek His guidance, so that we can safely navigate the treacherous waters in which we find ourselves. Our families and the Body of Christ are counting on us! Be bold and courageous. Stand firm. Have faith. Pray. If God be for us who can be against us?

SOME RELEVANT SCRIPTURE PASSAGES

Ephesians 6:17-20 “Take the helmet of salvation and the sword of the Spirit, which is the word of God. And pray in the Spirit on all occasions with all kinds of prayers and requests. With this in mind, be alert and always keep on praying for all the Lord’s people. Pray also for me, that whenever I speak, words may be given me so that I will fearlessly make known the mystery of the gospel, for which I am an ambassador in chains. Pray that I may declare it fearlessly, as I should.”

1 Thessalonians 5:16-19 “Rejoice always, pray continually, give thanks in all circumstances; for this is God’s will for you in Christ Jesus. Do not quench the Spirit.”

2 Corinthians 1:10-11 “He has delivered us from such a deadly peril, and he will deliver us again. On him we have set our hope that he will continue to deliver us, as you help us by your prayers. Then many will give thanks on our behalf for the gracious favor granted us in answer to the prayers of many.”

Romans 1:9-10 “God, whom I serve in my spirit in preaching the gospel of his Son, is my witness how constantly I remember you in my prayers at all times; and I pray that now at last by God’s will the way may be opened for me to come to you.”

Ephesians 1:16 “I have not stopped giving thanks for you, remembering you in my prayers.”

Colossians 1:3-6 "We always thank God, the Father of our Lord Jesus Christ, when we pray for you, because we have heard of your faith in Christ Jesus and of the love you have for all God's people— the faith and love that spring from the hope stored up for you in heaven and about which you have already heard in the true message of the gospel that has come to you. In the same way, the gospel is bearing fruit and growing throughout the whole world—just as it has been doing among you since the day you heard it and truly understood God's grace."

TAKEAWAY HIGHLIGHT

Learning to feel comfortable talking to God in prayer is important for our continued growth in intimacy of relationship with Christ. It is also absolutely crucial for prevailing in spiritual warfare!

Surely you sense the activity of principalities and powers all around you, and see all the evidence of the spiritual forces of wickedness running rampant in this dark world. But Satan is a defeated foe, and we are on the winning side! The devil is scared of a Christian who knows his delegated authority in Christ Jesus, and effectively wields the Word and prayer as his weapons. I am asking the Holy Spirit to give us all a burning desire to learn to pray more powerfully.

PRACTICAL APPLICATION

Make a list of family, friends and acquaintances for whom you want to pray regularly. Make some notes for each person as to specific prayer points. Start a prayer journal to keep track of what you have been praying and how God answers your prayer. This is powerfully faith-building!

WANT TO KNOW MORE?

Write to us to request the discipleship teaching on "The Pattern and

Purpose of Prayer". Mail it to: Freedom in Jesus Prison Ministries, Attn: Teachings, P.O. Box 939, Levelland, TX 79336.

Another spiritual discipline that helps us in our relationship with God is fasting. Read on...

Biblical Fasting

Biblical fasting can be an important way of seeking God in a deeper relationship experience. Denying ourselves something during a fast that our "flesh" craves strengthens us spiritually. It also trains us to say "no" to future temptations because we have confidence through personal experience that we can successfully resist the enemy.

Fasting is a topic I wanted to learn more about after I was saved and still incarcerated. Before I was released in December, 2010, I read what had been available to me at the time, and I wrote it down for myself and other prisoners to study. A number of times in prison I practiced the spiritual discipline of fasting and I believe it always resulted in me growing closer to, and experiencing deeper intimacy with, Father God.

Dr. Charles Stanley writes in his article, "Biblical Fasting", some of the important benefits:

"Before we go further, it is important to dispel a popular misunderstanding. Fasting doesn't serve to change God's mind, speed up His answer, or manipulate His will. Instead, it prepares us to hear from Him by temporarily laying aside something that vies for our attention or devotion—such as food, sleep, or a time of intimacy with a spouse.

"Denying ourselves in this way makes us better able to focus on Christ and hear Him clearly. His Spirit often starts by bringing to mind sin that needs to be confessed. In so doing, He sanctifies our thoughts—then He can use this precious time to intensify our desire for Him, reveal His Will, and grant understanding and peace. In essence, fasting binds us to Him in such oneness that we won't ever be the same again."

Kristen Feola, in her book *Spiritually Strong* writes:

"It truly is the 'path of pleasant pain,' as John Piper calls it. As you empty yourself physically and spiritually, you open the door for God to step in and do the miraculous. Your relationship with the Lord is taken to a whole new level. You also become more sensitive to the work of the Holy Spirit, which enables you to hear God's voice more clearly."

In an article Mary Fairchild wrote entitled, "What Does the Bible Say about Spiritual Fasting?", the purpose of fasting is clarified:

"While many people fast to lose weight, dieting is not the purpose of a spiritual fast. Instead, fasting provides unique spiritual benefits in the life of the believer.

"Fasting requires self-control and discipline as one denies the natural desires of the flesh. During spiritual fasting, the believer's focus is removed from the physical things of this world and intensely concentrated on God. Put differently, fasting directs our hunger toward God. It clears the mind and body of earthly attentions and draws us close to God. So, as we gain spiritual clarity of thought while fasting, it allows us to *hear God* more clearly. Fasting also demonstrates a profound need for God's help and guidance through complete dependence upon him."

In his "First15 Devotional", Craig Denison shares some of his insights on this topic:

"There's something powerful that takes place when we willingly surrender satisfaction in the world to make space for more of God. God loves to respond to our hunger. In his patience he waits for us to cry out to him to bring us into the fullness of what he has for us. But in his pursuit of us he constantly whispers from his Spirit to ours, beckoning us to give up the rags of this world for the riches that come through the life, death, and resurrection of Jesus.

"Whether you're fasting food, entertainment, relationships, or anything else to make space for more of God, the intention of God for fasting is to fill you up to overflow. It's his intention to realign your life to position you to consistently receive all he has for you. It's his intention to transform the pangs of separation from whatever you're fasting into deep prayers for more of his goodness. May you be honest with yourself and be filled with the desire to fast from that which stands in the way of you fully living the abundant life."

The Life in the Spirit Study Bible, by Zondervan, includes this section regarding the purpose of fasting with prayer:

"In Zechariah 7:1-5, we learn that fasting should be done out of a real hunger and thirst for God, not out of obligation or mere formality. Further, the people needed to pay attention to prophets such as Isaiah and to respond by fasting and praying for God's grace to live holy and just lives before God and others.

"Fasting relates to a time of confession (Psalm 69:10). It can be a time of seeking a deeper prayer experience and drawing near to God (Ezra 8:23; Joel 2:12).

"The purposes of fasting, with prayer and increased time in God's Word, are:

1. To honor God.
2. To humble ourselves before God in order to experience more grace and God's intimate presence.
3. To mourn over personal sin and failure.
4. To mourn over the sins of the church, nation and world.
5. To seek grace for a new task and to reaffirm our consecration to God.
6. To seek God by drawing near to Him and persisting in prayer against opposing spiritual forces.
7. To show repentance and so make a way for God to change His declared intentions of judgment.
8. To save people from bondage and evil.
9. To gain revelation and wisdom concerning God's will.
10. To open the way for the outpouring of the Spirit and Christ's return to earth for His people."

Fasting is one way that we can demonstrate to ourselves and God that we can deny ourselves at least one "desire of the flesh". It should give us more confidence that we can also successfully deny other desires of our "flesh" (e.g. addictions, bad habits, excessive attention to worldly pursuits, etc). There is no one "right way" (or length of time) to fast – it is between you and God.

Biblical fasting is also one small, sacrificial way we can recognize the much larger sacrifice Christ made for us. By humbly seeking God in increased prayer time and studying the Word during fasting, we achieve a victory of the spirit over the flesh; and, we get to know God in a deeper relationship experience.

SOME RELEVANT SCRIPTURE PASSAGES

Matthew 4:1-2 "Then Jesus was led by the Spirit into the wilderness to be tempted by the devil. After fasting forty days and forty nights, he was hungry."

Acts 10:30 NKJV "So Cornelius said, 'Four days ago I was fasting until this hour; and at the ninth hour I prayed in my house, and behold, a man stood before me in bright clothing...'"

Acts 14:23 "Paul and Barnabas appointed elders for them in each church and, with prayer and fasting, committed them to the Lord, in whom they had put their trust."

1 Corinthians 7:5 "Do not deprive one another except with consent for a time, that you may give yourselves to fasting and prayer; and come together again so that Satan does not tempt you because of your lack of self-control."

Ezra 8:23 "So we fasted and petitioned our God about this, and he answered our prayer."

Joel 2:12 "Even now, declares the LORD, return to me with all your heart, with fasting and weeping and mourning."

Matthew 6:16-18 "When you fast, do not look somber as the hypocrites do, for they disfigure their faces to show others they are fasting. Truly I tell you, they have received their reward in full. But when you fast, put oil on your head and wash your face, so that it will not be obvious to others that you are fasting, but only to your Father, who is unseen; and your Father, who sees what is done in secret, will reward you."

TAKEAWAY HIGHLIGHT

Biblical fasting can be an important way of seeking God in a deeper rela-

tionship experience. Denying ourselves something during a fast that our "flesh" craves strengthens us spiritually. It also trains us to say "no" to future temptations because we have confidence through personal experience that we can successfully resist the enemy.

Fasting is also one small, sacrificial way we can recognize the much larger sacrifice Christ made for us. By humbly seeking God in increased prayer time and studying the Word during fasting, we achieve a victory of the spirit over the flesh; and, we get to know God in a deeper relationship experience.

PRACTICAL APPLICATION

Ask the Holy Spirit to help you decide how and when to fast. Perhaps He will lead you to fast from food, but it could be something else your flesh normally craves, or maybe a habit that is not honoring God. Accompany this fast with prayer and the spending of more time studying God's Word.

WANT TO KNOW MORE?

Write to us to request the discipleship teaching on "Biblical Fasting". Mail it to: Freedom in Jesus Prison Ministries, Attn: Teachings, P.O. Box 939, Levelland, TX 79336.

Deepening our relationship with God can come by spending more quiet time with Him. What might this entail? Read on...

Quiet Time with God

If we want to cultivate a better relationship with someone we will want to spend quality time together on a regular basis. This commitment and follow-through is evidence of the relationship's importance to us. How much priority do we assign to spending time with God?

Many ask how to structure and enjoy a daily quiet time with God. I know first-hand how this requires patience, devotion and deliberate effort to block out the almost constant noise and distractions of entertainment, social media, the world, and especially in the chaotic and noisy atmosphere of prison. However, I can testify how much peace, calm, confidence and joy comes from intentionally starting and ending each day with quality time alone with God.

Having a "quiet time" with the Lord is not easy. Yet, when you purposefully tune-out the noise around you; take time to be still; intentionally quiet your mind and soul; and, prayerfully focus all your attention on God and His Word, you will experience incredible spiritual enrichment and peace.

Many Christians fall by the wayside when they neglect this very important time daily with God. This daily period will not solve all your problems, but it will certainly help.

Try to meet the Lord the first thing in the morning while your mind, soul and body are their best – before the demands of the day beset you (Proverbs 8:17; Psalm 63:1). It will set the whole tone for your day. Then when problems and situations arise, you are already prepared and empowered to deal with them in a Christ-like manner, with wisdom and patience.

Be diligent in this and do not let anything interfere. Satan knows how powerful this time is and will always try to keep you from your daily appointment with God. Satan does not want you putting on the whole armor of God (Ephesians 6:10-20), especially the most important covering – prayer. Do not allow the enemy to rush you or distract you. This is one of his favorite tricks (Ephesians 6:11; 1 Peter 5:8).

How much time should you spend? The amount of time is not the most important thing. An hour spent distractedly day-dreaming your way through the Word and prayer is mainly a waste of sixty minutes. On the other hand, fifteen minutes devoted to seriously seeking and praising God in prayer, and thoughtfully studying your Bible will be a wise and enriching investment.

What should you do during this devotional period? Many people agree that it could be divided three ways between Bible reading, prayer and Scripture memory work. Before you begin, prayerfully ask the Holy Spirit to give you wisdom, knowledge and understanding as you read the Word. Ask Him to reveal truth and how to specifically apply the Word to your life (Proverbs 1:2-4; Proverbs 30:5; John 14:26; John 16:13; James 1:5).

It is a good practice to read your entire Bible systematically through every year or so. There are many "plans" for doing this, but one suggestion is to start in Matthew and read 3-4 chapters a day through Revelation, then start with Genesis and go through the Old Testament the same way. The entire Bible can be read in about a year in this fashion.

Some people enjoy starting their quiet time with a daily devotion written for them, for example, from "Our Daily Bread", or even the daily discipleship book I wrote, *Diving Deeper*. The message is designed to teach and inspire you. Be sure to read the suggested Scripture passage for the day from which the idea for the devotion was drawn, and dive deeper into any related scriptures mentioned.

After you have received the Lord's message from His Word, seek God in prayer. This is the best time for cultivating and appreciating your intimate, personal relationship with Him. Worship, adoration and praise of God the Father, Jesus and the Holy Spirit, is an enriching way to begin your prayer time. Take time to consider all His attributes and appreciate the way He ministers to you in each aspect of the Trinity – the Father, Jesus, and the Holy Spirit.

Each personal prayer should include confession of specific, known and previously un-confessed sins, both intentional and unintentional. God does not move to answer the prayers of a sinner (Psalms 66:18; Isaiah 59:2), unless it is their sincere prayer of repentance. After confession, spend time thanking God for all your blessings, small and great. A grateful attitude of the heart is best developed intentionally.

Praying for others is a powerful privilege and responsibility. Focusing on the needs and concerns of others will make your own problems seem smaller. Pray and believe in faith that God meets all your needs. As you pray specifically for yourself, above all else surrender your will to His perfect Will and Divine plan for your life (Jeremiah 29:11-14a). Stand firm on His Word throughout your prayer time. There is real power and assurance that comes from praying God's Word back to Him.

Time spent daily in memorizing and meditating on Scripture not only transforms your mind and spirit, it enables you to pray with boldness and assurance that you are heard as the Spirit and Jesus intercede on your behalf with the Father. God always honors His Word.

During your quiet time, God will speak to your heart about a certain scripture. Write the verse down and carry it with you through the day. Read it over, meditate on each word, and consider how it applies to you. Look for opportunities to share it with others. Memorize the scripture reference as well as the verse. God promises you as you meditate daily on His Word that you will be fruitful, well-grounded, successful and prosperous (Psalm 1:1-3; Joshua 1:8)!

Andrew Murray, 19th century Christian writer and pastor once said,

"No person can expect to make progress in holiness who is not often and long alone with God."

As you plan your time of devotion with the Lord, consider this passage from an article by Cynthia Heald in Decision Magazine:

"The *dictionary* defines 'devotion' as religious fervor; an act of prayer or private worship; a religious exercise separate from corporate worship. Devotion is prayer, reverence, constancy and passion.

"My definition of devotion is taking time to sit at the feet of Jesus and to listen to His Word because I love Him. Living with a heart of devotion is about giving Him the best of my time and thoughts so that as I go about my day, my heart is centered on and devoted to Christ."

In his "First15 Devotional" entitled "God Speaks in Solitude", Craig Denison explains the importance of solitude with God:

"You can know that you need solitude for one reason— Jesus needed it. All over the New Testament we see examples of Jesus going off on his own to pray. One example, Mark 1:35, tells us that Jesus, *"rising very early in the morning, while it was still dark...departed and went out to a desolate place, and there he prayed."* Jesus, who practiced perfect communion with his heavenly Father while here on earth still needed to spend time in solitude. Jesus, who loved parties, loved people and was God and man simultaneously needed time alone. If he needed it, you and I can be sure we need it. When God incarnate was up against his hardest task, the Crucifixion, he didn't just toughen up and get through it. He spent time alone in the Garden of Gethsemane in conversation with his heavenly Father. He needed solitude to accomplish his purpose here on earth and so do you and I.

"Solitude is life-giving. It's necessary to the Christian spiritual life. Richard J. Foster said, 'Loneliness is inner emptiness. Solitude is inner fulfilment.' Solitude is one of the most important and life-giving spiritual disciplines. If you want to hear God, you must practice solitude. If you want fortitude in your life, a steadfastness that surpasses your circumstances, you must practice solitude. You are designed for time spent in the quiet, simply being with your heavenly Father."

Even in the loud and often chaotic conditions of daily life, it is possible to find a time to quiet your mind, body and spirit. You will be richly blessed when you make this your first priority daily.

Carefully implementing these suggestions fully could well be one of the most important aspects of developing and maintaining a lifelong, intimate relationship with Jesus.

SOME RELEVANT SCRIPTURE PASSAGES

Proverbs 8:17 "I love those who love me, and those who seek me find me."

Psalm 63:1 "You, God, are my God, earnestly I seek you; I thirst for you, my whole being longs for you, in a dry and parched land where there is no water."

1 Peter 5:8 "Be alert and of sober mind. Your enemy the devil prowls around like a roaring lion looking for someone to devour."

Ephesians 6:11 "Put on the full armor of God, so that you can take your stand against the devil's schemes."

Proverbs 30:5 "Every word of God is flawless; he is a shield to those who take refuge in him."

John 14:26 "But the Advocate, the Holy Spirit, whom the Father will send in my name, will teach you all things and will remind you of everything I have said to you."

John 16:13 "But when he, the Spirit of truth, comes, he will guide you into all the truth. He will not speak on his own; he will speak only what he hears, and he will tell you what is yet to come."

James 1:5 "If any of you lacks wisdom, you should ask God, who gives generously to all without finding fault, and it will be given to you."

Psalm 66:18 "If I had cherished sin in my heart, the Lord would not have listened..."

Isaiah 59:2 "But your iniquities have separated you from your God; your sins have hidden his face from you, so that he will not hear."

Jeremiah 29:11-14 "For I know the plans I have for you," declares the LORD, "plans to prosper you and not to harm you, plans to give you hope and a future. Then you will call on me and come and pray to me, and I will listen to you. You will seek me and find me when you seek me with all your heart. I will be found by you," declares the LORD, "and will bring you back from captivity. I will gather you from all the nations and places where I have banished you," declares the LORD, "and will bring you back to the place from which I carried you into exile."

Psalm 1:1-3 "Blessed is the one who does not walk in step with the wicked or stand in the way that sinners take or sit in the company of mockers, but whose delight is in the law of the LORD, and who meditates on his law day and night. That person is like a tree planted by streams of water, which yields its fruit in season and whose leaf does not wither—whatever they do prospers."

Joshua 1:8 "Keep this Book of the Law always on your lips; meditate on it day and night, so that you may be careful to do everything written in it. Then you will be prosperous and successful."

Mark 1:35 "Very early in the morning, while it was still dark, Jesus got up, left the house and went off to a solitary place, where he prayed."

TAKEAWAY HIGHLIGHT

"My definition of devotion is taking time to sit at the feet of Jesus and to listen to His Word because I love Him. Living with a heart of devotion is about giving Him the best of my time and thoughts so that as I go about my day, my heart is centered on and devoted to Christ." Cynthia Heald

PRACTICAL APPLICATION

Make a list of the positive benefits that might result if you allocated quiet time daily to spend with God. Ask the Holy Spirit to give you an idea of how you and God might spend this time together.

WANT TO KNOW MORE?

Write to us to request the discipleship teaching on "Quiet Time with God". Mail it to: Freedom in Jesus Prison Ministries, Attn: Teachings, P.O. Box 939, Levelland, TX 79336.

Relationship improvement is directly related to the level of quality and frequency of communication. Communication with God is a skill to be learned and practiced. Find out how...

Communication with God

Our relationship with God is directly impacted by how well we receive communication from Him and how willingly we obey and/or apply what He is saying.

Jesus said, "My sheep listen to my voice; I know them, and they follow me." John 10:27

My friend and former ministry partner, Carol Breeden, graduated to heaven in 2020. She wrote a book, Peace in Him, that is available in e-book form on Amazon. Of all the Christians I have known since my salvation in prison in 2009, Carol had the most profound sense of peace about her. She certainly knew how to communicate with God. The material in this chapter comes primarily from two teaching letters she wrote for our ministry in 2016.

"The first thing you must learn in order for this communication to take place is *your stillness, your silence.* Yes, that is right....practice being *still and silent.*

"When I first gave my heart to Jesus, I was not very knowledgeable of God or His Word. Oh, I had learned most of the Bible stories in a Sunday school class, but I did not know that the principles of the Bible were supposed to be applied to my life. And I certainly did not know that I could communicate with God!

"After several years of being a born-again Christian, a teacher in the adult Sunday school class I was attending challenged each of us to learn how to hear from God. I thought that was something only the most *spiritually-minded* were able to do. He shared how he began to hear from God, and I decided to do exactly what he did. I set my alarm clock for 4:30 a.m., a time when my husband and children were still asleep and I could be alone with God. I had pencil and paper close at hand and I asked God if He had anything to say to me. If He did, I was prepared to write it down on paper. Then, I silently waited for Him. He never disappointed me. Every morning, He had something to say to me.

"Over the next several months, my *silence before God* became even more rewarding. I learned to recognize His voice, what He cared about the most, and what He wanted from me. We began to develop a close relationship, one that would be very difficult to break. In fact, I had no desire to break this relationship. It became something I needed and looked forward to every day. Also, I began to have a better understanding of His Word and what He was saying to me through His Word, and I began to realize that He also spoke to me through other people around me.

"As time went on, I no longer set my alarm for 4:30 a.m. You see, God knew He could talk to me whenever He wanted. He could wake me up whenever He wanted. He also could talk to me during the day whenever He wanted. It became a very personal, intimate relationship.

"This communication is a little different with each person because with each it is a personal relationship. Just as your relationship and communication with one person will be different from one person to another, neither will another person share the exact same relationship and communication with God.

"In prison, where noise is almost constant, you will be rewarded to find a time of day or night when there are fewer distractions and it is easier for you to be still and silent. You must practice 'tuning out' the chatter and chaos of life around you so you can 'tune in' to communication with God! Then it will be easier to hear His Holy Spirit throughout the day. He is not only with you; He is in you!

"One thing you can always count on.....He does want to hear from you, and He does want to talk to you. His Word says: *'My sheep hear my voice, and another they will not follow.'"*

Gillis Triplett wrote a great teaching entitled, "The Five Fold Secret to Clearly Hearing God's Voice." He points out that "we must realize that there is more than one voice communicating with us. There are actually five voices communicating with us, and we must learn to recognize those five voices. Those five voices are: (1) The voice of God; (2) The voice of your conscience; (3) The voice of your reasoning; (4) The voice of your flesh; and (5) The voice of the devil."

"In most cases, each voice is going to lead you in the opposite direction of the voice of God. The sincere Christians who consistently miss God's voice, either: (a) don't know about all of these five voices, or (b) they have not learned how to discern which voice is speaking. Each voice has a distinct sound and is easily discernable once you know what to listen for."

How well we discern between these voices depends on what we are allowing into our minds a majority of the time. Proverbs 23:7 teaches us that whatever we habitually think about, that is who we are. And, what we habitually think about we will eventually speak forth, and then we act on it.

Mr. Triplett's teaching article ends with the *Seven Elements to Clearly Hearing God's Voice:*

"... there are the seven elements that must be in place in your life, if you are going to properly discern which voice is speaking.

1. You must study the Word of God for yourself, (See II Timothy 2:15)
2. You must meditate on the Word of God day and night, (Joshua 1:8)
3. You must spend time praying, (Mark 1:35)
4. You must spend time communing with the Holy Spirit, (II Corinthians 13:14)
5. You must be planted in a good church home, (Hebrews 10:24-25)
6. You must rationally consider all options, (Luke 14:28-30)
7. You must seek counsel from wise counselors, (See Proverbs 11:14)

If you follow those instructions, you will come to the place, where you quickly recognize which voice is speaking to you. That is an awesome feeling to know that you know that you know–*the voice of the Holy Spirit!*"

Blessings follow obedience: that is, obedience precedes blessings. Therefore, if we want a better life–if we want the enemy to be stopped from stealing, killing and destroying things in our lives–we must learn to recognize God's voice. Then, when we can hear His voice, we must act upon what we hear. We must be obedient to His voice. Hearing alone will get us nowhere. We must be a "doer of the Word". We must do what He says.

In his "First15 Devotional", "Tilling the Soil of the Heart: God's Voice", Craig Denison, teaches that God longs to talk to us even more than we long to listen:

"God promises to speak to you as his child. He longs to tell you his love for you even more than you long to hear it. He longs to tell you his plans even more than you want to know them.

"There hasn't been a single thing more impactful in my life than hearing the voice of God. His voice is so tender when I need tenderness, corrective when sin constricts my life, and powerful when only he can make the changes in my life that need to be made. He speaks perfectly, never a word out of place and always at the perfect time. You might hear God more than you think. I've never heard him speak audibly to me, but every day he whispers to my heart what I need to know. There are days I don't stop to listen. There are times I allow the weight of the world to crowd out his voice. But as I turn my heart back towards him, I find out that he was there—speaking all along. He whispers of his love for me when I feel crushed by the opinion of man. He tells me he's proud of me when I feel like everything I'm doing doesn't measure up. He whispers of his plans for me when I turn and go my own way. It's not because I'm gifted in some certain way that I hear his voice, but rather because God in his grace loves to speak.

"God has never made a spiritually deaf person. You can hear God because his voice is immeasurably more about his love than your abilities. You are his child; his love for you is vast, unchanging and unceasing. All it takes to hear him is simply inclining an ear to him and allowing his words to take root in you. As he speaks of his love, you will feel the chains of the world fall off. As he tells you of his purpose, you will discover that a plan has been in the works for you since before you were born. Choose to listen to his voice today; let it drown out the cares of the world and create a soil in you receptive to his seed, fertile and filled with the fruit of the Spirit."

Carol Breeden ended her teaching with, "These are valuable truths which, when we apply them to our lives, will greatly enrich our Christian walk and give us a closer, intimate relationship with our Heavenly Father; our Savior, Redeemer, Brother and Lord Jesus Christ; and the awesome and powerful Holy Spirit. I assure you, your life will never be the same once you learn to hear His voice. You will experience His love as never before, and you will gain a security in Him that you never knew before."

SOME RELEVANT SCRIPTURE PASSAGES

Psalm 46:10 "Be still, and know that I am God; I will be exalted among the nations, I will be exalted in the earth."

John 10:3-4 "The gatekeeper opens the gate for him, and the sheep listen to his voice. He calls his own sheep by name and leads them out. When he has brought out all his own, he goes on ahead of them, and his sheep follow him because they know his voice."

John 10:27 "My sheep listen to my voice; I know them and they follow me."

Jeremiah 33:3 "Call to me and I will answer you and tell you great and unsearchable things you do not know."

Psalm 4:3 "Know that the LORD has set apart the godly for himself; the LORD will hear when I call to him."

Psalm 119:147 "I rise before dawn and cry for help; I have put my hope in your word."

Psalm 63:1-2 "O God, you are my God, earnestly I seek you; my soul thirsts for you, my body longs for you, in a dry and weary land where there is no water. I have seen you in the sanctuary and beheld your power and your glory."

Proverbs 8:17 "I love those who love me, and those who seek me find me."

John 14:26 "But the Advocate, the Holy Spirit, whom the Father will send in my name, will teach you all things and will remind you of everything I have said to you."

John 16:13 "But when he, the Spirit of truth, comes, he will guide you into all the truth. He will not speak on his own; he will speak only what he hears, and he will tell you what is yet to come."

TAKEAWAY HIGHLIGHT

"God has never made a spiritually deaf person. You can hear God because his voice is immeasurably more about his love than your abilities. You are his child; his love for you is vast, unchanging and unceasing. All it takes to hear him is simply inclining an ear to him and allowing his words to take root in you. As he speaks of his love, you will feel the chains of the world fall off. As he tells you of his purpose, you will discover that a plan has been in the works for you since before you were born. Choose to listen to his voice today; let it drown out the cares of the world and create a soil in you receptive to his seed, fertile and filled with the fruit of the Spirit."
Craig Denison

PRACTICAL APPLICATION

Think about the fact that the Holy Spirit of God is with every Believer all the time. How much are you communicating with Him during the day? Do you seek His guidance for all your decisions? Do you try to obey His voice?

WANT TO KNOW MORE?

Write to us to request the discipleship teaching on "Communication with God – Parts 1 and 2". Mail it to: Freedom in Jesus Prison Ministries, Attn: Teachings, P.O. Box 939, Levelland, TX 79336.

The more familiar we are with God's attributes, the more inspired we will be to seek relationship with Him. Let's learn...

Knowledge of the Holy One

We are drawn ever closer to God in relationship as we get to know Him better. He is Holy.

"The fear of the LORD is the beginning of wisdom, and knowledge of the Holy One is understanding." Proverbs 9:10

As we gain more wisdom, knowledge and understanding of God our true worship of Him increases.

"Yet a time is coming and has now come when the true worshipers will worship the Father in the Spirit and in truth, for they are the kind of worshipers the Father seeks. God is spirit, and his worshipers must worship in the Spirit and in truth." John 4:23-24

To worship Him in spirit and in truth, we must come to the Father in complete sincerity. Our own spirit must be directed by the Holy Spirit within us. Worship must take place according to the truth that is revealed in the Son and received through the Holy Spirit.

To truly worship Him in spirit and truth we must gain knowledge and understanding of Him. God has revealed certain truths about Himself to us which we can begin to understand by reading His Word. In addition, we know Jesus is the Living Word, and we see His example for us. We also learn about God through His Holy Spirit who resides in us teaching us about His qualities and attributes.

God knows we cannot truly understand the Infinite with our comparatively feeble, finite brains. We can only begin to fathom some of His qualities and attributes through Spirit-inspired Word into our hearts. In this body on earth, we will never know or fully understand everything about Him. But as we seek Him diligently daily, He gradually reveals Himself to us. It is out of a deep knowing in our hearts, not the thoughts of our mind, that we are able to begin to truly worship Him in spirit and in truth.

As you begin to better appreciate the awesomeness, vastness and holiness of God, you will develop a different perspective of yourself and the challenges or problems you face daily. London Pastor F.B. Meyer once wrote, "The best answer to self-consciousness is God-consciousness. When I concern myself, not with the perceived inequities and injustices I face but rather with ministering the things that matter to God, I find myself feeling abundantly privileged and blessed. What changed? It was my vision. The surest way to lift a person's spirit is to lift his focus."

Pastor Meyer continues, "When I look, not only to the things of God, but to God Himself, I find that I have more reasons to rejoice than I have to mourn. I possess more than I've lost. I have more in my hand than has slipped through my fingers. I have more to thank God for than to petition Him for."

I summarized the following information about some of God's attributes from A. W. Tozer's book entitled *Knowledge of the Holy One*. As you prayerfully review these attributes, be careful to meditate on their meaning. Stop to appreciate their truth. Ask His Spirit to increase your knowledge and understanding of Him. When you pray during your daily quiet times, be sure to acknowledge and praise Him in light of His revelation to you of these truths describing His Holy nature and character. Your increased knowledge of the Holy One will enable you to worship and adore Him more fully.

A.W. Tozer, in his book, *The Knowledge of The Holy*, wrote,

"What comes into our minds when we think about God is the most important thing about us... The most important fact about any man is not what he at a given time may say or do, but what he in his deep heart conceives God to be like...Without doubt, the mightiest thought the mind can entertain is the thought of God...We can never know who or what we are till we know at least something of what God is...For while the name of God is secret and His essential nature incomprehensible, He in condescending love has by revelation declared certain things to be true of Himself. These we call His attributes."

Some Attributes of God (summarized from *The Knowledge of The Holy*, by A. W. Tozer):

The Holy Trinity–The Bible reveals that ***there is one eternal God, with one essence, existing in three persons who are equal yet distinct: God the Father and God the Son and God the Holy Spirit.*** All three are together in unity, equal and co-eternal. They are both one and three. They have one will. They always work together, and not even the smallest thing is done by one without the instant agreement of the other two. Tozer said, "The doctrine of the Trinity... is truth for the heart. The fact that it cannot be satisfactorily explained, instead of being against it, is in its favor. Such a truth had to be revealed; no one could have imagined it."

The Self-existence of God – ***God has no origin.*** Origin is a word that can apply only to things created. God was not created. He is self-existent. Aside from God, nothing is self-caused. Tozer writes, "Everything was made by Someone who was made of none...Man is a created being...who of himself possesses nothing but is dependent each moment for his existence upon the One who created him after His own likeness."

The Self-sufficiency of God – ***God requires no helpers and has no needs.*** God is what He is in Himself. All life is in and from God. Nothing is above Him. Nothing is beyond Him. Man is not necessary to God. He is not greater because we exist and He would not be less if we did not exist. God does not need our help. He does not need us to defend Him or His truths. His truth would still exist without us. God exists for Himself and man exists for His glory.

The Eternity of God – ***He is endless and everlasting***. Time marks the beginning of created existence, and because God was not created and never began to exist, time has no application to Him. He exists above and outside of time. Because God lives in an everlasting now, He has no past or future. When time-words occur in Scripture they refer to our time, not to His. God dwells in eternity, but time dwells in God. Time began in God and it will end in Him.

God's Infinitude – ***God has no limits in any thing or in any way***. Infinitude means limitless. Unfortunately, it is impossible for a limited mind to understand the unlimited. God is greater than mind itself. His greatness cannot be conceived. He knows no bounds. He is without limit. He cannot be measured. He is above, outside and beyond measurement. Because God's nature is infinite, everything that flows out of it is infinite also – for example, His love, grace, mercy and justice.

Those who are in Christ share with Him all the riches of limitless time and endless years. God never hurries.

The Immutability of God – ***God does not change.*** God never differs from Himself. He cannot change for the better. For example, since He is perfectly holy, he has never been less holy than He is now and can never be holier than He is and has always been. Similarly, neither can God change for the worse. Any deterioration within the holy nature of God is impossible. Nothing that God has ever said about Himself will ever be modified or rescinded. In all our efforts to find God, commune with Him and to please Him, we must remember that we must be the ones who change. God won't.

The Divine Omniscience – ***God knows all things perfectly and equally well.*** God possesses perfect knowledge and therefore has no need to learn. In fact, God has never learned and cannot learn. Since God is the source of all things, He knows all that can be known, instantly and effortlessly. He knows all things equally well. He never discovers any other thing. He is never surprised, never amazed and never wonders. God knows us completely. He knew us before we knew Him and He called us to Himself in the full knowledge of everything that was against us. No weakness in our character can ever come to light to turn God away from us. Whatever happens to us, God knows and cares as no one else can.

The Wisdom of God – ***His wisdom is perfect and infinitely pure, loving and good.*** His understanding is infinite. The idea of God as infinitely wise is at the root of all truth. Wisdom sees everything clearly, in proper relation to everything else. All God's acts are done in perfect wisdom, first for his own glory, and then for the highest good of the greatest number of people for the longest time. No matter how things may look, all God's acts are done in His perfect wisdom. We can count on God to know and do what's best.

The Omnipotence of God - ***God has all power - limitless and absolute.*** Omnipotent means having all power. The Bible often uses the more familiar word Almighty, but it is used only of God. He alone is almighty. God is infinite, without limit. Therefore God has limitless power. Nothing is too hard or difficult for God because He possesses absolute power, having command of all power in the universe.

The Divine Transcendence - ***His Being is exalted infinitely above all other being.*** This means that God is exalted far above the created universe, so far above that human thought cannot imagine it. "Far above" does not refer to physical distance but to quality of being. God is Spirit, and to Him magnitude and distance have no meaning. Forever God stands apart. It is God Himself who puts it into our hearts to seek Him and makes it possible in some measure to know Him, and He is pleased with even our feeblest efforts to make Him known to others.

God's Omnipresence - ***God is everywhere here, close to everything, next to everyone.*** In His presence is fullness of joy! God pervades His creation. There is no place in heaven or earth where men may hide from His presence. The Scriptures teach that God is at the same time far off and near, and that in Him men move and live and have their very being. Since He is infinite, there is no limit to His presence; He is omnipresent. God surrounds His finite creation and contains it. There is no place beyond Him for anything to be. God is near us, next to us, and He sees us through and through. Through Jesus Christ He is immediately accessible at all times to every loving and believing heart. The knowledge that we are never alone calms the troubled sea of our lives and speaks peace to our souls.

The Faithfulness of God – ***God is true to His Word. His promises are always honored.*** All of God's acts are always consistent with every one of His attributes. No attribute contradicts any other, but all harmonize and blend with each other. All that God does agrees with all that God is, He cannot act out of character with Himself. He is at once faithful and immutable, so all His words and acts must be and must remain faithful. There is no conflict among the divine attributes. God's being is unitary. He cannot divide Himself and act at any given time from one of His attributes while the rest remain inactive. All that God is must be in accord with all that God does. Justice must be present in mercy, and love in judgment. This is true with all His attributes. Because He is faithful, we are able to live in peace and look forward with assurance to all He has promised us here on earth, and later in eternity with Him.

The Goodness of God – ***He is infinitely kind and eternally blessing without partiality.*** The goodness of God is what disposes Him to be kind, cordial, benevolent and full of good will toward men. He is tenderhearted and quick in sympathy. He is always open, frank and friendly. By His very nature He is inclined to bestow blessings and He takes pleasure in the happiness of His people. God created us because He felt good in His heart and He redeemed us through Jesus for the same reason. The unmerited, spontaneous goodness of God is behind His every act of grace. His Divine goodness is self-caused, infinite, perfect, and eternal. Since God is immutable He has never been kinder than He is now, nor will He ever be less kind.

The Justice of God – ***God's judgment is His application of equity to moral situations, and may be favorable or unfavorable.*** The words for justice and righteousness as applied to God are used interchangeably in Scripture. They are forever intertwined. Justice embodies the idea of moral equity (or "rightness"), and iniquity is exactly the opposite; it is in-equity, the absence of equality from human thoughts and acts. Justice, when used of God, is a name we give to the way God is, nothing more; and when God acts justly He is simply acting like Himself in a given situation. Everything in the universe is good to the degree it conforms to the nature of God, and evil as it fails to do so. God is able to supply us mercy and compassion as sinners **only** because His justice was fully and forever satisfied when Jesus took all our sins away on the cross. In God's eyes, Jesus took our sins and gave us His righteousness. This is known as "the great exchange". However, God's justice stands forever against the unrepentant sinner. It can never be any other way.

The Mercy of God – ***This is God's pity and compassion for human suffering and guilt.*** We really have no right to ever enter Heaven. Yet, it is by God's mercy that we who have earned banishment shall instead enjoy communion with God in His presence; we who deserve the pains of hell shall know the bliss of Heaven. His mercy is His infinite and inexhaustible energy within His divine nature that causes Him to be actively compassionate. But we must realize He is just (full of justice) as well as merciful. He has always dealt in mercy with mankind, and will always deal in justice when His mercy is rejected and despised.

The Grace of God – ***Grace is His infinite goodness and unmerited favor directed towards human debt and demerit, given to us along with the power to do His will.*** It is the good pleasure of God to bestow benefits on the undeserving. It comes from the very heart of God, but the channel through which it flows out to us is Jesus Christ, crucified and risen! We who feel ourselves alienated from the fellowship of God can now raise our discouraged heads and look up. Through Christ's atoning death the cause of our banishment has forever been removed.

The Love of God – ***God's love is His eternal uncaused and undeserved good will to all.*** The words the Apostle John wrote, "God is love", mean that love is an essential attribute of God. Love is something true of God but it is not God. It expresses the way God is in His unitary being, as do the words holiness, justice, faithfulness and truth, but it is not all He is. His love always operates in harmony with all of His other attributes. He does not suspend one to exercise another. We may never know entirely what love is, but we can know it in the way it manifests itself. God shows us His love in His good will. Love wills the good of all and never wills harm or evil to any. Because of His holiness and righteousness, God hates sin and can never look with pleasure on iniquity, but where men in Christ seek to do God's will He responds in genuine affection.

The Holiness of God – ***His holiness is His infinite purity, moral excellence and absolute righteousness.*** No human can ever be qualified to fully appreciate or understand the holiness of God. We know nothing like it and have nothing to acceptably compare it with. It stands apart, unique, unapproachable, incomprehensible and unattainable. We may fear His power and admire His wisdom, but His holiness we cannot even imagine. Only His Spirit can impart to us the knowledge of the holy. Holy is the way God is. To be holy He does not conform to an objective standard. He is that standard. He is absolutely holy with an infinite, incomprehensible fullness of purity that is incapable of being other than it is. We must hide our un-holiness in the wounds of Christ. We must take refuge from God in God. We must believe that God sees us perfect in His Son and thereby allows us to be partakers of His holiness.

The Sovereignty of God – ***Sovereignty refers to God's absolute authority everywhere, forever.*** God's sovereignty is the attribute by which He rules His entire creation, and to be sovereign God must be all-knowing, all-powerful, and absolutely free. No one and no thing can hinder Him or compel Him or stop Him. He is able to do as He pleases always. In the moral conflict that rages constantly around us, whoever is on God's side is on the winning side and cannot lose; whoever is on the other side is on the losing side and cannot win. There is freedom to choose which side we shall be on but no freedom to negotiate the results of the choice once it is made. By the mercy of God we can repent a wrong choice and alter the consequences by making a new and right choice. We must all choose whether we will obey the gospel or turn away in unbelief and reject its authority. Our choice is our own, but the consequences of the choice have already been determined by the sovereign will of God, and from that there is no appeal.

THE KNOWLEDGE OF THE HOLY

The best counsel one can receive and implement is to "acquaint thyself with God". Our prayer life and relationship with God will be enriched as we meditate on His attributes. As we more fully understand His true nature and greatness we will naturally and enthusiastically worship, praise and adore Him in our daily quiet times with Him. Our faith will grow. Our witness will be more effective. We will remain humbly grateful.

As the knowledge of God becomes more real and wonderful to us we will feel a need for greater service to our fellow man. This blessed knowledge comes through the Holy Spirit pouring truth into our hearts, and such knowledge is not given to be enjoyed selfishly. The God who gave all ***to*** us will continue to give all ***through*** us as we come to know Him better. We must seek purposefully to share our increasing light with the fellow members of the household of God, and live in such a way that others may be brought out of darkness.

Remember: Stand in awe of God. Meditate on His beauty, wisdom, and love. Then praise Him!

Join me in praying: *Oh Lord, I choose to trust in who You are rather than who I am. In Jesus' Name. Amen.*

SOME RELEVANT SCRIPTURE PASSAGES

Proverbs 9:10-11 "The fear of the LORD is the beginning of wisdom, and knowledge of the Holy One is understanding. For through wisdom your days will be many, and years will be added to your life."

John 4:23-24 "Yet a time is coming and has now come when the true worshipers will worship the Father in the Spirit and in truth, for they are the kind of worshipers the Father seeks. God is spirit, and his worshipers must worship in the Spirit and in truth."

1 Corinthians 13:11-13 "When I was a child, I talked like a child, I thought like a child, I reasoned like a child. When I became a man, I put the ways of childhood behind me. For now we see only a reflection as in a mirror; then we shall see face to face. Now I know in part; then I shall know fully, even as I am fully known. And now these three remain: faith, hope and love. But the greatest of these is love."

Psalm 93:1-2 "The LORD reigns, he is robed in majesty; the LORD is robed in majesty and armed with strength; indeed, the world is established, firm and secure. Your throne was established long ago; you are from all eternity."

1 Chronicles 16:27 "Splendor and majesty are before him; strength and joy are in his dwelling place."

1 Chronicles 29:11 "Yours, LORD, is the greatness and the power and the glory and the majesty and the splendor, for everything in heaven and earth is yours. Yours, LORD, is the kingdom; you are exalted as head over all."

TAKEAWAY HIGHLIGHT

To truly worship Him in spirit and truth we must gain knowledge and understanding of Him. God has revealed certain truths about Himself to us which we can begin to understand by reading His Word. In addition, we know Jesus is the Living Word, and we see His example for us. We also learn about God through His Holy Spirit who resides in us teaching us about His qualities and attributes.

God knows we cannot truly understand the Infinite with our comparatively feeble, finite brains. We can only begin to fathom some of His qualities and attributes through Spirit-inspired Word into our hearts. In this body on earth, we will never know or fully understand everything about Him. But as we seek Him diligently daily, He gradually reveals Himself to us. It is out of a deep knowing in our hearts, not the thoughts of our mind, that we are able to begin to truly worship Him in spirit and in truth.

PRACTICAL APPLICATION

Choose one or two of God's attributes as summarized above to meditate upon each day. Include it as a matter of prayer and worship in your quiet time with God. Be intentional about getting to know Him better.

WANT TO KNOW MORE?

Write to us to request the discipleship teaching on "Knowledge of the Holy". Mail it to: Freedom in Jesus Prison Ministries, Attn: Teachings, P.O. Box 939, Levelland, TX 79336.

Our relationship with God becomes ever more important as we see the day approaching for the return of King Jesus! We are His ambassadors. Are we at the end of days? Read on...

TIME IS SHORT

The Last Days

Our relationship with God enables us as true believers to face a very uncertain future with hope, positive expectations, and faith. As we see end-times prophecies unfolding before our very eyes, I ask you to study the scriptures and examine the signs with an open spiritual mind and heart. This is necessary so that you may receive what the Holy Spirit wants you to know and understand, as He guides you through these perilous times in which we are now living.

The "end of the age" is drawing ever closer rapidly. Jesus speaks of it in Matthew 24, Mark 13 and Luke 21. Speculation, rumors, and theories abound as people everywhere become more anxious over what they are seeing, reading and hearing on the network news; and, as they "surf" YouTube and the rest of the internet. Many believe something is about to change drastically in our world. They are concerned about many things like:

> *Hamas; ISIS; Hezbollah; Iran's and North Korea's threats and nuclear capabilities; potential worldwide recession or depression; ongoing widespread murder of millions of children through abortions; the possible near passing of planet X (or Niburu), its moons*

and our sun's partner in a binary star system – a brown dwarf; the U.S. dollar's collapse and replacement as the World's trade currency; dramatic recent increases in the frequency of earthquakes and volcanic eruptions; rising intensity and frequency of unusual storms, floods, wildfires, tornadoes, hurricanes, typhoons, and tsunamis; severe droughts and famines in unexpected places; alarming increases in wars and other armed conflicts worldwide; outbreaks of Ebola, black plague, and other plagues; forced vaccinations with experimental, gene-altering drugs; calls for a New World Order and global governance; the establishment of a One-World Religion under the False Prophet; fear of unintended consequences of CERN's opening of portals to other dimensions from their renewed experiments at the Large Hadron Collider; concern about the possible return of the Nephilim; increased reports of alien influence in world affairs; concern about catastrophic asteroid collisions with Earth; resurgence of a boisterous Russia and China who are expanding their territories by force; legalization of same-sex "marriage"; transgender issues; scientists combining DNA of animals and humans; worldwide persecution and murder of Christians, etc.

People of the secular world are becoming anxious, fearful, hopeless and distraught. But how are we, as the Body of Christ, supposed to view these events? We submit to you that true believers face these uncertain times with eager anticipation, excitement, faith, peace, hope and confidence. How is this possible?

Messianic Rabbi Kirk Schneider shared a message on his "Seeds of Revelation" video encouragement August 14, 2020, entitled "God's Light will Shine Upon You", that I believe is particularly relevant. Here is the transcript:

"Arise, shine, for your light has come, and the glory of the Lord rises upon you. *See, darkness covers the earth and thick darkness is over the peoples, but the Lord* rises upon you *and his glory appears over you."* Isaiah 60:1-2

"Now I don't know about you, but that really encourages me because the older I get, the darkness is getting thicker and thicker on the Earth. In fact, I would have never believed that in such a short period, the darkness that is encircling the Earth right now would have gotten so severe and so thick. The rate at which darkness is over-taking the world is so powerful and is happening so quickly, that if we realized what is happening, it would literally take our breath away.

"Satan is gaining dominion on the Earth. The Bible tell us that in the last days, He that restrains (speaking of the Holy Spirit) will no longer restrain. In other words, the Holy Spirit, in these last days, is beginning to withdraw exercising His Dominion on the Earth. While the Holy Spirit is beginning to withdraw exercising His Dominion, what is happening in that vacuum is that evil is rising and becoming predominant. So, the Scripture says that darkness will cover the surface of the Earth, even deep, thick darkness. That is what is going on.

"It is going to get worse. It is going to get more intense than you can even realize right now, and it is going to happen quicker than you are expecting. But hear this, the Lord said His Light will shine upon you. So do not be afraid with what you see happening around you. The Bible says do not call a conspiracy what the world is calling a conspiracy. But you and I are to fear the Lord alone, and when we do, He will become our sanctuary.

"I want to encourage you today, as the world continues to spin out of control, as chaos increases, as corruption becomes more and more severe, as all the things spoken of in Scripture concerning the end times are now upon us, DO NOT BE AFRAID. Even though outside the darkness is getting deep and thick and quick, you have another destiny–His Glory will continue to be your portion and will shine upon you even in the midst of this darkened generation.

"I love you, beloved. We are more than conquerors in Messiah Jesus. In all these things we overwhelmingly conquer, so be of good cheer and do not be afraid."

Pastor Gary Delay, in his article, "God the Holy Spirit – Our Peace", writes to let us know how we can have peace in chaotic times:

"Jesus left us with HIS Peace – the Holy Spirit (see John 14:26-27). The same Peace Jesus had as He slept in the boat in the middle of a terrible storm, is the very Peace He says He left us. Paul described it as the 'peace that transcends all understanding', and the peace 'that will guard our hearts and minds in Christ Jesus' (Philippians 4:7). If we as believers abide and remain 'in Christ' we possess the same Peace Jesus had – the Holy Spirit.

"The Holy Spirit is given to us to be our Helper. He will teach us all things and tell us of things to come. Whatever true believers need to know about how to navigate through turbulent waters will assuredly be given to us by the instruction of the Holy Spirit.

"We must be careful to be led by the Spirit and maintain His peace within us; rather than being led by the flesh, and being overcome by the fear from the enemy that is prevalent in the world.

"As wars and rumors of wars abound, we need the Holy Spirit more than ever before. We need to rely on Him to lead, guide and teach us of things to come. This is our blessed assurance, that the Holy Spirit will be our peace in the days to come. He will do the job that the Father and Son sent Him to do. We can trust in Him."

Freedom in Jesus Ministries Founder, Rev. Don Castleberry, wrote an article entitled "The Latter Times" in which he encourages us to take a stand, and then stand strong:

"Demonic forces are loose on the earth and these forces want to deceive you!

'For the time will come when they (people) will not endure sound doctrine but according to their own desires, because they have itching ears (wanting to hear only good things) they will heap up for themselves teachers and they will turn their ears away from the truth, and be turned aside to (they will believe) fables, lies, and untruths (not from Holy Spirit).' 2 Timothy 4:3-4

"Now is the time for all of us to stabilize ourselves in the Word of God so diligently, so forcefully, being so persevering in the things of God, so that we will not be deceived and led astray by the 'demonic principalities, powers, rulers of the darkness of this age, and spiritual hosts of wickedness in the heavenly places.' (Ephesians 6:12)

"Ephesians 6:13 instructs us to 'take up the whole armor of God, that you (we) may be able to withstand in the evil day, and having done all, to stand.'

"This is not a day that we can put off for another day. The time to stand is now! Stand strong, saints of God!"

Pastor Johnny Davis, in his article, "Final Touches", spoke about making ourselves ready like a bride on the day of her wedding making some "final touches" to her make-up, hair and clothing before she walks down the aisle. In reference to the days we are facing, he asks:

"As a true believer and follower of Jesus Christ, what are some of 'the final touches' you might need to make? Is there an area of your life that you still need to surrender? Is there sin you have not confessed and of which you have not turned from (repented)? Are you holding un-forgiveness towards anyone for anything? Is there someone you offended or hurt from whom you need to ask forgiveness? Have you sincerely told your family recently how much they mean to you, and how much you love them?

"If there are any 'final touches' you need to make, do not delay. HE is coming soon!!! Today is YOUR DAY!!!"

Brothers and Sisters, I feel there is a sense of urgency for us to: make certain we came to salvation in Jesus Christ through true repentance; pray for our loved ones; pursue holiness; share the Good News of Jesus Christ with the lost and/or backslidden; be led by the Spirit instead of our flesh; and, be quick to confess sin daily. All of this we can do right where we are with the help of the Holy Spirit.

Stay calm. Stay focused. Stay close to Him.

SOME RELEVANT SCRIPTURE PASSAGES

Joel 2:28-32 "And afterward, I will pour out my Spirit on all people. Your sons and daughters will prophesy, your old men will dream dreams, your young men will see visions. Even on my servants, both men and women, I will pour out my Spirit in those days. I will show wonders in the heavens and on the earth, blood and fire and billows of smoke. The sun will be turned to darkness and the moon to blood before the coming of the great and dreadful day of the LORD. And everyone who calls on the name of the LORD will be saved..."

Isaiah 60:1-2 "Arise, shine, for your light has come, and the glory of the Lord rises upon you. See, darkness covers the earth and thick darkness is over the peoples, but the Lord rises upon you and his glory appears over you."

John 14:26-27 "But the Advocate, the Holy Spirit, whom the Father will send in my name, will teach you all things and will remind you of everything I have said to you. Peace I leave with you; my peace I give you. I do not give to you as the world gives. Do not let your hearts be troubled and do not be afraid."

Philippians 4:6-7 "Do not be anxious about anything, but in every situation, by prayer and petition, with thanksgiving, present your requests to God. And the peace of God, which transcends all understanding, will guard your hearts and your minds in Christ Jesus."

2 Timothy 4:3-4 "For the time will come when people will not put up with sound doctrine. Instead, to suit their own desires, they will gather around them a great number of teachers to say what their itching ears want to hear. They will turn their ears away from the truth and turn aside to myths."

2 Timothy 3:1-5 "But mark this: There will be terrible times in the last days. People will be lovers of themselves, lovers of money, boastful, proud, abusive, disobedient to their parents, ungrateful, unholy, without love, unforgiving, slanderous, without self-control, brutal, not lovers of the good, treacherous, rash, conceited, lovers of pleasure rather than lovers of God— having a form of godliness but denying its power. Have nothing to do with such people."

Ephesians 6:12-13 "For our struggle is not against flesh and blood, but against the rulers, against the authorities, against the powers of this dark world and against the spiritual forces of evil in the heavenly realms. Therefore put on the full armor of God, so that when the day of evil comes, you may be able to stand your ground, and after you have done everything, to stand."

Matthew 24:4-14 Jesus answered: "Watch out that no one deceives you. For many will come in my name, claiming, 'I am the Messiah,' and will deceive many. You will hear of wars and rumors of wars, but see to it that you are not alarmed. Such things must happen, but the end is still to come. Nation will rise against nation, and kingdom against kingdom. There will be famines and earthquakes in various places. All these are the beginning of birth pains.

"Then you will be handed over to be persecuted and put to death, and you will be hated by all nations because of me. At that time many will turn away from the faith and will betray and hate each other, and many false prophets will appear and deceive many people. Because of the increase of wickedness, the love of most will grow cold, but the one who stands firm to the end will be saved. And this gospel of the kingdom will be preached in the whole world as a testimony to all nations, and then the end will come."

TAKEAWAY HIGHLIGHT

Our relationship with God enables us as true believers to face a very uncertain future with hope, positive expectations, and faith. As we see end-times prophecies unfolding before our very eyes, we ask you to study the scriptures and examine the signs with an open spiritual mind and heart. This is necessary so that you may receive what the Holy Spirit wants you to know and understand, as He guides you through these perilous times in which we are now living.

PRACTICAL APPLICATION

Think about how you are feeling about things going on in the world in general, in your family, and in your immediate daily space wherever you happen to be. Are you feeling fear, anxiety, uncertainty or dread? Stop. Trust God. Review this chapter's encouragement and the scriptures immediately above. God is with you, and He will never leave or forsake you. Be the Light.

WANT TO KNOW MORE?

Write to us to request the discipleship teaching on "The Last Days". Mail it to: Freedom in Jesus Prison Ministries, Attn: Teachings, P.O. Box 939, Levelland, TX 79336.

If you have an intimate, personal relationship with Jesus you will always be looking forward expectantly and joyfully to His return. Are you ready? Be encouraged...

Jesus is Coming Again

Biblical prophecies concerning "The Day of the Lord" are being fulfilled quickly. Jesus will return for His Bride, the True Church, any moment. It could be today. Are you sure you're ready???

This subject is of utmost importance, and I ask you to study it with an open spiritual mind and heart so that you may receive what the Holy Spirit wants you to know and understand, as He guides you through these perilous times in which we are now living. Today, I beg you to examine yourself to see whether you are truly ready for the Second Coming of Christ Jesus!

Biblical scholars disagree about the timing of the "Rapture" when the Bible indicates Jesus is coming in the clouds and true believers will rise to meet Him in the air. This is discussed in its own chapter. But the Bible leaves little room for disagreement that He will come again to judge the nations and rule on Earth. At that time, the Bible indicates that Jesus descends to Earth in Jerusalem on the Mount of Olives. See Acts 1:11; Zechariah 14:4; Matthew 25:31-46.

No one knows the exact day and hour for the Return of Jesus; however, He told His disciples there would be certain things happening just before His return. We should be alert to the signs and season. Are you looking forward to His return? In 2 Timothy 4:8, we learn there is a crown for those who long for His appearing!

Jesus promised us He would come back to get us because He wants us to be with Him where He is. See John 14:1-3; 1 Thessalonians 4:15-18; Revelation 22:12-13. He first came as an innocent baby, a sacrificial lamb, and a suffering servant. This time, however, He will come as a conquering King, the Lion of the tribe of Judah, and the LORD of lords. Be certain of this–**Jesus is coming back for His People.**

When Jesus comes, it will be quickly, as in the blink of an eye, or as fast as lightning flashes from the east to the west. It will be a surprise, like a thief in the night comes without warning. See Matthew 24:27; Luke 21:34; Mark 13:32-37; 2 Peter 3:10. **Jesus is coming quickly, in an instant of time.**

The Disciples closest to Jesus went to Him privately to ask about the end of this age, and the "signs" that would point to His return. Please read carefully Matthew 24, Mark 13, and Luke 21 for His response. All of these signs are *now* happening. **Jesus is coming soon. It could be any day now.**

When He comes, will He know you? Study Matthew 7:21-23. You say you know Him...does Jesus KNOW you?

Jesus told us in Matthew 7:14 that the way is narrow that leads to life, and **few** find it. The Bible speaks of "the remnant" that remains. A remnant is a small piece that remains from a larger piece, for example a remnant of carpet. Please carefully study John 1:12; Romans 9:27, 29; Matthew 24:13-30; Deut. 4:27; Ezra 9:8,13; Zech. 8:6-12; Hag. 1:12-14; Amos 5:3; Isaiah 10:20-22; Isaiah 11:11; Isaiah 35:8-10; Isaiah 37:31-32; Isaiah 46:3-4. Will you be part of "the remnant"?

Every prophecy concerning His first coming was fulfilled exactly as Scripture predicted. We can be absolutely certain that the second coming of Jesus will fulfill every remaining prophecy just as precisely and completely.

Dr. David Jeremiah, in *The Jeremiah Study Bible* article "Prophecies Yet to be Fulfilled" states that, "Prophecy is never given to simply satisfy our curiosity about what the future holds. It is meant to motivate us to holy living in the present by edifying God's people, by exhorting them to stay committed to Christ and the truth, and by comforting those who are suffering trials... They are a powerful source of encouragement designed by God to motivate us to live holy lives in an unholy world."

Examine the scriptures for yourself. Stay ready. Pray for the lost. Jesus is coming again!

SOME RELEVANT SCRIPTURE PASSAGES

2 Peter 3:14 "So then, dear friends, since you are looking forward to this, make every effort to be found spotless, blameless and at peace with him."

2 Timothy 4:8 "Now there is in store for me the crown of righteousness, which the Lord, the righteous Judge, will award to me on that day—and not only to me, but also to all who have longed for his appearing."

Acts 1:11 "Men of Galilee, they said, why do you stand here looking into the sky? This same Jesus, who has been taken from you into heaven, will come back in the same way you have seen him go into heaven."

Zechariah 14:4 "On that day his feet will stand on the Mount of Olives, east of Jerusalem, and the Mount of Olives will be split in two from east to west, forming a great valley, with half of the mountain moving north and half moving south."

John 14:1-3 "Do not let your hearts be troubled. You believe in God; believe also in me. My Father's house has many rooms; if that were not so, would I have told you that I am going there to prepare a place for you? And if I go and prepare a place for you, I will come back and take you to be with me that you also may be where I am."

Revelation 22:12-13 "Look, I am coming soon! My reward is with me, and I will give to each person according to what they have done. I am the Alpha and the Omega, the First and the Last, the Beginning and the End."

Matthew 24:27 "For as lightning that comes from the east is visible even in the west, so will be the coming of the Son of Man."

Luke 21:34 "Be careful, or your hearts will be weighed down with carousing, drunkenness and the anxieties of life, and that day will close on you suddenly like a trap."

2 Peter 3:10 "But the day of the Lord will come like a thief. The heavens will disappear with a roar; the elements will be destroyed by fire, and the earth and everything done in it will be laid bare."

John 1:12 "Yet to all who did receive him, to those who believed in his name, he gave the right to become children of God..."

Romans 9:27-28 "Isaiah cries out concerning Israel: 'Though the number of the Israelites be like the sand by the sea, only the remnant will be saved. For the Lord will carry out his sentence on earth with speed and finality.'"

Ezra 9:8 "But now, for a brief moment, the Lord our God has been gracious in leaving us a remnant and giving us a firm place in his sanctuary, and so our God gives light to our eyes and a little relief in our bondage."

Isaiah 10:21-22 “A remnant will return, a remnant of Jacob will return to the Mighty God. Though your people be like the sand by the sea, Israel, only a remnant will return. Destruction has been decreed, overwhelming and righteous.”

Isaiah 11:1 “In that day the Lord will reach out his hand a second time to reclaim the surviving remnant of his people...”

TAKEAWAY HIGHLIGHT

Every prophecy concerning His first coming was fulfilled exactly as Scripture predicted. We can be absolutely certain that the second coming of Jesus will fulfill every remaining prophecy just as precisely and completely.

PRACTICAL APPLICATION

Meditate on the scriptures and concepts above. In light of the certainty of His coming, are you doing your best to live for Jesus every day? Do you look forward to His coming? Are you witnessing to the lost and praying for their souls?

WANT TO KNOW MORE?

Write to us to request the discipleship teaching on “Jesus is Coming Again”. Mail it to: Freedom in Jesus Prison Ministries, Attn: Teachings, P.O. Box 939, Levelland, TX 79336.

True intimacy of relationship with Jesus allows us to look forward to meeting Him in the clouds. Are you familiar with the concept of the Rapture? Read on...

The Rapture

The "end of the age" is drawing ever closer rapidly. Jesus speaks of it in Matthew 24, Mark 13 and Luke 21. The Bible says there is coming a day when Jesus returns in the sky and believers rise to meet Him in the air. Many scholars refer to this event as "The Rapture" of the Church.

Jesus assured us He would return for His Bride, the true body of believers, before the Father pours out His wrath on the unbelieving world. Biblical scholars disagree as to the timing but there is a little doubt among them that it will happen just as the Bible proclaims. Take a few minutes to read 1 Corinthians 15:50-58, 1 Thessalonians 4:13–5:11, 2 Thessalonians 2:1-4, and 1 Thessalonians 1:10, 5:9. We are not appointed to suffer the Father's wrath. At the Cross, Jesus took upon Himself the wrath we ourselves deserved.

In *The Life in the Spirit Study Bible* article entitled "The Rapture" the topic is introduced with this paragraph:

"The word 'rapture' is derived from the Latin word *raptu* which means 'caught away' or 'caught up'. This Latin word is equivalent to the Greek *harpazo* translated as 'caught up' in 1 Thessalonians 4:17. This event described here and in 1 Corinthians 15 refers to the catching up of the Church from the Earth to meet the Lord in the air. It involves only the faithful of Christ's churches."

The article continues, "Just prior to the rapture, as Christ is descending from Heaven for his church, the resurrection of the 'dead in Christ' will occur (1 Thessalonians 4:16)... At the same time as the dead in Christ rise, living believers will be 'transfigured'; their bodies will be clothed with immortality (1 Corinthians 15:51,53). This will happen in a very short time, 'in the twinkling of an eye' (1 Corinthians 15:52). Both the resurrected believers and the transfigured believers will be caught up together to meet Christ in the air, i.e. in the atmosphere between earth and heaven.

They will be visibly united with Christ (1 Thessalonians 4:16-17), taken to His Father's house in Heaven and united with loved ones who have died (1 Thessalonians 4:13-18)... The hope that our Savior will soon return to take us out of the world to 'be with the Lord forever' (1 Thessalonians 4:17) is the blessed hope of the redeemed (Titus 2:13) and a major source of comfort for suffering believers (1 Thessalonians 4:17-18, 5:10)."

Dr. David Jeremiah, in a devotional article entitled, "Ready to Go?" wrote:

"In biblical days, the bridegroom would travel in a procession to the home of his bride-to-be. The bride's family and friends would maintain a vigil, watching for the groom's arrival, so as to meet him with appropriate fanfare and welcome. Jesus used this very custom as the basis for a parable that carries a sober warning to all.

"In the parable (Matthew 25:1-13), ten virgins (think bridesmaids) were waiting with the family for the groom. When the groom was seen coming from afar at night, only five of the virgins had lamps with sufficient oil to go out and light the way for his arrival. The other five virgins had to go to buy oil, and when they returned, the door to the celebration was closed and they were shut out. Jesus' point was, 'Watch therefore, for you know neither the day nor the hour in which the Son of Man is coming' (Matthew 25:13). The Son of Man is coming for His Church at the Rapture — those not prepared will be left out of the celebration.

"Preparation means two things: Placing one's faith in Christ, and then living faithfully each day in anticipation of His return — which could be today! Amen. Even so, come, Lord Jesus! (Revelation 22:20)"

Jesus said only the Father knows when He will return. It seems the Bible differentiates two returns - one in the air, and His Second Coming where He sets His foot on the Mount of Olives to begin His 1,000 year reign on Earth. For His Second Coming at the end of the Great Tribulation, those previously caught away in the Rapture would be returning to rule with Him (see Revelation 19:11-14).

In the Rapture, Believers rise to meet Him in the air and many believe Jesus takes them to celebrate the Marriage Supper of the Lamb in Heaven while the Tribulation is completed on Earth. Most believe the timing of the Rapture will be either before the Great Tribulation of seven years, or half way through the Tribulation.

As Believers, we can look forward to His Return with an attitude of expectant hope! In the meantime, life on Earth may grow considerably worse. Do not fear. Be strong and courageous (see Joshua 1:7-9)! God is in control and His timing is perfect.

SOME RELEVANT SCRIPTURE PASSAGES

1 Corinthians 15:50-54, 58 "I declare to you, brothers and sisters, that

flesh and blood cannot inherit the kingdom of God, nor does the perishable inherit the imperishable. Listen, I tell you a mystery: We will not all sleep, but we will all be changed— in a flash, in the twinkling of an eye, at the last trumpet. For the trumpet will sound, the dead will be raised imperishable, and we will be changed. For the perishable must clothe itself with the imperishable, and the mortal with immortality. When the perishable has been clothed with the imperishable, and the mortal with immortality, then the saying that is written will come true: 'Death has been swallowed up in victory.' ... 58 Therefore, my dear brothers and sisters, stand firm. Let nothing move you. Always give yourselves fully to the work of the Lord, because you know that your labor in the Lord is not in vain."

1 Thessalonians 4:13-18 "Brothers and sisters, we do not want you to be uninformed about those who sleep in death, so that you do not grieve like the rest of mankind, who have no hope. For we believe that Jesus died and rose again, and so we believe that God will bring with Jesus those who have fallen asleep in him. According to the Lord's word, we tell you that we who are still alive, who are left until the coming of the Lord, will certainly not precede those who have fallen asleep. For the Lord himself will come down from heaven, with a loud command, with the voice of the archangel and with the trumpet call of God, and the dead in Christ will rise first. After that, we who are still alive and are left will be caught up together with them in the clouds to meet the Lord in the air. And so we will be with the Lord forever. Therefore encourage one another with these words."

1 Thessalonians 5:1-11 "Now, brothers and sisters, about times and dates we do not need to write to you, for you know very well that the day of the Lord will come like a thief in the night. While people are saying,

'Peace and safety,' destruction will come on them suddenly, as labor pains on a pregnant woman, and they will not escape.

"But you, brothers and sisters, are not in darkness so that this day should surprise you like a thief. You are all children of the light and children of the day. We do not belong to the night or to the darkness. So then, let us not be like others, who are asleep, but let us be awake and sober. For those who sleep, sleep at night, and those who get drunk, get drunk at night. But since we belong to the day, let us be sober, putting on faith and love as a breastplate, and the hope of salvation as a helmet. For God did not appoint us to suffer wrath but to receive salvation through our Lord Jesus Christ. He died for us so that, whether we are awake or asleep, we may live together with him. Therefore encourage one another and build each other up, just as in fact you are doing."

2 Thessalonians 2:1-4 "Concerning the coming of our Lord Jesus Christ and our being gathered to him, we ask you, brothers and sisters, not to become easily unsettled or alarmed by the teaching allegedly from us—whether by a prophecy or by word of mouth or by letter—asserting that the day of the Lord has already come. Don't let anyone deceive you in any way, for that day will not come until the rebellion occurs and the man of lawlessness is revealed, the man doomed to destruction. He will oppose and will exalt himself over everything that is called God or is worshiped, so that he sets himself up in God's temple, proclaiming himself to be God."

1 Thessalonians 1:10 "...and to wait for his Son from heaven, whom he raised from the dead—Jesus, who rescues us from the coming wrath."

1 Thessalonians 5:9 "For God did not appoint us to suffer wrath but to receive salvation through our Lord Jesus Christ."

Titus 2:13 "...while we wait for the blessed hope—the appearing of the glory of our great God and Savior, Jesus Christ..."

Revelation 22:20 "He who testifies to these things says, 'Yes, I am coming soon.' Amen. Come, Lord Jesus."

Joshua 1:5, 7-9 "No one will be able to stand against you all the days of your life. As I was with Moses, so I will be with you; I will never leave you nor forsake you... Be strong and very courageous. Be careful to obey all the law my servant Moses gave you; do not turn from it to the right or to the left, that you may be successful wherever you go. Keep this Book of the Law always on your lips; meditate on it day and night, so that you may be careful to do everything written in it. Then you will be prosperous and successful. Have I not commanded you? Be strong and courageous. Do not be afraid; do not be discouraged, for the Lord your God will be with you wherever you go."

TAKEAWAY HIGHLIGHT

"The Son of Man is coming for His Church at the Rapture — those not prepared will be left out of the celebration. Preparation means two things: Placing one's faith in Christ, and then living faithfully each day in anticipation of His return — which could be today!" David Jeremiah

PRACTICAL APPLICATION

Ask the Holy Spirit to illuminate the scriptures above. Are you living each day with eternity in mind? In your immediate circumstances and location daily are you allowing God to work in and through you to teach, help and encourage others who may not have an intimate, personal relationship with Jesus? Are you ready?

WANT TO KNOW MORE?

Write to us to request the discipleship teaching on "The Rapture". Mail it to: Freedom in Jesus Prison Ministries, Attn: Teachings, P.O. Box 939, Levelland, TX 79336.

Anyone who has an intimate, personal relationship with Jesus does not need to be concerned with the wrath of God soon to be poured out on this Earth. Judgment is coming...

Judgment is Coming

Wake up! It's one minute to midnight. We must repent. Judgment is coming. Soon. In this chapter I want to share with you exactly what God has put on my heart.

Ezekiel 33:1-11, 17-20, compel me to be direct and absolutely truthful. See also Ezekiel 3:10-11, and 27. For these purposes, God has appointed me a "watchman". Whether or not you listen and take action is up to you. *I believe we will be accountable to God for what we do with this information.* I cannot stand the thought of someone not knowing the imminent danger of judgment; and, I do not want their blood on my hands because I gave no warning.

After reading what God has to say about false, un-caring shepherds in Ezekiel 34, I know I want to be a caring under-shepherd to the Great Shepherd, Jesus. Frankly, I believe every true believer is charged by God to be both a "watchman" and a caring shepherd. We must pray for the lost, and warn everyone of the coming judgment. We are ambassadors for Christ Jesus, and we have the sobering responsibility to represent Him well.

I cannot over-emphasize how crucial this message is for both believers and unbelievers. Every person who has ever lived on this planet will, in fact, face Jesus as Judge. As individuals, every knee will bow, and every tongue confess Jesus as LORD. The remnant of true believers will be judged for rewards. Unbelievers will be judged based on their life and works, and eternally separated from God. Each person stands alone, and the judgment is final.

Whether someone dies before "the last days", or is alive to see Jesus return in the clouds for His Bride, every person will be judged. This is individual judgment.

However, over the centuries past, God has repeatedly judged nations, and His own people. Prophetic scriptures guarantee there is a final future judgment on all the nations and people groups living in this world at the time of the end. In my opinion, no nation deserves judgment more than the United States of America. *How much longer will God withhold His Hand?*

Repeatedly in the Bible we learn that God judges rebellious people and nations. A good passage to illustrate this is Isaiah 30:8-14.

"Go now, write it on a tablet for them,
   inscribe it on a scroll,
that for the days to come
   it may be an everlasting witness.
9 For these are rebellious people, deceitful children,
   children unwilling to listen to the LORD's instruction.
10 They say to the seers,
   'See no more visions!'
and to the prophets,
   'Give us no more visions of what is right!
Tell us pleasant things,
   prophesy illusions.'

11 Leave this way,
get off this path,
and stop confronting us
with the Holy One of Israel!"

12 Therefore this is what the Holy One of Israel says:
"Because you have rejected this message,
relied on oppression
and depended on deceit,
13 this sin will become for you
like a high wall, cracked and bulging,
that collapses suddenly, in an instant.
14 It will break in pieces like pottery,
shattered so mercilessly
that among its pieces not a fragment will be found
for taking coals from a hearth
or scooping water out of a cistern."

Here are a few examples of God's past judgments of nations – Noah's day (Genesis 6:1-7); the Tower of Babel (Genesis 11:1-9); Aaron and the Golden Calf (Exodus 32:7-35); during the time of the Judges (Judges 2:6-23); the Northern Kingdom of Israel taken captive by Assyria (2 Kings 18:9-12); the Southern Kingdom which was primarily Judah was taken into captivity by Babylon (2 Kings 24:18-20 and 2 Kings 25:1-21), and Jerusalem was destroyed by the Romans in 70 A.D.

God does not change. He is the same yesterday, today and tomorrow! See Malachi 3:6-7, Hebrews 13:8, James 1:17, Psalm 102:25-28, Psalm 90:2. Before she graduated to heaven, Ruth Graham, wife of Billy Graham, said, "If God does not judge America, He will have to apologize to Sodom and Gomorrah."

Do you think America deserves judgment? Consider these facts:

1. We have removed God and prayer from our schools, courthouses, public events, government & even some churches.
2. We have "offended" the children, and surely deserve the "millstone". See Matthew 18:6; Revelation 18:21. Consider these facts:
   a. In the U.S., in the early 1960's, we took God and prayer away from our children in the schools.
   b. In the U.S., since 1973, 65 Million babies have been murdered in the womb (worldwide, 42 Million in 2018 alone).
   c. Now in New York, and 7 other states, babies can be murdered up until birth. In Virginia, they considered a bill to allow the murder of a child after it has been born. **Infanticide**. Aborted baby body parts are **SOLD**.
   d. The U.S. has legalized a form of "marriage" that will not even produce children.
   e. We are allowing access to our children in restrooms by "transgender" men, and libraries by "drag queens", at least one of which in Houston was a registered sex offender.
   f. Income from **child** sex industry and human trafficking is third largest source of illegal funds behind only counterfeiting and drugs. It is estimated that 5.5 million children under 18 are enslaved worldwide. As of 2019, there were 44 children per day sold into slavery (per *www.vets4childrescue.org*).
   g. Almost the entire world has turned their backs on God's original children, Israel, through whom we were given the precious Child of God, Jesus!
3. We celebrate sin and perversion of every sort; and, many of the world's most powerful, influential and richest people openly worship Satan/Lucifer.

4. We worship almost every worldly idol above God–for example, sports, Hollywood, material possessions, jobs, etc.
5. Almost the entire world despises the Name of Jesus Christ. See Psalm 2.
6. "Christian" denominations ordain ministers who live in open and direct rebellion to the Word of God.

There is always time for individual repentance as long as a person is still living. However, does America as a whole have the motivation and time to repent on a national scale? I'm doubtful. Jesus said in John 9:4, "As long as it is day, we must do the works of him who sent me. Night is coming, when no one can work." Isaiah prophesied of a time like today in Isaiah 60:2, "See, darkness covers the earth and thick darkness is over the peoples..."

Ask God to show you how to apply these truths in your particular circumstances. Pray for courage and boldness to share it with others as you discharge your responsibility as a "watchman" and caring shepherd. Pray diligently for the lost. Be prepared to suffer persecution for your faith. In 2018, 4,136 Christians were killed worldwide for faith-related reasons. *Are you willing to give up your life rather than deny Jesus?* It may come to that.

I pray you will personally rededicate your life to go "all in, and all out" for Jesus. Ask the Holy Spirit to set you apart from the world, and make you ever more holy daily. Make up your mind to do the best you can to be obedient in every area of your life, and repent quickly if you fall. ***This is absolutely not the time to be "lukewarm", "on the fence", or "playing with God".***

SOME RELEVANT SCRIPTURE PASSAGES

Ezekiel 33:1-11 "The word of the Lord came to me: "Son of man, speak to your people and say to them: 'When I bring the sword against a land,

and the people of the land choose one of their men and make him their watchman, and he sees the sword coming against the land and blows the trumpet to warn the people, then if anyone hears the trumpet but does not heed the warning and the sword comes and takes their life, their blood will be on their own head. Since they heard the sound of the trumpet but did not heed the warning, their blood will be on their own head. If they had heeded the warning, they would have saved themselves. But if the watchman sees the sword coming and does not blow the trumpet to warn the people and the sword comes and takes someone's life, that person's life will be taken because of their sin, but I will hold the watchman accountable for their blood.'

7 "Son of man, I have made you a watchman for the people of Israel; so hear the word I speak and give them warning from me. When I say to the wicked, 'You wicked person, you will surely die,' and you do not speak out to dissuade them from their ways, that wicked person will die for their sin, and I will hold you accountable for their blood. But if you do warn the wicked person to turn from their ways and they do not do so, they will die for their sin, though you yourself will be saved.

10 "Son of man, say to the Israelites, 'This is what you are saying: "Our offenses and sins weigh us down, and we are wasting away because of them. How then can we live?"' Say to them, 'As surely as I live, declares the Sovereign Lord, I take no pleasure in the death of the wicked, but rather that they turn from their ways and live. Turn! Turn from your evil ways! Why will you die, people of Israel?'"

Ezekiel 33:17-20 "Yet your people say, 'The way of the Lord is not just.' But it is their way that is not just. If a righteous person turns from their righteousness and does evil, they will die for it. And if a wicked person turns away from their wickedness and does what is just and right, they will live by doing so. Yet you Israelites say, 'The way of the Lord is not just.' But I will judge each of you according to your own ways."

Ezekiel 3:10-11 "And he said to me, 'Son of man, listen carefully and take to heart all the words I speak to you. Go now to your people in exile and speak to them. Say to them, 'This is what the Sovereign Lord says', whether they listen or fail to listen.'"

Ezekiel 3:27 "But when I speak to you, I will open your mouth and you shall say to them, 'This is what the Sovereign LORD says. 'Whoever will listen let them listen, and whoever will refuse let them refuse; for they are a rebellious people.'"

Ezekiel 34:10 "This is what the Sovereign LORD says: I am against the shepherds and will hold them accountable for my flock. I will remove them from tending the flock so that the shepherds can no longer feed themselves. I will rescue my flock from their mouths, and it will no longer be food for them."

Malachi 3:6-7 "I the LORD do not change. So you, the descendants of Jacob, are not destroyed. Ever since the time of your ancestors you have turned away from my decrees and have not kept them. Return to me, and I will return to you, says the LORD Almighty."

Hebrews 13:8 "Jesus Christ is the same yesterday and today and forever."

James 1:17 "Every good and perfect gift is from above, coming down from the Father of the heavenly lights, who does not change like shifting shadows."

Matthew 18:6 "If anyone causes one of these little ones—those who believe in me—to stumble, it would be better for them to have a large millstone hung around their neck and to be drowned in the depths of the sea."

Revelation 18:21 "Then a mighty angel picked up a boulder the size of a large millstone and threw it into the sea, and said: 'With such violence the great city of Babylon will be thrown down, never to be found again.'"

TAKEAWAY HIGHLIGHT

I cannot over-emphasize how crucial this message is for both believers and unbelievers. Every person who has ever lived on this planet will, in fact, face Jesus as Judge. As individuals, every knee will bow, and every tongue confess Jesus as LORD. The remnant of true believers will be judged for rewards. Unbelievers will be judged based on their life and works, and eternally separated from God. Each person stands alone, and the judgment is final.

Whether someone dies before "the last days", or is alive to see Jesus return in the clouds for His Bride, every person will be judged. This is individual judgment.

However, over the centuries past, God has repeatedly judged nations, and His own people. Prophetic scriptures guarantee there is a final future judgment on all the nations and people groups living in this world at the time of the end.

PRACTICAL APPLICATION

Take a few minutes to think about the current state of our nation and the world. Make a list of reasons why we deserve God's judgment. Why do you think God has so far stayed His Hand? Are you warning others?

WANT TO KNOW MORE?

Write to us to request the discipleship teaching on "Judgment is Coming". Mail it to: Freedom in Jesus Prison Ministries, Attn: Teachings, P.O. Box 939, Levelland, TX 79336.

If you do not have an intimate personal relationship with God, and do not repent before you die, your eternal destination is Hell instead of Heaven. If that's you, please make sure you are right with God today. Read on...

Hell–Real, Fearful, and Forever

In pulpits across America, the stark reality of Hell is almost never mentioned–much less taught. Yet, Jesus taught a lot about Hell. The Bible makes it clear that Hell is real, fearful and forever. **As true believers, we must be concerned about the eternal destination of those who do not have an intimate, personal relationship with Jesus.**

We must choose, in this life, where we will spend eternity. There are only two options and they are direct opposites of one another – Heaven or Hell. *A person who wants nothing to do with God in this temporal existence on Earth will be forever separated from Him. Our Father will not make a person choose Heaven.* A person must willingly receive the love, mercy and grace from the Father through Jesus and the Holy Spirit in order to be saved from sin, condemnation and judgment.

Robert Velarde wrote an article, "Is Hell Real?", which in part is defining who goes to hell, "Despite God's offer of redemption and salvation through Christ, not everyone will be redeemed, resulting in those who reject God being destined for hell." It is important to note that hell was never made for humans, rather for the devil and his fallen angels (Matthew 25:41).

Robert Velarde's article discusses hell and the nature of God in this way:

"Christ, then, had much to say about hell. Rather than being cruel, however, His intention then and now is to offer a way out of such a horrible destiny. But people must be willing to embrace this opportunity.

"Another aspect of the doctrine of hell that is key to understanding it has to do with the nature of God. He is all-loving, but also completely sinless, holy and just. This means that anything unholy cannot enter His direct presence. As a result, those who fail to accept His truths must reside somewhere else (i.e., hell). God is also loving, but this characteristic means that He does not force belief upon anyone, but instead seeks to persuade us."

Tim Bertolet, in his article entitled "Hell: Who Goes There?" writes, "The simplest answer to the question 'who goes to hell?' is to answer: 'unrepentant sinners who do not have saving faith in the Lord Jesus Christ will go to hell.' In fact, when the Philippian jailer asked the most basic question: 'what must I do to be saved?' Paul and Silas responded, 'Believe in the Lord Jesus, and you will be saved...' (Acts 16:31). This is salvation from judgement, condemnation, and hell.

"Likewise, at the end of Revelation, Jesus showed that those who are cleansed having their robes washed in Jesus' blood and righteousness inherit the blessings of the eternal city and the tree of life. Those who are immoral are outside this city (Rev. 22:15). Elsewhere, Revelation is clear:

> **Rev. 20:15** '*And if anyone's name was not found written in the book of life, he was thrown into the lake of fire.*'
>
> **Rev. 21:8** '*But as for the cowardly, the faithless, the detestable, as for murderers, the sexually immoral, sorcerers, idolaters, and all liars, their portion will be in the lake that burns with fire and sulfur, which is the second death.*'

"Likewise, Paul describes it as sinners who face the judgment and do not inherit the kingdom of God:

> **1 Cor. 6:9-10** *'Or do you not know that the unrighteous will not inherit the kingdom of God? Do not be deceived: neither the sexually immoral, nor idolaters, nor adulterers, nor men who practice homosexuality, nor thieves, nor the greedy, nor drunkards, nor revilers, nor swindlers will inherit the kingdom of God.'*
>
> **Gal. 5:19-21** *'Now the works of the flesh are evident: sexual immorality, impurity, sensuality, idolatry, sorcery, enmity, strife, jealousy, fits of anger, rivalries, dissensions, divisions, envy, drunkenness, orgies, and things like these. I warn you, as I warned you before, that those who do such things will not inherit the kingdom of God.'"*
>
> "The sinner is sent to hell because of the guilt of their sin. The sin of an individual leaves them as guilty and condemned before God. The fair and just punishment of any offense against the holiness of the eternal God is sentencing the sinner to hell. The Bible says, '[for] all have sinned and fallen short of the glory of God' (*Rom. 3:23*)."

In her article, "What is Hell Like", Salem Web Network Editor, Emily Hall shares this:

"The reality of hell, like heaven, is hotly debated in large part because no human has visited and returned with first-hand knowledge of the place. In Christianity, followers of Jesus Christ believe he is the incarnation of the all-knowing God (Matthew 1:23) and the 'Word [of God] made flesh,' (John 1:14). With this understanding, we the living can best know what hell is like by studying how God's word as a whole describes it and what Jesus, specifically, said about it in the Gospels.

We can know from what Jesus said that hell is an eternal (Matthew 25:41), physical (Matthew 10:28), and horrifying (Mark 9:43) place where those who've sinned (Romans 3:23) are headed, and from where Jesus Christ came to rescue all who would believe in him (John 3:16-18)."

Emily Hall's article cites many scripture references which describe Hell as:

1. **Darkness** (Nahum 1:8, Matthew 8:12, Matthew 22:13, Matthew 25:30, Jude 1:13, revelation 16:10.
2. **Gnashing of Teeth** (Matthew 13:41-43, Matthew 8:12, Matthew 13:50, Matthew 22:13, Matthew 24:51, Matthew 25:30, Luke 13:28).
3. **Fire** (Isaiah 66:24, Matthew 13:42, Matthew 13:50, Matthew 5:22, Matthew 18:8-9, Matthew 25:41, Mark 9:43, Mark 9:48, Revelation 14:10).
4. **Separation from God** (2 Thessalonians 1:9, Matthew 25:41, Matthew 25:46).

In a devotional article, "A Loving God and Eternity", Dr. Charles Stanley cites Matthew 25:31-46 and writes:

"God's Word clearly speaks about existence after death—people will spend eternity in either heaven or hell. Yet many individuals consider this truth inconsistent with other facts about the Lord. While their objections are understandable, the Bible provides the answers to their questions:

"How can the Lord be good if He lets some people spend their afterlife in hell? God is love and doesn't want anyone to live without Him (1 John 4:8; 1 Tim. 2:4). Everyone can turn from sin and receive the Savior, thereby avoiding eternal separation from Him. But some reject Christ

and live apart from Him all their days on earth. Because of that choice, they'll exist apart from His presence for eternity.

"Why would the Lord create certain individuals, knowing they would never turn to Him? To some, this seems unloving. Yet the alternative would be worse. God created us with free will—we can choose to obey and follow Him. If our Father gave us no choice, we would be mere robots, unable to truly respond, love, and worship.

"Isn't an endless penalty unfair, particularly if non-Christians never heard a clear presentation of the gospel? As long as unbelievers are alive, the heavenly Father does everything He can to keep them from eternal punishment—except violate their free will. He gives enough time and evidence so that nobody has a valid excuse for rejecting the one path to salvation (Rom. 1:20; John 14:6).

"Do you know Jesus as your Lord and Savior? He wants you to spend eternity with Him."

Everyone in Hell still has their sins forgiven through the finished work of Jesus. Everyone in Hell is still loved by the Heavenly Father. However, they rejected this unconditional love and forgiveness by deciding they did not want a relationship with God while on Earth. God respects their free will, and they will be forever separated from Him. As one Christian institution has wisely asserted, ***"there is such a thing as Hell, but nobody will go there because God doesn't love them...they will go there precisely because they have willingly chosen to reject His love."***

Although we may be uncomfortable with the reality of Hell, it should compel us to action. *"For those who don't know Christ, it should motivate them to redouble their efforts to seek Him and to find Him. For those of us who know Him, it should cause us to redouble our efforts to extend His message of mercy and grace to those who need it."* (J.P. Moreland, Ph.D., as quoted by Lee Strobel, *The Case for Faith*)

Ask God to show you how to apply these truths. Pray for courage and boldness to share the truth with others. Pray diligently for the lost. We are seeing prophecy unfold before our eyes, and witnessing all of the signs preceding the soon coming return of King Jesus!

Hell is real, fearful and forever. No-one should go there.

SOME RELEVANT SCRIPTURE PASSAGES

Matthew 25:41 "Then he will say to those on his left, 'Depart from me, you who are cursed, into the eternal fire prepared for the devil and his angels.'"

Galatians 5:19-21 "The acts of the flesh are obvious: sexual immorality, impurity and debauchery; idolatry and witchcraft; hatred, discord, jealousy, fits of rage, selfish ambition, dissensions, factions and envy; drunkenness, orgies, and the like. I warn you, as I did before, that those who live like this will not inherit the kingdom of God."

1 Corinthians 6:9-10 "Or do you not know that wrongdoers will not inherit the kingdom of God? Do not be deceived: Neither the sexually immoral nor idolaters nor adulterers nor men who have sex with men nor thieves nor the greedy nor drunkards nor slanderers nor swindlers will inherit the kingdom of God."

Revelation 21:8 "But the cowardly, the unbelieving, the vile, the murderers, the sexually immoral, those who practice magic arts, the idolaters and all liars—they will be consigned to the fiery lake of burning sulfur. This is the second death."

Revelation 20:15 "Anyone whose name was not found written in the book of life was thrown into the lake of fire."

Ephesians 2:1-3 "As for you, you were dead in your transgressions and sins, in which you used to live when you followed the ways of this world and of the ruler of the kingdom of the air, the spirit who is now at work in those who are disobedient. All of us also lived among them at one time, gratifying the cravings of our flesh and following its desires and thoughts. Like the rest, we were by nature deserving of wrath."

John 3:16-18 "For God so loved the world that he gave his one and only Son, that whoever believes in him shall not perish but have eternal life. For God did not send his Son into the world to condemn the world, but to save the world through him. Whoever believes in him is not condemned, but whoever does not believe stands condemned already because they have not believed in the name of God's one and only Son."

TAKEAWAY HIGHLIGHT

Everyone in Hell still has their sins forgiven through the finished work of Jesus. Everyone in Hell is still loved by the Heavenly Father. However, they rejected this unconditional love and forgiveness by deciding they did not want a relationship with God while on Earth. God respects their free will, and they will be forever separated from Him.

PRACTICAL APPLICATION

Look up all the scripture references cited in this chapter. Ask the Holy Spirit to let you see others with a heart of compassion and concern for their eternal destination. Boldly but lovingly share the truth about hell with unbelievers; and pray that God gives them a heart to listen and respond.

WANT TO KNOW MORE?

Write to us to request the discipleship teaching on “Hell – Real, Fearful and Forever”. Mail it to: Freedom in Jesus Prison Ministries, Attn: Teachings, P.O. Box 939, Levelland, TX 79336.

True believers who maintain an intimacy of personal relationship with Jesus will spend eternity with Him in Heaven! What is Heaven like? Read on . . .

Heaven – What It's Like

Although there are many current benefits in this life from cultivating and maintaining an intimate personal relationship with Jesus, the eternal reward we look forward to is living forever in Heaven with Him when our brief time on Earth is over.

I can only imagine the joy and gratitude we will feel when we hear Him say, "... *'Well done, good and faithful servant! You have been faithful with a few things; I will put you in charge of many things. Come and share your master's happiness!'"* Matthew 25:21

Once we are "born again" or "born from above", this Earth is no longer our home. We belong to another Kingdom and we are just passing through on our way to Heaven. The Bible says we are aliens and strangers in this world, and that our physical life here is so temporary compared to our eternal spiritual life in Heaven.

With this truth in mind our perspective should change daily to focus more and more on things that matter for eternity. John Bevere's book, *Driven by Eternity*, makes this very point so well in that it uses an allegory of several people who appear before Jesus upon their arrival in Heaven. There they discover what things in their life had eternal significance and what was relatively meaningless. If you can get a copy, I know you will enjoy it.

I found a sermon by Pastor Ray Pritchard given January 19, 1998, entitled "What is Heaven Like?" Although it is too lengthy to present in its entirety here, I know you will be blessed with these excerpts:

"I begin this sermon with two statements that I believe to be almost universally true: Everyone wants to know about heaven and everyone wants to go there. Recent polls suggest that nearly 80% of all Americans believe there is a place called heaven. I find that statistic encouraging because it tells me that even in this skeptical age there is something deep inside the human heart that cries out, 'There's got to be something more.'

"The most important fact is that heaven is a real place. Listen to the words of Jesus on the night before he was crucified:

"*Do not let your hearts be troubled. Trust in God; trust also in me. In my Father's house are many rooms; if it were not so, I would have told you. I am going there to prepare a place for you. And if I go and prepare a place for you, I will come back and take you to be with me that you also may be where I am.*" (John 14:1-3).

"Twice in three verses Jesus calls heaven a place. He means that heaven ('my Father's house') is a real place, as real as New York, London or Chicago. The place called heaven is just as real as the place you call home. It's a real place filled with real people, which is why the Bible sometimes compares heaven to a mansion with many rooms (John 14:1-3) and sometimes to an enormous city teeming with people (Revelation 21-22).

"Heaven is a real place, it's where Jesus is right now, and it's not far away from us.

"What is heaven like? Here are some biblical facts about heaven. It is ...

1. God's dwelling place (Psalm 33:13).
2. Where Christ is today (Acts 1:11).
3. Where Christians go when they die (Philippians 1:21-23).
4. The Father's house (John 14:2).
5. A city designed and built by God (Hebrews 11:10).
6. A better country (Hebrews 11:16).
7. Paradise (Luke 23:43).

"Most of us have heard that heaven is a place where the streets are paved with gold, the gates are made of pearl, and the walls made of precious jewels. Those images come from Revelation 21-22, which offers us the most extended picture of heaven in the entire Bible. If you ask me if I believe those things are literally true, the answer is yes and no. Yes, they are literally true but no, heaven won't be anything like we imagine. It will be much greater.

"Heaven is a real place filled with real people. The Bible pictures it as a great city filled with all of God's people.

"What would such a city look like? It would be a city with ...

1. No pollution for the skies would always be crystal clear.
2. No crime or violence for no criminals would ever enter.
3. No greedy politicians, no drug pushers, no child molesters.
4. No potholes and no power outages either.
5. It would be filled with abundant parks, rivers, rolling meadows, and flowing streams. Lining the streets would be flowers in constant bloom, fruit trees of every kind, every species of plant life growing free from pestilence and disease.

6. The gates would be made of pearl, the walls of jasper, the streets of gold. Precious stones would lie on the ground like playthings–emeralds, rubies, diamonds galore.
7. On every hand there would be children laughing, bright conversation, music floating from every direction.

"In the city that God builds, there are no tears, there is no sorrow ... no regret ... no remorse. Bitterness gone forever, failure left far behind, suffering redeemed and rewarded. There are no eyeglasses, no braces, no wheelchairs, no false teeth, no bald heads, no hearing aids, and no crutches. There are no more hospitals, no more nursing homes, no paramedics, no CPR. Doctors have to find a new job, they aren't needed anymore. Aspirin gone, accidents over, cancer disappeared, heart attacks banished, AIDS a distant memory. In heaven no one grows old and feeble.

"Who is in heaven right now? This question is not difficult to answer. God is in heaven because heaven is his dwelling place. The Lord Jesus has been in heaven ever since he ascended from the earth shortly after his resurrection (Acts 1:9-11). The Bible tells us that angels are in heaven. In fact there are myriads of angels-uncountable numbers of heavenly beings-all of them serving the Lord in various ways.

"And the saints of God who died on this earth are in heaven. [Note: I mean by this that heaven includes the Old Testament Saints who by faith trusted in God's Word and looked forward to God's redemption at Calvary (which they did not fully understand). It also includes every true believer from every continent and every denomination. Everyone who has genuinely trusted in Christ as Lord and Savior will be there. I also think that children who died before the 'age of accountability' go to heaven and I would also include those born with such mental limitations that they cannot understand the gospel.]The Bible teaches that the moment we die we go directly into the presence of the Lord Jesus Christ. Paul spoke of this in 2 Corinthians 5:7-8 and Philippians 1:21-23.

"But I do not want to be ambiguous on this point. Not everyone is in heaven now. Some people won't make it. The Bible speaks of the saved and the lost. The saved are those who trust Jesus Christ as their eternal Savior. The lost are those who do not trust Christ as Savior. This is the great dividing line of humanity-you are either saved or you are lost. And there is no middle category. You will either spend eternity in heaven or eternity in hell.

"What will we do in heaven? One of our more honest junior highers put the question this way: 'Worshipping God forever in heaven sounds boring-is it wrong to feel this? Is heaven going to be fun?' Again, the Bible doesn't tell us everything we would like to know, but of this we can be sure: Heaven won't be boring and it will be more fun than the best party you ever attended.

"I can guarantee you this: No one will be sitting around on a cloud eating grapes and polishing his halo. No, we'll all be too busy for that. Here are five things that will occupy us in heaven. We will ...

1. Worship without distraction.
2. Serve without exhaustion.
3. Fellowship without fear.
4. Learn without fatigue.
5. Rest without boredom.

"How can I be sure I am going to heaven? This is the most important question of all. Here is a wonderful truth: God has made it easy for you to go to heaven. He did the hard part when he sent his Son to die on the Cross for you. He paid the price for your sins so that you could one day stand before God in heaven. Jesus said, 'I am the way and the truth and the life. No one comes to the Father except through me' (John 14:6). He also said, 'I am the door; if anyone enters through Me, he shall be saved' (John 10:9 NASB). Jesus is not only the way to heaven, he is also the door to heaven. If you want to go to heaven, you've got to go through the door marked 'Jesus Christ.' There is no other entrance.

"Let me make this very personal. If you were to die tonight, do you know for certain that you would go to heaven? I've already said that this is too important to say 'I think so' or 'I hope so.' If you're wrong, you're going to be wrong for a long, long time.

"What we need is solid ground on which to stand. And we have it in the death and resurrection of Jesus Christ. Our entire hope of heaven is wrapped up in what Jesus did when he died on the cross for the sins of the world and rose from the dead on Easter Sunday morning.

"One final word and I am done. No one goes to heaven by accident. Heaven is God's prepared place for prepared people. We prepare for heaven and then God prepares heaven for us. I've already told you that most people believe in heaven and most people think they are going there. But are they on the right road? Are they building their lives on Jesus Christ-the solid rock? Too many, I fear, are standing on sinking sand and do not know it.

"What is your hope for heaven? Mine is Jesus Christ. I've staked everything I have on him. If he can't take me to heaven, then I'm not going there. What about you? When the dark night falls, the lights go out, and the waters of death swirl around you, what will happen to you then? If you know Jesus, you have nothing to fear. Put your trust in Jesus. Run to the Cross. Stand with your full weight on the Solid Rock of our salvation. May God help you to trust in Jesus Christ and him alone for your salvation. And may God grant that we will all meet one day in heaven.

"Safe at home. In heaven at last. I'll be there. What about you?"

In his book, *Where I Am: Heaven, Eternity and Our Life Beyond*, Rev. Billy Graham wrote:

"Many people teach today that the blood of Jesus covers all sin, regardless of whether the sinner repents or not. This is Satan's great lie. Some believe they will automatically walk into Heaven when this earthly life is over because God is love. That would negate the sacrifice Jesus made on the cross. Don't be deceived, for God is not mocked. God is also a God of justice and righteousness. He is not preparing a place in Heaven for unrepentant sinners. While we have contributed nothing to God's free gift of salvation, there is a condition to possessing it-we must confess our sin, turn from it, and receive Christ on His terms.

"This truth is repulsive to many. The pride that flaunts our self-proclaimed innocence is the very evidence of our guilt. Continuing in rebellion against God, whether the sin be pride or murder, will send souls to Hell. Then there will no turning back, no second chances. There is no afterthought in the afterlife. Today is the time to decide where you will live forever-either Heaven or Hell. This may very well be an unpopular teaching, but popularity polls do not determine destiny for anyone."

Brothers and sisters in Christ, it is only in this life that we can make a decision where we will spend eternity. We are eternal spiritual beings.

We will all live eternally in only one of two places. With all my heart, I pray you will choose Heaven.

The Bible seems very clear that each of us is required to have an intimate, personal relationship with God the Father, because of the finished work of Jesus, by and through His Holy Spirit. The more we comprehend and receive the unconditional, sacrificial love of God we will be motivated to obey Him, and we will desire to do our best to please Him. Although we will never be perfectly obedient during this lifetime, we have the Holy Spirit Who empowers us to do our best every day, and Who will gently convict us to repent when we miss it. Then when we get to Heaven, we will hear, "Well done, good and faithful servant. Enter in to the joy of the Lord."

SOME RELEVANT SCRIPTURE PASSAGES

John 14:1-3 "Do not let your hearts be troubled. You believe in God; believe also in me. My Father's house has many rooms; if that were not so, would I have told you that I am going there to prepare a place for you? And if I go and prepare a place for you, I will come back and take you to be with me that you also may be where I am."

Philippians 3:20-21 "But our citizenship is in heaven. And we eagerly await a Savior from there, the Lord Jesus Christ, who, by the power that enables him to bring everything under his control, will transform our lowly bodies so that they will be like his glorious body."

Luke 23:43 "Jesus answered him, 'Truly I tell you, today you will be with me in paradise.'"

Hebrews 12:22-24 "But you have come to Mount Zion, to the city of the living God, the heavenly Jerusalem. You have come to thousands upon thousands of angels in joyful assembly, to the church of the firstborn, whose names are written in heaven. You have come to God, the Judge of all, to the spirits of the righteous made perfect, to Jesus the mediator of a new covenant, and to the sprinkled blood that speaks a better word than the blood of Abel."

John 14:6 "Jesus answered, 'I am the way and the truth and the life. No one comes to the Father except through me.'"

2 Corinthians 5:7-8 "For we live by faith, not by sight. We are confident, I say, and would prefer to be away from the body and at home with the Lord."

Philippians 1:21-23 "For to me, to live is Christ and to die is gain. If I am to go on living in the body, this will mean fruitful labor for me. Yet what shall I choose? I do not know! I am torn between the two: I desire to depart and be with Christ, which is better by far..."

TAKEAWAY HIGHLIGHT

Brothers and sisters in Christ, it is only in this life that we can make a decision where we will spend eternity. We are eternal spiritual beings. We will all live eternally in only one of two places. With all my heart, I pray you will choose Heaven.

The Bible seems very clear that each of us is required to have an intimate, personal relationship with God the Father, because of the finished work of Jesus, by and through His Holy Spirit. The more we comprehend and receive the unconditional, sacrificial love of God we will be motivated to obey Him, and we will desire to do our best to please Him. Although we will never be perfectly obedient during this lifetime, we have the Holy Spirit Who empowers us to do our best every day, and Who will gently convict us to repent when we miss it. Then when we get to Heaven, we will hear, "Well done, good and faithful servant. Enter in to the joy of the Lord."

PRACTICAL APPLICATION

Ask the Holy Spirit to help you think of the aspects of Heaven you are looking forward to the most. Who are you excited to see again that may have gotten there before you? How do you think you will feel when you see Jesus? What will you want Him to say to you?

Are you absolutely sure where you will spend eternity? If there is any doubt in your mind, review pages 333-336, and then be led by the Holy Spirit how to respond.

WANT TO KNOW MORE?

Write to us to request the discipleship teaching on “Heaven - What It’s Like”. Mail it to: Freedom in Jesus Prison Ministries, Attn: Teachings, P.O. Box 939, Levelland, TX 79336.

TAKE ACTION

You Can Have "The Real Thing"

"The Real Thing" has nothing to do with "religion." Rather, it is an intimate personal relationship with our Heavenly Father, because of the finished work of Jesus at the Cross. The Holy Spirit comes and seals us as His very own, and begins an ongoing work in us to conform us to the image of Christ Jesus.

You can begin this exciting and abundant life today. It will continue throughout all eternity.

First, acknowledge and confess that you have sinned against God.

Second, renounce your sins – determine that you are not going back to them. Turn away from sin. Turn to God.

Third, by faith receive Christ into your heart. Surrender your life completely to Him. He will come to live in your heart by the Holy Spirit.

You can do this right now.

Start by simply talking to God. You can pray a prayer like this:

"Oh God, I am a sinner. I'm sorry for my sin. I want to turn from my sin. Please forgive me. I believe Jesus Christ is Your Son; I believe

He died on the Cross for my sin and You raised Him to life. I want to trust Him as my Savior and follow Him as my Lord from this day forward, forevermore. Lord Jesus, I put my trust in You and surrender my life to You. Please come into my life and fill me with your Holy Spirit. In Jesus' Name. Amen."

If you just said this prayer, and you meant it with all your heart, we believe you just got Saved and are now Born Again in Christ Jesus as a totally new person.

"Therefore, if anyone is in Christ, he is a new creation; the old has gone, the new has come!" (II Corinthians 5:17)

We urge you to go "all in and all out for the All in All"! (Pastor Mark Batterson, *All In*)

We suggest you follow the Lord in water baptism at your earliest opportunity. Water baptism is an outward symbol of the inward change that follows your salvation and re-birth.

The grace of God Himself gives you the desire and ability to surrender completely to the Holy Spirit's work in and through you (Philippians 2:13).

The Baptism in the Holy Spirit is His empowerment for you.

You Can Receive the Baptism in the Holy Spirit

The Baptism in the Holy Spirit is a separate experience and a Holy privilege granted to those who ask. This is God's own power to enable you to live an abundant, overcoming life. The Bible says it is the same power that raised Jesus from the dead (Romans 1:4; 8:11; II Cor. 4:13-14; 1 Peter 3:18).

Have you asked the Father for Jesus to baptize you (immerse you) in the Holy Spirit (Luke 3:16)? If you ask the Father, He will give Him to you (Luke 11:13). Have you allowed the "rivers of living water" to flow from within you (John 7:38-39)? Our Father desires for us to walk in all His fullness by His Holy Spirit.

The power to witness, and live your life the way Jesus did in intimate relationship with the Father, comes from asking Jesus to baptize you in the Holy Spirit. To receive this baptism, pray along these lines:

Abba Father and my Lord Jesus,

Thank you for giving me your Spirit to live inside me. I am saved by grace through faith in Jesus. I ask you now to baptize me in the Holy Ghost with Your fire and power. I fully receive it through faith just

like I did my salvation. Now, Holy Spirit, come and rise up within me as I praise God! Fill me up Jesus! I fully expect to receive my prayer language as You give me utterance. In Jesus' Name. Amen.

Now, out loud, begin to praise and glorify JESUS, because He is the baptizer of the Holy Spirit! From deep in your spirit, tell Him, "I love you, I thank you, I praise you, Jesus."

Repeat this as you feel joy and gratefulness bubble up from deep inside you. Speak those words and syllables you receive – not in your own language, but the heavenly language given to you by the Holy Spirit. Allow this joy to come out of you in syllables of a language your own mind does not already know. That will be your prayer language the Spirit will use through you when you don't know how to pray (Romans 8:26-28). It is not the "gift of tongues" for public use, therefore it does not require a public interpretation.

You have to surrender and use your own vocal chords to verbally express your new prayer language. The Holy Spirit is a gentleman. He will not force you to speak. Don't be concerned with how it sounds. It is a heavenly language!

Worship Him! Praise Him! Use your heavenly language by praying in the Spirit every day! Paul urges us to "pray in the Spirit on all occasions with all kinds of prayers and requests." (Ephesians 6:18)

Contact Us

We would love to hear your feedback or answer your questions.

- We would especially like to know if you made a decision to receive Jesus into your heart and prayed the prayer of Salvation on page 333. Or maybe you had prayed a similar prayer before, but this is the first time you really meant it from your heart. Tell us about your decision.
- Perhaps you made a decision to rededicate your life to Christ – to go "all in and all out" for Jesus! If so, we would like to know so we can encourage you. Please write to us.
- If you prayed the prayer to ask Jesus to baptize you in the Holy Spirit, please tell us.

As a further aid and encouragement, we would like to teach you more about how to follow Jesus – how to be a true disciple. A disciple is a "disciplined learner" and we want to share many truths with you about how to have an intimate relationship with God the Father, by the Holy Spirit. Jesus came to reconcile us to the Father. We want to help you develop a meaningful relationship with Him.

Please ask us to include you in our Discipleship Program whereby you will receive an encouraging teaching every two months or so. This is not the kind of lesson you are required to fill in and send back to us. You must only desire to be encouraged regularly in the Lord, and be willing to prayerfully study the materials. That's all.

Please send your comments, questions and feedback to:

Freedom in Jesus Prison Ministries
Attn: Stephen – KJI
P.O. Box 939
Levelland, TX 79336

Ask your loved ones to check out our ministry website at *www.fijm.org*

They can learn more about Stephen Canup's books and read previews of them, at *www.stephencanup.com*

We pray you are blessed abundantly by our Father every day, in every way, in Christ Jesus as you seek Him daily in and by the Holy Spirit!

I Challenge You!!!

God is able to transform your life in the same way He did mine. Understanding and receiving God's love is key; and, willing obedience is necessary.

But you must understand that He rewards those who diligently and earnestly seek Him (Hebrews 11:6); and, that you are transformed by renewing your mind through applying the principles in His Word to your daily life (Romans 12:1-2).

I challenge you to:

- Start every day with the Word and the Spirit. Ask the Holy Spirit to help you apply His Truth to your life. Let the Spirit use the Word to transform you.
- Look up every scripture reference in this book. Mark the verses in your own Bible. Memorize the ones that mean the most to you.
- Study the scriptural principles in this book in small groups. Sharing concepts from the Word with others helps you learn and apply them to your life.
- Show this book to others. As an ambassador for Christ (see II Corinthians 5:18-20), please use this book as a tool to reach the lost and encourage the Body of Believers. After sharing it with them, encourage them then to contact me to request their own copy of the book so they can study it and loan it to others. Each person who wants one must write me individually because I can only send one book to each person.

- Pray daily for us and for our ministry. We need your prayers.
- Do you want to help us continue to provide books like these free to prisoners? At your first opportunity, begin a program of regular giving to us so we can better minister to others who want to be free from every form of bondage. Former prisoners helping prisoners is what we are all about.

INFORMATION FOR FURTHER REVIEW AND APPLICATION

Spiraling Down to Depravity

By Stephen Canup

Outwardly, in the world's eyes, I was at the top of the ladder of success, the pinnacle of prosperity, and living the dream. With an office on Park Avenue in New York City, and making nearly $250,000 a year in 1985, I had it made. However, deep inside I had begun to delve into an entirely different life which would later lead to the very depths of depravity, perversion and reprobation.

Part of my destruction was revealed in my previously published personal testimony contained in my first book, *Jail-House Religion: From Park Avenue... to Park Bench... to Prison.*

Today, I am able to fill in some of the sordid details for the purpose of bringing more glory to God believing that more personal transparency will bring increased hope and freedom to others if they too turn their lives totally over to Jesus Christ as Lord and Savior. If God can change me, and He has, He can change anybody!

Having risen close to the very top of the business world as a Certified Public Accountant with the world's largest accounting firm, I maintained an outward persona necessary to achieve and quickly climb the corporate ladder. However, my darkest inner secrets of twisted thinking and behavior were well hidden for a time, and I deceived my very own self–destroying my career, my family and my morals by descending into an ever deepening pit of darkness.

Although I was raised in a Christian home, I was exposed to pornography through childhood friends around age 10. Earlier, at age 6 or so, an older boy was in the woods with me behind my house, and in the process of committing sodomy with me, when my mother's voice rang out from the back door that supper was ready, interrupting him and saving me from his designs.

Both of these events introduced darkness in my soul at a young age giving the enemy a foothold he would use on and off for nearly fifty years to lead me into a secret life beginning with lustful imagination and self-gratification, eventually immersing me in triple XXX theatres and bookstores, and sexual immorality of every kind.

Since being saved in prison at age 57, I praise God that He has delivered me from darkness and from deep bondage to a prior lifestyle of sin, depravity and sexual perversion. Among the many addictions I once had, it was pornography, drugs and alcohol that fueled an immoral lifestyle. This was heightened by the fact that I never consistently took the psych meds prescribed for the bipolar diagnosis I received in 1989 at age 37.

It was as if there was a big, black pit in my soul that constantly demanded chemical and sexual indulgences; but it was never filled or satisfied in spite of everything I tried. Over the twenty years between Park Avenue and Prison, I was empty, bored, searching, seeking and restless. I felt powerless to resist almost every enticement presented me. Although I was once very ashamed of the behaviors to which I was led, I am forever grateful to Jesus Christ for finding me and setting me forever free (see Romans 6:16-23).

Where did it all lead? Without details, here are some of the things I struggled with or participated in over the years before I was saved: bisexual encounters, gender confusion, illicit hook-ups with strangers of both sexes, activities in back rooms of adult bookstores, gay bars, indecent exposure, and compulsive self-gratification. The shame and guilt I felt as a result of this lifestyle contributed to constant hopelessness, depression and several suicide attempts.

Jesus took all my shame so that I could have His righteousness; He took all my rejection upon Himself at Calvary so that I could have His acceptance by the Father. The saving work of Jesus, the love of the Father, and the power of the Holy Spirit are the only things that filled that deep pit inside me. The peace, joy, wholeness and abundance I have in place of the emptiness is impossible to adequately describe; and, I am humbly grateful daily that I am now forever free of the condemnation, torment, guilt, embarrassment, shame, perversion and depravity that dominated my soul and life before I was born again. I am a totally new man in Christ Jesus (2 Corinthians 5:17-21). Praise God!!!

I will say it again, if God can save, deliver, heal and change me; He can save, deliver, heal and change anyone! I have learned to take the wrong kind of thoughts captive quickly so that I do not give in to the almost daily temptations the devil brings (2 Corinthians 10:4-5).

But before I was saved, I fell a mighty long way. I was unemployed for seven years, and homeless for three years, leading up to being sent to prison for the first (and last) time at age 56. My crime was solicitation of a minor and I thought my life would be forever ruined because of the label I now carried of "sex offender". I was sent to a medium security, medium term facility managed by CCA (now CoreCivic) in Nashville, TN, to serve my time.

At Davidson County Jail, before I was sent to prison, I requested something to read and the Chaplain sent me a pocket-size Gideon's New Testament. Reading was something I did often to "escape" when I was homeless, helpless and hopeless. Until I finally was able to go to the prison library, the Bible was the only thing I had to read. Since I had already heard men being made fun of for reading their Bible or going to chapel classes or services, I read mine out of the way of others while on my bunk, both in jail, and later in prison.

For the first ten or twelve months in prison, I stayed pretty much to myself and experienced a lot of fairly severe depression. I was not given any meds for bipolar illness so I was essentially stuck in the manic-depressive phase. No one knew where I was so I had no money on my books and did not receive any visits or letters. Sometimes I got out of my depression and despair enough to play some cards or dominos or watch television., but most of the time I was a loner. I kept reading my Bible a little late at night and in the early morning, but I primarily read spy novels, murder mysteries, and westerns. I did not attend chapel. My time drug by.

As I read my Bible more, I remembered what I had learned in the Baptist church growing up about Jesus forgiving all my sins and that He has a plan for everyone's lives. I had a very hard time believing that still applied to me based on all I had done and how far I had fallen, but I could sense a small glimmer of hope. Could God really accept me, forgive me, and love me? The Bible made it clear that He could and does!

Certainly I blamed myself for where I ended up and for the charges I had. I hated myself and could not bear to look into the mirror when shaving or brushing my teeth. I was overcome with guilt, shame, regret and embarrassment. I began to understand that God forgave me, but I couldn't forgive myself. I thought my past was so bad that I had no future.

In my addictions and sin, I had pushed away every family member and friend. My family didn't even know where I was nor if I was even alive. I had not tried to contact them in five or six years. The fact that I had always been so prideful made it impossible for me to reach out to them while I was homeless and unemployed. Now I was in prison where none of my family had ever been.

A major breakthrough began in February, 2009, when I felt God encouraging me to reach out to and ask forgiveness from my family. Humbling myself enough to write that first letter was so very hard, but I felt a huge burden begin to lift as soon as I mailed it. In a short time, I heard from my two older brothers. They said they weren't holding anything against me and both wanted to know what they could do to help me. Wow, what a miracle!

Then the Lord impressed in my spirit that if my family could forgive me, and He could forgive me, then I needed to forgive myself. Oh my goodness, what a sense of freedom from bondage began to grow in me as I decided to put my past in the past, forgive myself, and trust God with my future one day at a time. I reveal much more about this part of my "awakening" in my longer testimony book, *Jail-House Religion: From Park Avenue... to Park Bench... to Prison.*

I began to have more of a hunger for the Word and much less desire for the all the other books I was using to avoid dealing with my feelings and situation. On my 57th birthday, April 20, 2009, I attended my first Chaplaincy class that would last three months. I declare this date as my official "re-birth" date! Being "born again" is the very best thing that has ever happened to me. If it took going to prison to get my attention, so be it.

Soon after, I started going to Chapel when they called out for "church". People were surprised and made fun of me but I didn't care. I was being progressively filled with hope little by little. Having been absolutely hopeless for years of suicidal depression, this was a very welcome feeling. Then I learned from Jeremiah 29:11-14 that God really did have a plan and a future for me. Yes, even me, a sex offender!

I went "all in" for Jesus. I have never looked back and I have never regretted my commitment, not even for a minute. I began to do every Bible Correspondence course I could get my hands on. I started a Bible study and prayer group in my housing area. For me, "Jail-house Religion" was "the real thing".

My two brothers committed to help me get back to Texas as soon as I discharged my sentence. One of them knew the founder of Freedom in Jesus Prison Ministries, Don Castleberry, who began to correspond with me prior to release. Because I felt God had a call on my life for prison ministry, I moved to Levelland, TX, where Don lived and started volunteering in his ministry. He then agreed to mentor me and we were accountability partners. We spent a lot of quality time together and we have become best friends. I am now President of Freedom in Jesus Prison Ministries., after having been Executive Director for about four years.

After a year under Don Castleberry's supervision, in 2012 I asked him to ordain and license me into the Gospel ministry. In prison, I made the commitment to serve God with all of my heart for all of my days. So on February 23, 2012, in front of fifty or so friends and family members, I publically submitted myself to a higher standard of lifetime accountability to God and the Body of Christ as an ordained minister and a licensed teacher of the Word.

My purpose and passion is to share the love and hope of the Gospel of Jesus Christ with every prisoner and inmate I can.

I will say it again, if God can change me (and He surely has), He can change anyone who will surrender their lives, seek Him with all their heart, and be willing to follow hard after Jesus!

The "Old Man"

Six Months before Prison (2007)

Stephen Canup

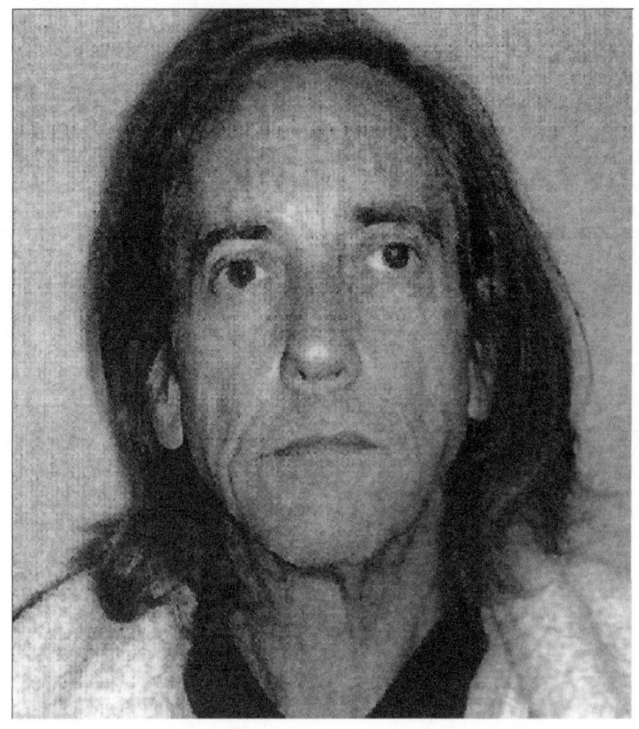

Guilty and condemned by sin to death

Romans 6:23 "For the wages of sin is death...

GUILTY OF THESE SINS AGAINST GOD, OTHERS AND SELF:

Addictions to drugs, alcohol, sex, pornography, praise of men, work

Pride	Perversion	Depravity	Confusion
Worry	Idolatry	Reprobation	Lying
Fear	Selfishness	Un-forgiveness	Conceit
Depression	Judgment	Immorality	Intellectualism
Hopelessness	Self-hate	Self-abuse	Humanism
Anxiety	Resentment	Bitterness	Shame
Profanity	Regret	Thievery	Remorse
Fornication	Anger	Adultery	Guilt
Lustful desires	Covetousness	Sexual identity	Offense

THE SINFUL AND CURSED LIFE I WAS LIVING BEFORE PRISON RESULTED IN ME BEING:

- Homeless, living on the streets of Nashville, TN, for 3 years prior to prison.
- Unemployed for 7 years prior to incarceration.
- Broke after having filed for bankruptcy twice.
- Destitute with all my earthly possessions contained in 1 hanging garment bag in the prison's property room awaiting the day of my release.
- Desolate having abandoned all family and friends, leaving me lonely and utterly forsaken.
- Depressed so deeply by these life conditions that I had attempted suicide several times.
- Hopeless and absolutely convinced nothing would ever change or get better in any way.

The "New Man"

One Year after Prison (2012)

Stephen Canup

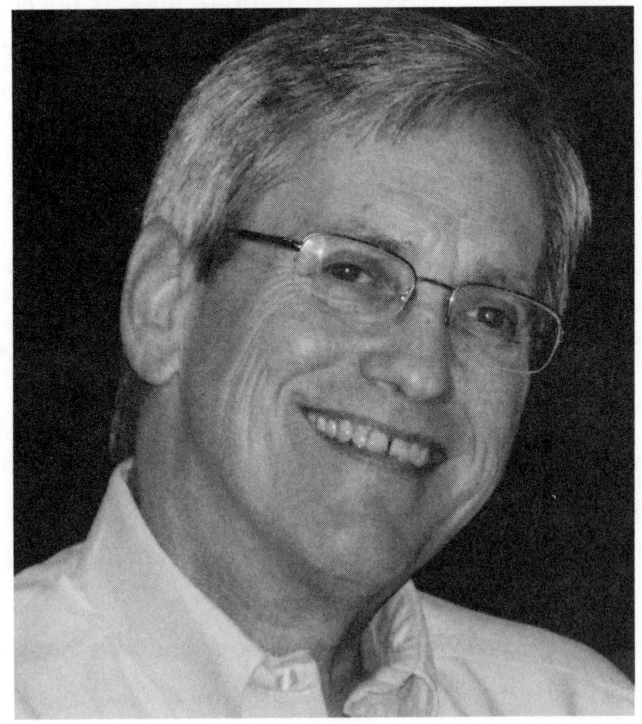

A Free Man – Alive in Christ

...but the gift of God is eternal life in Christ Jesus our Lord."

Romans 6:23

"I have been crucified with Christ and I no longer live, but Christ lives in me. The life I now live in the body, I live by

faith in the Son of God, who loved me and gave himself for me." (Gal. 2:20)

"Therefore if any is (ingrafted) in Christ, the Messiah, he is (a new creature altogether), a new creation; the old (previous moral and spiritual condition) has passed away. Behold, the fresh and new has come!" (II Cor. 5:17, AMP)

"So if the Son sets you free, you will be free indeed" (John 8:36)

The new life in Christ that began in prison in 2009 has brought many blessings. As of early 2023, some of these abundant life realities include:

- My spiritual re-birth April 20, 2009!!!
- Restored relationships with every family member.
- A mentor and accountability partner, Don Castleberry, who speaks the truth in love.
- Acceptance instead of rejection.
- Joy and hope instead of depression and hopelessness.
- Purpose and passion to help set others free.
- Peace, boldness and confidence instead of anxiety and fear.
- The righteousness of Christ Jesus instead of perversion and depravity.
- Love and compassion for others instead of selfishness and self-hate.
- Freedom from addictions to alcohol, drugs, pornography, smoking and gambling.
- A tongue of blessings and respect instead of pride, criticism and profanity.

- A beautiful, three bedroom, two bath home provided rent-free except for utilities.
- Three late-model vehicles have been provided to me free, in great condition, with low mileage.
- A house full of good furniture, and a closet full of good clothes.
- Debt-free, with also some money in savings.
- A renewed mind free of all the bad effects of addictions and depression.
- Good health.
- Mature Christians I can call for prayer or advice anytime about anything.
- Licensed and ordained in 2012 as a minister of the Gospel of Jesus Christ.
- President of Freedom in Jesus Prison Ministries.

Prayers of Submission

DAILY PRAYER OF SURRENDER AND SUBMISSION

Father God, I humbly surrender and submit myself fully to You and your leadership by Your Holy Spirit.

Lord, please forgive me for both my willful and my unintentional sins. Help me to freely and fully forgive others as You forgive me.

Father, I submit willingly and completely to your Hand as The Potter. Re-make me into the person You want me to be for the plan You have for me in Your perfect will. As You do, conform me to the image of Jesus by the sanctifying work of Your Holy Spirit.

Father, by Your grace help me to always be a grateful, humble heir of all Your promises; an obedient, faithful servant of all Your commands; a persistent, bold witness of Your salvation through Jesus; and, a loving, trusting child full of Your love. I surrender to Your Holy Spirit's leadership.

Let me be patient and persevering in prayer, ever watchful and responsive for opportunities to bless others as You have blessed me. Empower me Father with Your grace, through the Spirit of Jesus in me, to diligently seek You and Your eternal Kingdom, so that I will not be distracted and overcome with the temptations and temporary pleasures of this alien world. In everything I think, say and do today, Father, let me continually glorify and honor You.

I love You, Jesus. I praise You and adore You for first loving me. Thank You for being made sin for me so that I am made righteous in You.

Please love and bless others through me today as I seek to know and do Your perfect will for my life. I want to be led today by Your Holy Spirit in me.

In the power of the blood of Jesus, and the authority of His Name I pray. Amen.

PRAYER OF SUBMISSIVE OBEDIENCE IN A PARTICULAR AREA

Father, You are worthy of all praise, honor, and glory. I adore You. I worship You. I praise Your Holy Name.

Lord, You have been so patient with me, and I thank You. I also recognize Your still, small voice, speaking to me about an area of my life that needs resolution. You have been reminding me of my need to move ahead in this certain area, and I confess that I have not yet obeyed You. Please forgive me for my hesitation.

Today, I declare that I will take the step of faith You have spoken to me about. Lord, in regard to this step that I have been hesitant to take, I put away all my reluctance now, and I pledge to You that I will obey You.

And Lord, in those matters where I have been doing what You would prefer that I not do, I lay them aside, so that I can make room to do what You want me to do.

This is the way I choose to walk with you from now on. Laying aside my hesitancy and stubbornness, I step boldly, choosing You and Your purposes for my life. I declare that I will follow You in obedience.

Thank You, Lord! In Jesus' Name I pray. Amen.

Note: "The Prayer of Submissive Obedience in a Particular Area" was from a teaching by Derek Prince, www.derekprince.org.

Baptism in the Holy Spirit–Scriptural Basis and Authority

JOHN THE BAPTIST TAUGHT ABOUT THE HOLY SPIRIT:

Matthew 3:11 "I baptize you with water for repentance. But after me will come one who is more powerful than I, whose sandals I am not fit to carry. He will baptize you with the Holy Spirit and with fire."

JESUS CHRIST HAD TO HAVE THE HOLY SPIRIT:

Matthew 3:16-17 As soon as Jesus was baptized, he went up out of the water. At that moment heaven was opened, and he saw the Spirit of God descending like a dove and lighting on him. And a voice from heaven said, "This is my Son, whom I love; with him I am well pleased."

JESUS NEEDED TO BE LED BY THE HOLY SPIRIT:

Matthew 4:1 Then Jesus was led by the Spirit into the desert to be tempted by the devil.

Luke 4:1 Jesus, full of the Holy Spirit, returned from the Jordan and was led by the Spirit in the desert...

JESUS WAS EMPOWERED BY THE HOLY SPIRIT:

Luke 4:14 Jesus returned to Galilee in the power of the Spirit, and news about him spread through the whole countryside.

Luke 4:18-19 "The Spirit of the Lord is on me, because he has anointed me to preach good news to the poor. He has sent me to proclaim freedom for the prisoners and recovery of sight for the blind, to release the oppressed, to proclaim the year of the Lord's favor."

Acts 10:38 ...how God anointed Jesus of Nazareth with the Holy Spirit and power, and how he went around doing good and healing all who were under the power of the devil, because God was with him.

YOU CAN HAVE THE HOLY SPIRIT AS A GIFT:

Luke 11:11-13 "Which of you fathers, if your son asks for a fish, will give him a snake instead? Or if he asks for an egg, will give him a scorpion? If you then, though you are evil, know how to give good gifts to your children, how much more will your Father in heaven give the Holy Spirit to those who ask him!"

John 7:37-39 On the last and greatest day of the Feast, Jesus stood and said in a loud voice, "If anyone is thirsty, let him come to me and drink. Whoever believes in me, as the Scripture has said, streams of living water will flow from within him." By this he meant the Spirit, whom those who believed in him were later to receive. Up to that time the Spirit had not been given, since Jesus had not yet been glorified.

Revelation 22:17 The Spirit and the bride say, "Come!" And let him who hears say, "Come!" Whoever is thirsty, let him come; and whoever wishes, let him take the free gift of the water of life.

John 14:16-17 "And I will ask the Father, and he will give you another Counselor to be with you forever— the Spirit of truth. The world cannot accept him, because it neither sees him nor knows him. But you know him, for he lives with you and will be in you."

Acts 1:4-5 On one occasion, while he was eating with them, he gave them this command: "Do not leave Jerusalem, but wait for the gift my Father promised, which you have heard me speak about. For John baptized with water, but in a few days you will be baptized with the Holy Spirit."

Acts 2:1-4 When the day of Pentecost came, they were all together in one place. Suddenly a sound like the blowing of a violent wind came from heaven and filled the whole house where they were sitting. They saw what seemed to be tongues of fire that separated and came to rest on each of them. All of them were filled with the Holy Spirit and began to speak in other tongues as the Spirit enabled them.

THE BAPTISM OF THE HOLY SPIRIT IS SEPARATE FROM WATER BAPTISM:

John 20:21-22 Again Jesus said, "Peace be with you! As the Father has sent me, I am sending you." And with that he breathed on them and said, "Receive the Holy Spirit."

Acts 8:14-17 When the apostles in Jerusalem heard that Samaria had accepted the word of God, they sent Peter and John to them. When they arrived, they prayed for them that they might receive the Holy Spirit, because the Holy Spirit had not yet come upon any of them; they had simply been baptized into the name of the Lord Jesus. Then Peter and John placed their hands on them, and they received the Holy Spirit.

Acts 19:1-6 While Apollos was at Corinth, Paul took the road through the interior and arrived at Ephesus. There he found some disciples and asked them, "Did you receive the Holy Spirit when you believed?" They answered, "No, we have not even heard that there is a Holy Spirit." So Paul asked, "Then what baptism did you receive?" "John's baptism," they replied. Paul said, "John's baptism was a baptism of repentance. He told the people to believe in the one coming after him, that is, in Jesus." On hearing this, they were baptized into the name of the Lord Jesus. When Paul placed his hands on them, the Holy Spirit came on them, and they spoke in tongues and prophesied.

The Holy Spirit

The Holy Spirit is the third person in the Trinity. He is fully God. He is eternal, omniscient, omnipresent, has a will, and can speak. He is alive. He is a person. He is not as visible in the Bible as the Son or Father because His ministry is to bear witness of them (John 15:26). However, as you begin to focus on Him, you will see how very important He is to us!

In the Old Testament the Hebrew word ruwach (pronounced roo'-akh) was used when talking about the Spirit. This word literally means WIND or BREATH. In the New Testament the Greek word pneuma (pronounced pnyoo'-mah) was used which means the BREATH or a BREEZE. We can literally think of the Holy Spirit as the "BREATH OF GOD."

Throughout the ages, many people have thought of the Holy Spirit as more of a "thing", or a "force", than a "Person." Nothing could be further from the truth. In fact, as we begin to know the Person of the Holy Spirit, we will want to have a closer relationship with Him just as we would the Father or Son.

The truth is that the Holy Spirit is a Person the same as the Father and Son are Persons within the Trinity.

By careful study of the following scriptures about the Person of God the Holy Spirit, you will be able to better understand His Presence and Power living in you:

HIS NAMES	HIS ATTRIBUTES	SYMBOLS OF	SINS AGAINST	POWER IN CHRIST'S LIFE
God *Acts 5:3-4*	Eternal *Heb. 9:14*	Dove *Matt. 3:16*	Blasphemy *Matt. 12:31*	Conceived of *Matt. 1:18,20*
Lord *2 Cor. 3:18*	Omnipotent *Luke 1:35*	Wind *Acts 2:1-4*	Resist (Unbelief) *Acts 7:51*	Baptism *Matt. 3:16*
Spirit *1 Cor. 2:10*	Omnipresent *Psalm 139:7-10*	Fire *Acts 2:3*	Insult *Heb. 10:29*	Led by *Luke 4:1*
Spirit of God *1 Cor. 3:16*	Will *1 Cor. 12:11*	Living Waters *John 7:38-39* *1 Cor. 12:13*	Lied to *Acts 5:3*	Filled with Power *Luke 4:14,18*
Spirit of Truth *John 15:26*	Loves *Rom. 15:30*	•••••	Grieved *Eph. 4:30*	Witness of Jesus *John 15:26*
Eternal Spirit *Heb. 9:14*	Speaks *Acts 8:29; 13:2*	•••••	Quenched *1 Thess. 5:19*	Raised Jesus *Rom. 8:11*
The Person of God the Holy Spirit				

Although the word Trinity is not mentioned in the Bible, we know God is three in one. There are three very distinct Persons that make up the Godhead. They are all equal in every way. The Holy Spirit is a Person the same as the Father and the Son are Persons within the Trinity. There are some who believe the Holy Spirit is merely a force. If this were true, then He could not speak (Acts 13:2); He could not be grieved (Eph. 4:30); and He would not have a will (I Cor. 12:11).

It is important to understand the Holy Spirit is truly God because of the fact that if we are born again He lives in us. What we allow ourselves to become a part of we are inviting God to be part of. I Cor. 6:19.

FOUR IMPORTANT PRINCIPLES TO REMEMBER:

1. The Holy Spirit is God. Like the Father and the Son, He is a Person, not a "force", a "thing", or an "it".

2. We cannot focus on the Holy Spirit too much. Why? What is the Holy Spirit's mission? To reveal Jesus. What is Jesus' mission? To reveal the Father. What about the Father.....to send Jesus and the Holy Spirit so we can come to Him. Perfect Harmony. They never had a crisis management meeting in Heaven. They never tried to sit down and work things out. They never had a power struggle amongst themselves.

3. The Holy Spirit gives gifts for use in ministry and empowers effective ministry. I Cor. 12:7-11

4. The Holy Spirit gives us fruit which develops in us Christ-like character. Gal. 5:22-23

QUALITIES THAT A PERSON HAS....
(A "FORCE" OR "THING" DOES NOT):

1. The Holy Spirit has intellect. I Cor. 2:10
2. The Holy Spirit has knowledge. I Cor. 2:11
3. The Holy Spirit has emotions. Ephesians 4:30
4. The Holy Spirit has his own will and he makes decisions. Acts 16:6
5. The Holy Spirit loves. Romans 15:30

THINGS ONLY A PERSON WOULD DO
(A "FORCE" OR "THING" DOES NOT):

1. He teaches you things about God and yourself. John 14:26
2. He tells the truth. John 15:26
3. He guides. John 16:13
4. He convinces. John 16:8
5. He prays for you. Romans 8:26-27
6. He commands. Acts 13:2

THE HOLY SPIRIT WAS ON THE SCENE LONG BEFORE THE DAY OF PENTECOST:

- He moved upon the face of the waters and was the active agent in creation. Jesus was the Word, the Holy Spirit moved. John 1:1,14; Genesis 1:2
- The Holy Spirit gave us the Word of God. 2 Peter 1:20-21

- The Holy Spirit regenerates our spirit when we accept Jesus Christ into our life. John 3:6

IN FACT, THE HOLY SPIRIT HAS ALWAYS WORKED HAND-IN-HAND WITH JESUS CHRIST:

- His birth. Matthew 1:20
- The life and ministry of Jesus. Luke 4:1; Luke 4:18
- His death and offering Himself as the perfect sacrifice. Hebrews 9:14
- The resurrection of Jesus – Actually all 3 members of the Godhead had a part in the resurrection! FATHER (Eph. 1:19-20); SON (John 10:18); HOLY SPIRIT (Romans 1:4).
- The main purpose of the Holy Spirit is to tell us about Jesus and Glorify Him. John 16:13-14

PENTECOST:

- Jesus said it was imperative that He go or the Spirit would not be sent. John 16:7
- Jesus felt it important enough for them to wait until the Spirit came to empower them. Acts 1:4-8
- Jesus' own mother needed the baptism of the Holy Spirit to be an effective witness. Acts 1:14
- On the day of Pentecost, the believers who were assembled in the Upper Room experienced a new Baptism, the one which John referred to. Acts 2:1-4

Ministry of the Baptism of the Holy Spirit

Hebrews 6:17 **Malachi 3:6**	God's purpose is unchanging, confirmed and guaranteed.
Matthew 28:20	He is always with us through His Holy Spirit.
John 14:12 **Matthew 28:18**	The Holy Spirit enables us to do greater works than Jesus through the authority of Jesus given to us.
Hebrews 13:8	"Jesus Christ is same yesterday, today, and forever."

WHO IS THE HOLY SPIRIT?

Genesis 1:2,26	The Holy Spirit is the 3rd person of the Trinity.
1 Corinthians 12:11	He has a will.
Ephesians 4:30	He has feelings.
Luke 1:35	He conceived Jesus.

THE HOLY SPIRIT'S MINISTRY

John 14:15-18 **John 15:26-27** **John 16:13-15**	The Holy Spirit has been given to us that we may let Jesus work in and through us (our sole purpose in life is to carry the Holy Spirit in our body and let Him work through us that the Father might be glorified in the Son).
Romans 8:26-27	He makes intercession for us when we don't know how to pray.
John 14:16	He is our Helper and Teacher.

John 16:8	The Holy Spirit convicts. It is not our place to judge others; we are to let the Holy Spirit convict them.
Ephesians 4:30	He seals us for the day of redemption.
1 Corinthians 12:7-11	He distributes His manifestation gifts to us.
Hebrews 10:15	He witnesses to us (bears witness).
Romans 8:11	The Holy Spirit dwells in us and gives life to our mortal bodies
Acts 9:31	He comforts and encourages us.
Galatians 5:22-23	He bears fruit in us.
John 16:14	The Holy Spirit always glorifies Jesus.
1 Corinthians 12:13 and Acts 1:5	He baptizes.
Acts 1:8 and Luke 24:49	He endues power.

FIVE ACCOUNTS IN THE BOOK OF ACTS OF THE BAPTISM OF THE HOLY SPIRIT

Acts 2:4, Acts 8:14-25, Acts 9:17-20,
Acts 10:44-48, Acts 19:1-7

HOW TO RECEIVE THE BAPTISM OF THE HOLY SPIRIT

Jesus is the Baptizer of the Holy Spirit: Matthew 3:11, Mark 1:8, Luke 3:16

Believe, Pray, Ask, Receive

MORE INFORMATION ON THE BAPTISM IN THE HOLY SPIRIT

SCRIPTURE REFERENCES

The Day of Pentecost	Acts 2
Spirit of power, love and a sound mind	2 Timothy 1:7
Sending another Counselor	John 14:15-20; John 16:7
Quenching the Spirit	1 Thessalonians 5:19-22
Receive the Holy Spirit	John 20:22
Joel's Prophecy	Joel 2:28-32
Test the Spirits	1 Thessalonians 5:21; 1 John 4:1
You will know them by their fruit	Matthew 7:15-20

SOME HOLY SPIRIT MANIFESTATIONS IN SCRIPTURE

- There is no comprehensive list... the Bible does not record all possible experiences (John 21:25).
- Falling under the influence of the Spirit (Revelation 1:17; Matthew 17:6; John 18:6; Acts 9:4-8; Ezekiel 1:28; 3:23, 43:3, 44:4; Daniel 8:17-18; Daniel 10:8-9).
- Drunk in the Spirit (Acts 2:15; Ephesians 5:18).
- Laughter and joy (Romans 14:17; Galatians 5:22; Psalm 126:2-3; Genesis 21:3,6; 1 Peter 1:8).
- Trembling and terror (Daniel 8:17-18, 10:7-11; Matthew 17:6; Matthew 28:4).

- Shaking (Exodus 19:16-18; Acts 4:31; Isaiah 6:4).
- Speechless (Daniel 10:15-19; Ezekiel 3:26; Luke 1:22).
- Weeping (2 Chronicles 34:27; Hosea 12:4; Matthew 26:75; Luke 19:41; 2 Corinthians 7:10; Revelation 5:4; Hebrews 5:7).
- Trances (Acts 10:10, 22:17; Numbers 24:3-4).
- Pockets of power (1 Samuel 19:19-24).
- Traveling by the Spirit (Acts 8:39-40; Ezekiel 3:14, 8:3, 11:24; 2 Corinthians 12:1-4, Revelation 4:1-2).
- Fire (Exodus 3:2, 24:17, 40:38; Leviticus 9:24; Luke 3:16; Acts 2:3; 1 Thessalonians 5:19; Hebrews 12:29).

Confessions for Every Day

Loved One in Christ–Build your faith and claim God's promises for yourself by reading these confessions of God's Word aloud (thoughtfully and prayerfully – with conviction) every day. Keep doing it until they are your thoughts so that you can use the Word against Satan to "take every thought captive" when he attacks your mind! To "confess" is to say the same thing as God, so that as the Word transforms your mind, His thoughts become your thoughts! Confess these daily at least once – early morning is best so you are "armed and dangerous" when Satan attacks during the day! Before bedtime is good too so you are protected as you rest.

- I am not just an ordinary man/woman. I'm a child of the living God.
- I am not just a person; I'm an heir of God, and a joint heir with Jesus Christ. I'm not "just an old sinner", I am a new creation in Jesus, my Lord. I'm part of a chosen generation, a Royal Priesthood, a Holy Nation. I'm one of God's people. I am His. I am a living witness of His grace, mercy and love!
- I have been crucified with Christ and I no longer live, but Christ lives in me! The life I live in the body, I live by the faith of the Son of God, who loved me, and gave Himself for me. When the devil tries to resurrect the "old man", I will rebuke him and remind him sternly that I am aware of his tricks, lures, lies and deception. The "old man" is dead. My "new man" knows all old things are passed away–all things have become new!
- I'm not under guilt or condemnation. I refuse discouragement, for it is not of God. God is the God of all encouragement. There is therefore

now no condemnation for those in Christ Jesus. Satan is a liar. I will not listen to his accusations.

- I gird up my loins of my mind. I am cleansed in the Blood. No weapon formed against me shall prosper, and I shall condemn every tongue rising against me in judgment. I am accepted in the beloved. If God be for me, who can be against me?
- My mind is being renewed by the Word of God. I pull down strongholds; I cast down imaginations; I bring every thought captive to the obedience of Christ.
- As the Father loves Jesus, so Jesus loves me. I'm the righteousness of God in Christ. I'm not slave of sin; I am a slave of God and a slave of righteousness. I continue in His Word; I know the truth and I practice it, so the truth sets me free.
- Because the Son sets me free, I am free indeed. He who is born of God keeps me, therefore the evil one does not touch me. I've been delivered out of the kingdom of darkness. I am now part of the Kingdom of Light, the Kingdom of God. I don't serve sin any longer. Sin has no dominion over me.
- I will not believe the enemy's lies. He will not intimidate me. He is a liar and the father of lies. Satan is defeated. For this purpose, the Son of God came into this world – to destroy the works of the devil. No longer will he oppress me. Surely, oppression makes a wise person mad. I will get mad at the devil. I defeat him by the Blood of the Lamb, by the word of my testimony as to what He has done for me, not loving my life, even to death.
- I will submit to God. I will resist the devil and he will flee. No temptation will overtake me that is not common to man. God is Faithful

and True; He will not let me be tempted beyond my strength, but with the temptation He will also provide the way of escape (Jesus) that I may be able to endure.

- I will stand fast in the liberty with which Christ has made me free. Where the Spirit of the Lord is, there is liberty – not liberty to do what I "want", but freedom to do as I "ought". The law of the Spirit of Life in Christ Jesus has set me free from the law of sin and death.
- Nothing can separate me from the love of God that is in Christ Jesus, my Lord. His Holy Spirit is my guide, comforter, teacher and best friend! Jesus is my Protector, my Deliverer, my Rewarder, my Refuge, my Strong Tower, my Shepherd, my Light, my Life, my Counselor, my Rock, my Freedom! He is everything to me!
- Christ causes me to triumph. I will reign as a king in life through Christ Jesus. As a young man/woman I am strong. The Word of God abides in me, and I have overcome the evil one. I am more than a conqueror through Christ who loves me. I am an overcomer. I am invincible. I can do all things through Christ who strengthens me. Thanks be to God who gives me the victory through Jesus Christ, my Lord!

WISDOM AND GUIDANCE CONFESSIONS

- The Spirit of Truth abides in me and teaches me all things, and He guides me into all truths. Therefore, I confess I have perfect knowledge of every situation and circumstance I come up against, for I have the wisdom of God. (John 16:13; James 1:5)
- I trust in the Lord with all my heart and I do not lean or rely on my own understanding. In all my ways I acknowledge Him, and He directs my path. (Proverbs 3:5-6)

- The Lord will perfect that which concerns me, and fulfill His purpose for me. (Psalm 138:8)
- I let the Word of Christ dwell in me richly in all wisdom. (Colossians 3:16)
- I do follow the Good Shepherd, and I know His voice. The voice of a stranger I will not follow. (John 10:4-5)
- Jesus is made unto me wisdom, righteousness, sanctification, and redemption. Therefore, I confess I have the wisdom of God, and I am the righteousness of God in Christ Jesus. (I Cor. 1:30; II Cor. 5:21)
- I am filled with the knowledge of the Lord's will in all wisdom and spiritual understanding. (Colossians 1:9)
- I am a new creation in Christ. I am His workmanship created in Christ Jesus. Therefore, I have the mind of Christ and the wisdom of God is formed within me. (II Cor. 5:17; Ephesians 2:10; I Cor. 2:16)
- I receive the Spirit of wisdom and revelation in the knowledge of Him, the eyes of my understanding being enlightened. I am not conformed to this world but I am transformed by the renewing of my mind. My mind is renewed by the Word of God. (Ephesians 1:17-18; Romans 12:2)

I AM...

- I am forgiven. (Col. 1:13-14)
- I am saved by grace through faith. (Eph. 2:8)
- I am delivered from the powers of darkness. (Col. 1:13)

- I am led by the Spirit of God. (Rom. 8:14)
- I am kept in safety wherever I go. (Psalm 91:11-12)
- I am getting all my needs met by Jesus. (Phil. 4:19)
- I am casting all my cares on Jesus. (I Peter 5:7)
- I am not anxious or worried about anything. (Phil. 4:6)
- I am strong in the Lord and in the power of His might. (Eph. 6:10)
- I am doing all things through Christ who strengthens me. (Phil. 4:13)
- I am observing and doing the Lord's commandments. (Deut. 28:13)
- I am blessed going in and blessed going out. (Deut. 28:6)
- I am above only and not beneath. (Deut. 28:13)
- I am blessed with all spiritual blessings. (Eph. 1:3)
- I am healed by His stripes. (I Peter 2:24)
- I am more than a conqueror. (Romans 8:37)
- I am an overcomer by the Blood of the Lamb and the word of my testimony. (Rev. 12:11)
- I am not moved by what I see. (II Cor. 4:8-9)
- I am walking by faith and not by sight. (II Cor. 5:7)
- I am daily overcoming the Devil. (I John 4:4)
- I am casting down vain imaginations. (II Cor. 10:4)
- I am bringing every thought into captivity. (II Cor.10:5)

- I am not conformed to this world, but I am being transformed by renewing my mind. (Romans 12:1-2)
- I am blessing the Lord at all times and continually praising the Lord with my mouth. (Psalm 34:1)
- I am a child of God. (Romans 8:16)

Personalized Daily Prayers

LOVED ONE IN CHRIST:

These passages of scripture from Paul, David, and Isaiah have been personalized for you. They are powerful prayers, by powerful men, to the Most Powerful! As you pray God's Word back to Him, He is pleased, for He has told us to put Him in remembrance of His Word. Do you think He needs to be reminded? Like He forgot? No, we are the ones who need to be reminded. We claim these awesome promises for ourselves. Pray these daily as the Spirit leads you. You will be richly blessed in doing so.

IN THE NAME OF JESUS,

I praise you Lord from my soul. From my inmost being I praise your Holy Name. I praise you Lord from my soul. I will not forget all your benefits – you forgive all my sins and heal all my diseases. You redeemed my life from the pit and crowned me with your love and compassion. You satisfy my desires with good things so that my youth is renewed like an eagle's. Amen. (Psalm 103:1-5)

IN THE NAME OF JESUS,

As I dwell in the shelter of the Most High I will rest in the shadow of the Almighty. I will say of you Lord, "You are my refuge and my fortress. You are my God and I will trust in you." Surely you will save me from the fowler's snare and from the deadly pestilence. You will cover me with your feathers, and under your wings I will find refuge; your faithfulness will be my shield and rampart.

I will not fear the terror of night nor the arrow that flies by day, nor the pestilence that stalks in the darkness, nor the plague that destroys at midday. A thousand may fall at my side, ten thousand by my right hand, but it will not come near me.

I will observe with my eyes and see the punishment of the wicked. I will make the Most High my dwelling – the Lord is my refuge – so that no harm will befall me, no disaster will come near my tent. God, you will command your angels concerning me to guard me in all my ways; they will lift me up in their hands, so that I will not strike my foot against a stone. I will tread upon the lion and the cobra; I will trample the great lion and the serpent.

Lord, you said because I love you, you will rescue me. You will protect me, for I acknowledge your name. I will call upon you and you will answer me; you will be with me in trouble, you will deliver me and honor me. With long life will you satisfy me and show me your salvation. Amen. (Psalm 91)

IN THE NAME OF JESUS,

No weapon forged against me will prevail and I will refute every tongue that accuses me. This is my heritage as a servant of the Lord, and this is my vindication from you. Amen. (Isaiah 54:17)

IN THE NAME OF JESUS,

I keep asking that you, God of my Lord Jesus Christ, my glorious Father, may give me the Spirit of wisdom and revelation that I may know you better. I pray also that the eyes of my heart may be enlightened in order that I may know the hope to which you have called me, the riches of your glorious inheritance in the saints, and your incomparably great power for us who believe. That power is like the working of your mighty strength, which you exerted in Christ when you raised Him from the dead and seated Him at your right hand in heavenly realms, far above all rule and authority, power and dominion, and every title that can be given, not only in the present age but also in the one to come. And you, God, placed all things under His feet and appointed Him to be over everything for the church, which is His body, the fullness of Him who fills everything in every way. Amen. (Ephesians 1:17-23)

IN THE NAME OF JESUS,

I pray that out of your glorious riches you may strengthen me with power through your Spirit in my inner being, so that Christ may dwell in my heart through faith. And I pray that as I am rooted and established in love, I may have power, together with all the saints, to grasp how wide and long and high and deep is the love of Christ, and that I may know this love that surpasses knowledge – that I may be filled to the measure of all your fullness.

Now to you, God, who is able to do immeasurably more than all I ask or imagine, according to your power that is at work within me, to you be glory in the church and in Christ Jesus throughout all generations, forever and ever! Amen. (Ephesians 3:16-21)

IN THE NAME OF JESUS,

This also is my prayer: that my love may abound more and more in knowledge and depth of insight, so that I may be able to discern what is best and may be pure and blameless until the day of Christ, filled with the fruit of righteousness that comes through Jesus Christ – to the glory and praise of you, God. Amen. (Philippians 1:9-11)

IN THE NAME OF JESUS,

I pray that you fill me with the knowledge of your will through all spiritual wisdom and understanding. I pray this in order that I may live a life worthy of the Lord Jesus and please Him in every way: bearing fruit in every good work, growing in the knowledge of you, God, so that I may be strengthened with all power according to your glorious might so that I may have great endurance and patience and joyfully give you thanks. Amen. (Colossians 1:9b-11)

NOTES

NOTES

NOTES

NOTES